OF COSTLIEST EMBLEM:

Paradise Lost
and the Emblem Tradition

Shahla Anand

University Press
of America™

مُناظرہ

فردوسِ گُم شدہ

از

شہلا آنند

'OF COSTLIEST EMBLEM':

PARADISE LOST AND THE EMBLEM TRADITION

Contents:

ILLUSTRATIONS

FOREWORD

'Of Costliest Emblem': Paradise Lost and the

Emblem Tradition

Taking Mario Praz's premise that "every poetical image
contains a potential emblem," the thesis explores
spiritual and temporal images and ideologies in Para-
dise Lost in relation to the English emblem books. The
emblem books used are: Geoffrey Whitney, A Choice of
Emblemes, 1586; Henry Peacham, Minerva Britanna, 1612;
Henry Hawkins, Partheneia Sacra, 1633; George Wither,
A Collection of Emblemes, 1635; Francis Quarles,
Emblems, 1635 and Hieroglyphikes of the Life of Man,
1638; John Hall, Emblems with Elegant Figures, 1658;
E. M. Ashrea: or the Grove of Beatitudes, 1665; and
St. Robert Bellarmine, A Shorte Catechisme, 1614.

   After defining the emblem as a literary genre and
noting its popularity in the seventeenth century, the
thesis argues Milton's familiarity with emblem literature. Although Milton uses the word "emblem" once in
its sense of an ornate inlay, he has verbal pictures,
replete with mottoes, which can be equated with the
emblem. Milton's unmatched learning, poetic excellence, and sophistication far outshine the emblematists, but do not bar his use of the emblematic mode.
The epic has a sensuous quality that recalls Renaissance paintings and sculpture. Milton's dense word
pictures carry symbols, which could be overlooked.
Aldrich and Medina, the first to illustrate Milton's
works, caught the essence of his pictorial style.
It also fired the imagination of Dore and Blake.

   Milton is not unique in his pre-occupation with
the spiritual as well as the sensuous. Praz states,
"In need as he was of certainties of the senses, the
seventeenth-century man did not stop at the purely
fantastic cherishing of the image: he wanted to externalize it, to transport it into a hieroglyph, an
emblem." Both Milton and the emblematists take upon
themselves to "externalize" scriptural truths and
their own thoughts in pictures.

   Milton's literary pictorialism encompasses emblems of the Creator, the angelic world, the Creation,

i

the Devil and hell. From the mediaeval times symbolic
modes of expression had interested artists and men of
letters. Early illuminations, bestiaries, allegorical
fantasies are examples. The early seventeenth-century
is still medieval in much of its outlook, though Janus-
like, it faces the age of science and reason as well.
Like the medievalists the emblem writers often depict
God as a monarch seated in a canopied throne, his feet
resting on clouds, his angels around him. At times he
appears as a symbol: a benign Sun, a lit cloud carrying the hieroglyphics for "Yahweh," a hand lowered
from the sky pouring streams of life-giving grace into
a parched soul. In Paradise Lost God appears in full
refulgence to his Son alone. Others, angels and man,
see his skirts, hear his voice or feel his presence.
The angels are seen both by the emblem writers and
Milton as God's emissaries and loyal subjects. They
worship God in song and music and have their appointed
missions. Creation in both the emblematists and Milton
is drawn largely from Ovid and Genesis 1-3. The Devil
is God's once trusted Archangel, now apostate. He
takes on many forms both male and female in the emblem-
artists. In Milton he is the glorious archangel
tainted; metamorphosing to the diabolic both in body
and soul. Hell is the yawning, medieval mouth of the
mythical dragon for the emblematists, where souls and
devils wallow in contorted forms. Milton's hell is a
cavernous cosmos in itself. Its bituminous lake and
plain and frigid hills contain the tarnished angels,
who bristle with power and often argue "in reason's
garb." At God's will, when most proud and elated,
they change to reptiles of many varieties, symbolically, hydra-headed evil. Milton and the emblem writers'
ideas of Heaven and Hell have much in common, but
Milton's lines remain unexcelled.

Emblems of war, madness and degeneracy in connection with Satan, Sin and their human victims stem
from holocausts and aftermath of wars. Both Milton
and the emblematists dwell on physical and psychological war as pernicious to mental health. A good example is envy. For the emblematists she is a horrifying
virago consuming her heart, or wound with snakes. In
Milton envy is best seen in the distorted face and
demeanor of Satan as spied by Uriel.

The temptation and Fall of Adam and Eve are favorite subjects of the emblematists. They treat the
event in pictures, as laments, as combined miracle and

morality plays, and at times only as exempla. The temptation and Fall, along with their corollary, redemption, are the core of Milton's epic. They lead to religious and ethical ideas in Milton and the emblem writers and become a point of departure for moralizing, based on inspirational psalms, proverbs, other scriptural passages, and the Church fathers.

The liturgical and dramatic icons in Paradise Lost are equated with the liturgy of the Book of Common Prayer and illustrated from Bellarmine. In spite of Milton's Independent religious stance, he is well versed in the Anglican form of worship, a form best known to him; and Milton teaches as he sings.

Milton's epic has been studied for its pictorial quality, but seldom associated with iconology. This thesis has tried to show that Milton was not averse to the emblematic mode when it could elucidate a point or teach a lesson, for, as W. R. Parker has stressed, Milton was a teacher par excellence.

N.B.   The quotations are from Mario Praz, Studies in Seventeenth-Century Imagery. 2nd. ed. Rome: Edizioni Di Storia E Letteratura, 1964.

S.A.

Paradise Lost, like Lycidas or Samson Agonistes,
reveals Milton's discriminating sense of who his greatest predecessors were: Homer, Virgil, Dante, poets
worthy of admiration and also strong enough to be
fought with as Milton twists traditional genres and
themes to his own ends. But Milton did not hesitate
to borrow his materials from smaller writers, such as
du Bartas, whenever it suited his purpose. Although
the poetry of England's emblem books seldom transcends
the serviceable, the emblems themselves represent something more than the merely popular. It is (I think)
hard to read through these books without being at
once disappointed by most of the poetry yet nevertheless repeatedly fascinated by the idea of creating
an equal symbiosis between engraving and text, cry-
stalizing a poem in a picture and a picture in a poem.
If poetry strives toward the condition of music, it
also strives toward Aristotelian exemplary mimesis.
In their sometimes simple-minded way, this is precise-
ly what the emblem books attempt: to educate not by
didacticism but by pictorial examples that sway the
feelings through the senses, as Sidney describes the
process in his Defense of Poetry. Just because they
approach this central preoccupation of literature with
such simple directness, the emblem poets may help us
understand the subtler, deeper, and less easily de-
tachable images of such major poets as Milton.

As Shahla Anand's study shows, the connections
between the emblem writers and Milton are by no means
simple or obvious. When George Herbert takes an emblem, he customarily makes it his own by dramatizing
and humanizing it and putting it into motion; yet the
original emblem is often still recognizable. Milton,
although he once refers explicitly to the emblem in
Paradise Lost, does not reveal influences so easily.
It is hard to be sure whether, in any particular case,
he derived an image or a scene from the emblematists
or from some other source. (Indeed, it is hard to
find anything in Milton that does not seem to have
multiple sources.) Nevertheless, Milton, like the
emblem writers, is deeply committed to teaching "by
ensample," and his fit readers were accustomed to
thinking and feeling similarly. If, as Jung thought,
ours is an age that has neglected the image for the
abstraction, then the emblem writers can teach us

something we need to know before we approach Milton or
any great poet. Of course, modern criticism is thor-
oughly aware of the importance of imagery; yet, with
its tendency to value the image for its own sake, it
has perhaps learned only half the lesson.

If the connections between Milton and the emblem
writers are seldom simple, they have a certain fascination that teases us out of thought and touches the
heart of poetic method. Mrs. Anand's study, as it
treats both individual figures and large-scale pictorial effects, from Milton's God and his angelic world
to Satan and hell, suggests how emblematic methods
may convey a doctrine, an emotion, or a perception.
As is so often the case, the attempt to see Paradise
Lost in a seventeenth-century context at the same time
may give readers new insights into the poetry itself.

                              Anthony Low
                    Professor, Department of
                              English
                        New York University

   This book is addressed to lovers of Milton--es-
pecially those who delight in the infinite variety of
his pictorial style. Dr. Shahla Anand finds emblems
in every nuance of this variety. For Paradise Lost,
as she abundantly proves, "is a mine of emblems."
The early chapters pursue analogues of Milton's emblematic themes among such predecessors and contemporaries as Whitney, Peacham, Wither, and Quarles. The
emblematists, according to Dr. Anand, prepared the way
for, or shared the spiritual climate of, Milton's
pictorial style.

   But OF COSTLIEST EMBLEM is more than a sequence
of parallel passages. From the more concrete types of
emblem Dr. Anand ascends in the manner of Plato to the
most abstruse symbols of Milton's epic, arriving finally at Milton's central problem: "Of man's first disobedience." God endowed man with right reason and a
free will:

          "But God left free the will, for what
          obeys
          Reason, is free, and Reason he made
          right. . ." (IX. 351-2)

Thus Adam was created:

     "Sufficient to have stood, though free to fall,"
(III.99). Milton, as Dr. Anand stresses, was a man of
his age, far more than has generally been thought.
And his was the age of Descartes, Spinoza, and Hobbes.
To the seventeenth century rationalist the concepts of
reason had their counterparts in existence. To the
mentality of the twentieth century, however, Milton
set Adam adrift in the universe with two unreliable
pilots: free will and reason. Free will has lost
much of its dignity, if not its very identity, under
the investigations of depth psychology. "Reason,"
writes Ernst Cassirer in his Essay on Man, "is a very
inadquate term with which to comprehend the forms of
man's cultural life in all their richness and variety."
To be sure, it was not reason but emotion which brought
on Adam's fall:

          "Against his better knowledge, not deceiv'd,
          But fonduly overcome with female charm."
                                        (IX.998-9)

Some scholars have felt that Milton deals harshly
with Eve. They argue that her insistence on culti-
vating her own part of the garden reflected the actual
status of many Puritan housewives who became de facto
partners in their husbands' businesses. From Milton's
viewpoint Eve disobeyed her husband on the day she met
the serpent and was suborned. And this is the view we
find in Samson Agonistes:

> "Therefore God's universal Law
> Gave to the man despotic power
> Over his female in due awe,
> Nor from that right to part an hour."
> (1053-56)

Dr. Anand sees Eve as a link in the long chain of
female temptresses. Even before the Fall, Dr. Anand
finds signs of weakness in Eve, though "In her pristine innocence, Eve typifies the virgin." While she
is quicker to find an argument than Adam, yet her intellect is "less keen than Adam's." She has all that
is required of a 'worthy' woman," says Dr. Anand,
"but the lure of a Siren." And Adam's fall has much
in common with the fate of the many men whom Circe
with her evil drugs turned into swine. Moreover,
every Milton student will see in Dalila, betrayer of
Samson, a fallen Eve.

The label "Puritan" as applied to Milton has
turned the attention of many students away from the
Anglican roots of Milton's religious training. Dr.
Anand's discussion of the many uses Milton makes of
the Anglican Book of Common Prayer is, therefore, both
refreshing and enlightening. The author shows that
Milton's epic is permeated in both style and content
with this basic document of the Anglican faith. Quite
modestly, she sums up her case by stating that many
passages in Paradise Lost "seem convincingly influenced by the rites and ceremonies and verbal turns of
the Book of Common Prayer." While Dr. Anand's arguments are mainly based on internal evidence found in
the epic, the external evidence supporting this view
has been most impressively compiled by Harris F.
Fletcher in the first volume of his Intellectual Development of John Milton. As is well known, John
Milton attended All Hallows Church in Bread Street
London in his formative years. His father was an in-
fluential member of the parish, and probably, as
Fletcher intimates, took a leading role in bringing
the Reverend Richard Stock to All Hallows. Stock was

an Anglican with liberal leanings, inclining to Calvinism. According to Fletcher, ". . . perhaps no other person ever connected with the poet at any age of his life contributed more permanently and so variously to the boy's development as Stock did."* Dr. Anand assesses the far-reaching effects of Stock's religious instruction upon Milton.

In the abundance of studies of Paradise Lost one rarely comes upon a treatment of what the poem certainly meant primarily to its author. To review De doctrina christiana is to marvel again at the intensity of Milton's religious views--and at the perseverance with which he sought divine inspiration. To this reader, Dr. Anand's treatment of Paradise Lost as religious experience is sensitive, scholarly, and beautifully expressed. This is not a book for the rapid reader. Many and many a time the reader must pause to refresh his mind with the relevant passages of the epic. Milton's poem is as replete with religious symbolism as The Divine Comedy. The fountain from which these symbols flowed was the poet's ever-burning zeal for godliness. As Dr. Anand expresses it, "Milton's extended narrative poem, then, becomes a massive act of devotion."

---

*Harris F. Fletcher, The Intellectual Development of John Milton (Urbana: University of Illinois Press, 1956), p. 60.

James P. Pettegrove
Professor, Department of
English
Montclair State College

DEDICATION

Recorded my gratitude to theologian, scholar, author and linguist, the Right Reverend Kenneth D. W. Anand, Bishop of the Diocese of Amritsar (Kashmir, Punjab, Himachal), India, and Assistant Bishop of the Diocese of Newark, New Jersey, U.S.A.; my mentor, counsellor, friend, husband, without whose aid, understanding and patience this work would have remained in the nascent stage.

'OF COSTLIEST EMBLEM':

PARADISE LOST AND THE EMBLEM TRADITION

CHAPTER ONE

MILTON IN THE EMBLEM TRADITION

It may be irreverent to search for emblems in
Milton's magniloquent and monumental epic, for rhap-
sodists like the emblem writers may not have appealed
to him; yet the work of the emblem writers is of considerable literary merit. It lacks the eminence Milton
expected of true vates; the kind of eminence he had
schooled himself to achieve, but in its use of both
spiritual and temporal images and ideologico, the emblem is a genre of the Renaissance, and is known to
have had great popularity in the sixteenth and seventeenth centuries. To a student of seventeenth-century
literature it is evident that in Milton's avid thirst
for all available knowledge, he encountered this art
form in England and probably in his travels abroad.
Being a classicist, he may have been intrigued by the
emblem's epigrammatic and succinct compression and its
simplicity. Research shows that emblems abound in
Paradise Lost, and can afford hours of painstaking delight. They spring up unexpectedly in the epic, and
prove that Milton was either consciously or unconsciously following a mode of expression which puts
him in line with the emblematists as with the great
artists of his time. Both Milton and the emblem
writers were committed artists and aesthetes of the
Renaissance, and gave poetic expression to graphic
art. If Milton takes all knowledge as his province,
so in a humbler way do the emblematists. They too
cover the whole expanse of the Aristotelian-Neoplatonic
universe from the throne of God to the inert "atomies"
of matter.

Rosemary Freeman points out that works of the
continental emblem writers were imported into Elizabethan England and became very popular. Andrea Alciati's Emblematum Liber fired the imagination of lit-
erateurs and artists after its first appearance in
1531. According to Rosemary Freeman, Alciati culled
the word "emblem" from G. Bude's Annotationes in
Pandectas where it appears in its original sense of

1

a mosaic.[1] The only time that Milton uses the word
"emblem" in Paradise Lost is in that particular sense
of a formal, patterned mosaic. He sees the flower-
covered bower of Adam and Eve as a mosaic floor "more
color'd than with stone / Of costliest Emblem." (IV.
702).[2] Apart from this use of the word "emblem," it
is possible that Milton read Alciati in the original
and was familiar with the works of Italian, French,
Spanish, German, Dutch and Flemish emblem writers,
such as Gabriele or Giovio Symeoni and Girolamo Rus-
celli,[3] and works such as Perrière's Le theatre de
bons engins, 1539; Gilles Corrozet's Hecatomagraphie,
1540; Maurice Sceve's Delie, Object de plus haulte
vertu, 1544; Claude Paradin's Devises heroiques, 1557;
Hadrianus Junius' Emblemata, 1565; Theodore de Beze's
Icones, 1580; Nicolaus Reusner's Emblems, Frankfort,
1581; Cesare Ripa's Iconologia, 1603; Daniel Heinsius'
Emblemata amatoria, 1608; Otho Vaenius' Amorum emblemata , 1608; Jacob Cats' Silenus Alchiadis, 1618;
Herman Hugo's Pia desideria Emblematis Elegiis et
Affectibus ss. Patrum illustrata, 1624;Diego Fajardo's
Idea de un Principe politico cristiano, 1640, and other
works.[4]

Among the English emblem writers whom Milton may
have known was the popular and fascinating Whitney.
He was known to the Elizabethans from 1586, when his
A Choice of Emblemes, and Other Devices was published.
The book was a compilation of Whitney's rendition in
English of European emblems as well as his own original devices and poesies. Henry Peacham's Basilikon
Doron appeared between 1603 and 1606 with reprints in
1608 and 1610. In 1632 and 1635 Henry Hawkins published Parthenia Sacra and Emblems. Emblem books published about the time Milton was at Horton were George
Wither's A Collection of Emblemes Ancient and Modern
(1635), and Francis Quarles' Hieroglyphikes of the
Life of Man (1638). Harvey's Schola Cordis appeared
in 1647. John Hall, who like Milton was a secretary
and pamphleteer to Oliver Cromwell, published Emblems
with Elegant Figures in 1658, while Milton was at
work on his great epic. E. M.'s Ashrea (1665) was
published the year before Paradise Lost was completed
in the serene seclusion of Chalfont St. Giles, Buck-
inghamshire. Philip Ayres, one of the last emblematists of the period, was writing his Emblemata Amatoria
during the Restoration. His book did not appear until 1683, nine years after Milton's death.

Emblems in the seventeenth century were present

2

not only in literature, but were the leitmotiv of the
artists in almost all media. Imprints, emblems and
decorations were part of the murals on walls and ceil-
ings of manorial homes and castles, of monasteries,
refectoria and churches. They were present in mosaic
floors of courtyards and halls, in tapestries, arti-
facts and armour; on carvings and lapidary work of
master craftsmen. Emblems appear in the drawings and
pictures of artists like Leonardo Da Vinci, and the
portraits of Titian and Tintoretto. All this was due
to the unprecedented interest in the new hieroglyphics
of the sixteenth and seventeeth centuries, the era to
which Milton belonged.

Emblems have been defined variously. The most
comprehensive description of emblems hails back to
Whitney, the best known of the early English emblem
writers. He calls emblems:

> suche figures, or workes, as are wrought
> in plate, or in stones in the pavements,
> or on the waules, or such like, for the
> adorning of the place: having some
> wittie devise expressed with cunning
> woorkemanship, somethinge obscure to be
> perceived at the first, whereby, when
> with further consideration it is under-
> stood, it maie the greater delighte the
> bohoulder.[5]

In the seventeenth century the word "figure" was used
interchangeably with impress, emblem and hieroglyphic;
the last suggesting sacred carving. The Oxford Companion to Art states that emblem books are "books of
symbolic pictures accompanied by explanatory texts.
And emblems give . . . symbolic expression to a moral
adage. The emblematic concept arose through the
attempts of Italian humanists to create a modern
equivalent of the Egyptian Hieroglyph, an attempt
which was triggered off by the discovery in 1419 of
the Hieroglyphica of Horapollo. Its background was
Renaissance Platonism, which laid stress on the visual
image as a vehicle for hidden philosophic mysteries.
. . . The vitality of the emblematic formula as a
vehicle moralizing in the visual arts lasted through
the 17th and well into the 18th c."[6] Webster's Third
New International Dictionary stresses the "inlaid
work, the tesselated work," of the emblem, though it
defines it as "A visible sign of an idea."[7] These
definitions make it clear that Milton is conscious of

3

the significance of emblems, for he uses the word "emblem" (IV. 703) in its sense of rich, decorative, figured inlay; and when he brings in the idea of emblems and emblazoning and impresses (I.538; II. 511; IX.31-36), the impact is that of the seventeenth-century emblems; the verses become pictures with covert meanings.

Rosemary Freeman states that the English emblem books were derivatives of the Continental emblems and that their popularity and appeal in England never reached the "emblem-mania" of the Continent. She points out that almost all of Whitney's emblems can be traced to Alciati, though Whitney may have owed his emblems to Samuel Daniel who published his translation of Paolo Giovio's emblems with a prefatorial letter by N. W. A statement made in the letter by the unidentified N. W. is worth quoting for the emblematists and Milton, like N. W., see visible nature symbolic of spiritual and profound verities:

> But concerning the arte of Impresse I
> neede not draw the petigree of it, sith
> it is known that it descended from the
> auncient Aegiptians and Chaldeans, in
> the Schoole of Memphis; who devised
> meanes before characters were founde
> out, to utter their conceiptes by formes
> of Beaste, Starres, Hearbes, . . .
> drawing these characters from the world
> as from a volume wherein was written
> the wonders of nature. This was the
> first foundation layd of Impresse:
> From hence was derived by succession
> of pregnant wittes Stemmata Coates of
> Armes Insignia Ensignes, and the olde
> Images, which the Romanes used as
> witnesses of their Auncestors, Emblems
> and Devises . . . . Iamblicus saieth
> that they were conceiptes by an ex-
> ternall forme representing an inward
> purpose.[8]

For Sir Thomas Browne "the finger of God hath left an Inscription upon all his works, not graphical or composed of letters, but of their several forms, constitutions, parts and operations, which aptly joyned together do make one word that doth express their natures. By these letters God calls the stars by their names; and by this Alphabet Adam assigned to

4

every creature a name peculiar to its Nature."[9]
Milton expresses similar thoughts in Of Education,
when he cogitates on the purpose of education; the
imperative of right knowledge being knowledge of God
and re-establishing the relation which Adam had severed
from God. Man depends on sensate things to understand psycological and philosophical issues; and Milton
confirms it, "because our understanding cannot in this
body found itself but on sensible things, nor arrive
so clearly to the knowledge of God and things invisible
as by orderly conning over the visible and inferior
creature, the same method is necessarily to be followed
in all discreet teaching."[10] Milton's God thus can
only be understood by his impress on Man, who, except
for his fallen nature, is the epitome of God's creation and God's image. The abstract can only be
grasped by knowing and studying the visible. This was
the emblematists' greatest claim to importance.
Francis Quarles, who graduated from Christ's College,
Cambridge, the year Milton was born, was sixteen years
his senior, and like Milton, eschewed the church to
serve his countrymen through "the just practice of
law", tried to justify God to man in Emblems (1658)
with Miltonic and evangelistic zeal. Like many of
his contemporaries he was inspired by the numinous,
but had need of the concrete to illustrate the unseen.
Many of his emblems are appropriate to the thoughts
they express, but some illustrative impresses and devices are grotesque and cluttered with images. Often
they are distinctly different from the verses, and
at times, at odds with them. Much imagination is
needed to formulate their message, and envision their
original appeal.

Milton was undoubtedly familiar with the emblem
books. He refers to the intricate frontispiece of
Eikon Basilike, which carries the emblematic picture
of the unfortunate Charles I, symbolically enshrined
among the disasters which led to his decapitation.[11]
Other than mentioning "costliest Emblem" (IV. 703),
Milton makes no overt comment on emblems in Paradise
Lost. However, he does refer to "emblazon'd Shields,
/ Impreses quaint," (IX. 34-5) when describing mediaeval pageantry and heraldic insignia on shields and
banners. Long before Paradise Lost Milton had
abandoned the idea of writing an Arthuriad; thus when
he mentions mediaeval heraldic pomp, he contemptuous-
ly adds he is not skilled to write a standard epic
based on the romance of the period; his mission is
to justify God to man and especially to post-lapsarian

man. Uriel's gliding through the atmosphere to warn
Gabriel of a malign, alien presence in Eden, strikes
Milton as the impress left in the sky from the light
of a shooting star (IV. 558). The prelapsarian fruit
in the Garden bear a golden impress, left on their
rind by the sun (IV. 150). The most glorious emblem
is seen in God's Son who carries on his face the impress of God's effulgent glory, while the angels sing
their songs of praise (III. 388). The Son alone can
be viewed by creatures who cannot face the unveiled
luminosity of God; God only reveals himself by his
impress on the Son. Nature being the reflection of
the macrocosmic God, also reveals itself in signs.
These signs, emblem-like, are impressed on its creatures and even on inanimate air: "Nature first gave
Signs, imprest / On Bird, Beast, Air," (XI. 182-3).
Milton is aware of signs, emblems and impresses that
reveal ultimate truths through their linear and symbolic forms. Interpreted, they are a storehouse of
verities. This belief of his era Milton reiterates
in his tractate Of Reformation. In it he affirms that
emblematic signs disturb some of his contemporaries:
"Let the Astrologer be dismay'd at the portentous
blaze of comets, and impressions in the aire as fore-
telling troubles and dangers to states;" but for Milton, different kinds of signs forebode doom, signs
such as the mass migration of Englishmen on account
of the country's intolerance and lack of sympathy for
their religious rights and liberties.[12] The exodus
was alarming for Milton, as it spelt the end of freedom of choice; a thing of greater import to man than
any "nova" or sign in the sky.

    Milton is also aware that poets enjoy an intel-
lectual license that allows their fancy to colour
their ideas. This license is more than evident in the
emblem writers. Milton resorts to it in using emblems
for didactic as well as aesthetic reasons. He states,
"Poets are wont to give a personal form to what they
please."[13] Paradise Lost revels in its emblems; each
beautiful and majestic, and each part of the tradition that took Europe and England by storm, for the
literary climate of the sixteenth and seventeenth centuries was receptive to the genre. Helen C. White
points out that emblematists provided patterns for
metaphysical conceits, and asserts the emblem was
"the major source of metaphysical poetry." Crashaw
leaned on the emblem tradition for both his secular
and religious verse, and according to Helen C. White,
followed the Ignatian technique of meditation. St.

6

Ignatius for his Spiritual Exercises suggested visual
aids: "'composition' for a visual meditation, that is,
an imaginative reconstruction in which the aspirant
to contemplation tries to bring before his eyes some
episode or scene in sacred history or the appropriate
physical setting for an illustration of some theme in
dogmatic theology . . . . Usually such a reconstruction is brief, precise, definite to bring the theme
of the meditation so vividly before the mind that the
thoughts will be elevated and concentrated."[14] Milton's satiric warning to the Parliament in the Areopagitica appears as a conceit, where he uses the word
"impression" with printing in mind. He warns the
Parliament to be wary of spilling the life-blood of
writers, for the destruction could "extend to the
whole impression, it would be a kind of massacre."[15]
His figurative and emblematic language has a distinct
motto that tampering with individual liberty can spell
destruction of potential and creativity. He uses
another emblem to emphasize it, "And thus ye have the
Inventors and the originall of Book-licensing ript
up, and drawn as lineally as any pedigree."[16] The
motto is implicit in the remark. Milton refers to emblems in the Areopagitica when calling attention to
frontispiece of books, some lewd and "dangerous" yet
impractical to be banned. J. Max Patrick in his note
on the subject quotes Phillips' dictionary, where
"Frontispieces" are "Emblems or Pictures set before
the Title of a Book to show the Design of it."[17]
However objectionable, no books or emblems, according
to Milton, can be censored. Man alone can censor his
choices through right training and self discipline.
The emblems provide the designs.

    Although in the "Seventh Prolusion" Milton boldly
stated that he had little use for metaphysical conceits, in studying his works it is evident that the
claim was the bravado of a youthful Cantabrigian.
Like the metaphysicals and the emblematists Milton
often juxtaposes unusual images, such as the oxymoronic "darkness visible" and "palpable obscure;" and
startles. The mystical flights of fancy and emotional
fervour that mark the work of Donne and Herbert are
not absent from Milton. Like his contemporary metaphysical poets Milton also follows the Ignatian technique of concentration on emblems in sacred books and
mystical icons. References to the numinous appear
in his invocations and dedications, in his hymn to
light, and the morning Litany of Adam and Eve. The
technique is also present in Eve's adulation of the

7

Tree of Knowledge, and Adam's acquiescence in God's
final judgment and edict. One of the finest examples
of this technique is in the opening invocation of the
Epic, where Milton, with the icon of God in mind, is a
suppliant for God's sapience and guidance:

> And chiefly Thou O Spirit, that
>   does prefer
> Before all Temples th' upright
>   heart and pure,
> Instruct me, . . .
>   What in me is dark
> Illumine, what is low raise and support;
> (I. 17-23)

In Emblems with Elegant Figures (1658) John Hall, addressing God, makes a similar plea for God's supporting
grace:

> Still may I rise, still further clime
>   Till that I lie
>
> Swath'd in Eternity.   18

The device shows Anima shooting her enkindled heart
with bow and arrow toward God's Spirit, seen descending in rays of light. Both Milton and Hall are seeking
God's supernal inspiration and grace.

Paradise Lost is a mine of emblems. The symbolic
and detailed word pictures that Milton has delineated
in the epic are all essential to his design and purpose. The poem shows a constant interplay between the
linear and graphic icons and the thoughts that Milton
expresses. Many of Milton's emblems lack, no doubt,
the mystical and contemplative quality of those of
Hawkins and Hall, and hardly conform to the epigrammatic style of Ayres, or to the trite and commonplace
renderings seen frequently in Whitney, Peacham,
Quarles, Wither and Ashrea, but what Milton does have
in common with the English emblem writers is an identical literary heritage, which enables him to create
his graphic pictures like them, and to symbolize his
ideas of a vast incomprehensible universe in direct
relation to deep religious and ethical convictions.
Like the emblem writers Milton exploits the Hebraic-
Christian Scriptures, classical mythology, legends,
mediaeval romance and allegory, the bestiaries, folk-
lore, fables, heraldic devices and insignia, contemporary cosmology, and the exciting new sciences, to

etch his emblems; and interweaves the emblems with erudite knowledge and peerless poetic genius. Milton's emblems have the Miltonic aura. He does not have woodcuts to adorn his devices, or mottoes to codify his ideas. He has no need of either, for "the poem can create and carry within itself its own visual referent."[19] Paradise Lost yields emblems that enthrall, as did the popular emblem books in the sixteenth and seventeenth centuries. With his emblems Milton embellishes and illuminates his ideas as he instructs. His "emblazon'd Shields, / Impreses quaint" (IX.34-6), are mentioned in a catalogue of other graphic pictures, but for Milton these images of the emblems conjure up thoughts profound and deep. To endite poems of abstract heroism, he claims, is his forte; the qualities of the true "heroic" left unsung by others--"the better fortitude / Of Patience and Heroic Martyrdom / Unsung," (IX.31-4). Though he dismisses the "emblazon'd Shields" and "impreses quaint," they become the graphic panoply and paraphernalia that direct the mind toward the inward grace embodied and embedded in Milton's "higher Argument" (IX. 42). This argues Whitney's point: "something obscure to be perceived at first, whereby, when with further consideration it is understood, it may the greater delight". Milton instructs and delights. He stresses the idea of the Renaissance Platonists that the visual is a means of comprehending invisible philosophic mysteries.

Seriously motivated artists like Milton may have questioned the decorum of emblem literature, yet the format of the emblems, with their drawings and mottoes attached to the verses, appealed to aesthetic sensibility and aroused intellectual curiosity. The unusual juxtaposition of icons in the devices and in the attached poems entertain and cunningly focus the issues. Many times the significance of an emblem, that is of both the picture (figura) and of the word (the vox and poema), is covert, as George Wither mentions in "A Preposition to this Frontis-piece":

> If any thinke this Page will, now, declare
> The meaning of those Figures, which are there,
> They are deceiv'd. . . .
>   tis ordain'd,
> That, none must know the Secrecies contain'd,
> Within this Piece; but, they who are so wise
> To finde them out, by their prudencies;
> And, hee that can unriddle them, to us
> Shall stiled be, the second Oedipus. 20

9

Milton's great allegory, Paradise Lost, deals with the
reader in a similar way. One has a feeling it asks
for a willing suspension of disbelief through the
great myth, and for the great Jungian desire to probe
each archetypal image to its very root, and uncover
the labyrinthian heights and depths of the master's
imagination and belief.

Several devotional vignettes of Paradise Lost
stem from mediaeval and monastic traditions and heritage. In their breviaries and Books of Hours, the
monastics concentrated on images and devices for contemplation and meditation. Some of the most pictorial
parts of the epic are orisons and glosses on psalms,
where Milton's spirit soars far above any "middle
flight." Many of the sixteenth and seventeenth-century
devotional emblems, though simple in form and structure,
were meant to serve deep and complex religious aspirations. Allegory, the mediaevalists' stock in trade,
was a powerful aid to the emblematists in elucidating
religious concepts and spiritual verities. It was
often used to give reality to "hell-fire" or heaven
and to make abstractions like sin and death concrete.
Milton was not averse to the use of allegory. His Sin
with her bestial tail and siren-lure, and his horrifying, crowned, amorphous Death, are not only legacies
of the mediaeval Morality tradition, but embody emblems that have their poetical and pictorial counterparts in the devices of the emblem writers. In devotional literature, the emphasis of both Milton and
the emblem writers is on moral and ethical values.
Their method of approach to truth and goodness is that
of the devotee. The picture and the poem become offerings to God or to the aesthetic principle.

Milton's appeal in his emblematic pictures is to
the sight and sense as well as to the intellect. His
description of Eve in her naked majesty, like Raphael's
Venus rising from the sea, shows the skill of a consummate artist depicting innocence in its glory. The
symbolic sensuousness of the picture is enhanced in
grandeur when Eve appears distraught and repentant
in later pictures. The comparison is implicit rather
than explicit, being visual and intellectual. Unconsciously Milton has created poetry in the mode of
the emblematists. "The poets' unrelenting efforts to
vie with painters in the sensuousness of their descriptions,"21 reveal their aesthetic as well as
ethical concerns; concerns which make emblematic

10

literature potent. Milton shows a preoccupation with
many of the concepts evident in the work of the emblem
writers. His Commonplace Book reveals that during the
five years at Horton, his concerns for study were religious, ethical, economic and political. In his
methodical and oratorical way he categorizes his study
under three heads: "ethical: moral evil, avarice, glut-
tony, suicide, the knowledge of literature, curiosity,
music, sloth, lying; economic: food, conduct, matrimony, the education of children, poverty, alms, usury;
and political: the state, kings (two pages), subjects,
nobility, property and taxes, athletic games, public
shows."[22] These very motifs appear in the emblem
books, and many of them are reiterated in one form or
another in Paradise Lost. The difference is that Milton achieves in words and rhythm and literary conceito,
what the emblem writers do in a comparatively simple
way, with linear pictures and mottoes and attached
verse; the last often of little poetic merit. Like
the emblematists Milton uses symbols and verbal in-
terpretations to convey complementary parts of unified
ideas. Similes, parallels in themes and correspondences are essential tools for Milton as for the emblem writers; and paradoxes help to intensify the
chiaroscuro nuances of their icons and their ideas.
Artists like Blake and Paul Doré caught some of the
emblems of Paradise Lost in their stylized etchings
and illustrations of the epic, though Milton's poetic
art had already sculpt the pictures as his language
laid bare their meaning.

"Emblem writing as conceived by Alciati and generally practised in the Renaissance was essentially
literary in character even though the illustrations
were theoretically important."[23] In England "their
very ingenuousness and their popularity proves how
deeply the emblematical way of thinking had penetrated
the consciousness of the country, and that good poets
used it as a means to an end rather than an end in
itself."[24] Milton, the greatest literary artist of
the century, emulates the genre's concise, cryptic,
codified form in his epic. The inordinate artistry
of his emblems and the elevated literary style in
which they are presented aid their religious and philosophical significance. Milton's sole mention of
"emblem" (IV.703) belongs in the utopian conception
of perfection, where each piece fits a perfect inlay.
It is only in God's prelapsarian Eden that there can
be such faultless workmanship. It can also be seen

in some of the pictures based on the Book of Revelation: the gem-encrusted portals and towers, and heaven's golden pavements.[25] These exquisite emblems are to please and to stress the absolute excellence of God's abode, for anything dissociated from God is either evil or marred. Hell and Tartarean fires, however majestic, are diabolic.

Milton's sketches often excel the work of limners and could illuminate "costliest emblems." The complexity of Milton's art is closely related to intricately wrought emblematic pictures that convey the baroque style of the period. Some of Milton's pictures are miniatures, others vast canvases, but all portray the ethos of the times. In giving the vignettes of the minims of nature, creatures "Perfect in lineaments and wings" (VII.477), Milton shows an exceptional power of observation and amazing recall. He gives intricate details of these "minims," their shapes and forms and habits; in doing so he enters the domain of the miniaturist. Milton, like Sir Thomas Browne, displays interest in natural objects; and like him is enthralled with the new science that was shaking beliefs and values. To him as to Browne "Nature was the Book of God where God's fingers had given his hieroglyphics to be read and digested and assimilated."[26] Raphael reiterates the idea when he states, "for Heav'n / Is as the Book of God before thee set, / Wherein to read his wond'rous Works," (VIII. 67). For Milton an ordered world, the work of a Master Architect, was theocentric, and in God's Book of Nature emblems abounded. The blind Milton recalled the emblems in his mind's eye and recorded them in verse. Milton, the classicist, is a true romantic in his fidelity to nature.

Roger Daniel, in dedicating Hall's _Emblems with Elegant Figures_ (1658) to Mrs. Dorothy Stanley and her husband, Thomas Stanley, avers that "...that the book is not an example of 'high Discourses of the best Philosophy (whether Ancient or Modern,) or choice pieces of Philologie,' but hopes it will grow venerable by the Dedication."[27] Milton writing his _Paradise Lost_ at this period was using "high discourses of best philosophy" and "choice pieces of philologie" to present his emblemata, but required no patron to make his work live. As Milton and his contemporaries were exposed to this calligraphic and symbolic mode of expression and were aware of the significance underlying it, they made their verbal pictures adhere to

12

Horace's adage ut pictura poesis. They believed that
the picture and the verse were integral and inseparable
entities of total expression, and each essential to
the comprehension of the other. Milton's poetical
philosophy in the epic cannot be separated from his
word pictures. There is a wedding of the arts. John
Quarles makes a similar comment in the preface to John
Hall's Emblems with Elegant Figures (1658): "Divine
love so enamored with humane Wit and Art, that by an
holy copulation they have both together brought forth
(without adultery,) that happie Child of such heavenly
beauty, that it wounds the Reader not as other poesies
with darts of wanton sensuality, but with the influence
of that Divine love wherewith it self is replenished."28

    Milton's pictures capture the concrete as well as
the abstract minutiae of ideas, in keeping with the
Ramist movement of the Renaissance. "At the heart of
the Ramist enterprise is the drive to tie down words
themselves . . . in simple geometrical patterns, . . .
where the nonspatial world of sound is reduced to the
sphere of a graph."29 Peter Ramus' thesis like the
emblematists' emphasised that mental processes can be
visualized spatially; an idea that appealed to poets
and literati, such as Herbert. Its popularity is evident in the graphic methodology of the emblem writers.
In Milton word pictures and often single words give
symbolic and significant images, as though to codify
the Ramist theory. Milton follows the Ramist and emblematic mode at times. He poses ideas like captions,
then pursues them in verse until the thought is entirely explored, and ends with an appropriate resolu-
tion or motto. He uses analogy to vitalize his
points of view and metaphysical juxtapositions to
catch the attention. If the emblem was considered
"metaphysical conceit in little,"30 Milton has exploited the idea in his verbal pictures. His God, for
example, is tantalizingly complex. He is heard but
not seen; his glory is refulgent, but he veils himself
in clouds. His Son, on the other hand, appears with
the compression of a mediaeval illumination and a
Mughal miniature. In exploring Paradise Lost for emblems, the words of St. Augustine act as a directive:
"Wherever you turn wisdom speaks to you through the
imprint it has stamped upon its works."31 John Hall
borrowed copiously from the Augustinian emblem books;
Milton may have been aware of them, for he was conscious of the emblematic nature of wisdom.

    Whitney's work leaned on Alciati's and was in

direct tradition of Ovid and Pliny and Aesop's fables,[32]
yet showed originality; his religious imagery was distinctly Christian. In the third plate of A Choice of
Emblemes he shows a wayfarer uncertain of his direction,
turning to Hermes, who, caduceus in hand, points him
to the right path; while a third figure in the background beckons the pilgrim alluringly. The verse to
the emblem ends with the precept, "Then happie those,
whom God doth shew the waye." This is the central
theme of Paradise Lost. The virtues of moderation and
knowledge, which Henry Peacham (taking his ideas from
Cesare Ripa's Iconologia) celebrates in Minerva Britanna, correspond to the heroic virtues of Milton's
Adam. Adam's moderation and quest for knowledge, are
part of man's prelapsarian rationality and postlapsar-
ian goal. Crowned with hope, these virtues were dear
to Renaissance man. Ripa's icon of Hercules slaying
the dragon coiled round an apple tree, is a symbol of
hope. In coming to terms with himself while learning
the natural law of obedience, is symbolic of Adam's
conquest over the demonic; and it spells hope for mankind. Mythology, both Christian and pagan, provides
symbols for Milton and the emblem writers.

Milton's sophistication did not allow him to use
poetic formats to resemble or convey his subject pictorially. He could not resort to structures like Herbert's "Easter wings" and "The Altar," "The Church
Floor" and "Church Monuments;" neither could he use
hieroglyphics as visual symbols of devotion; nor like
Quarles could he use the terminology "hieroglyphics"
in his tirade against women or pun on woman's function
as a rib, Adam's rib, although Milton does condemn
Eve as "a Rib / Crooked by nature," a sign "sinister"
and as "supernumerary" (X. 884-7). Milton's words
though sardonic, unlike Quarles, have a ring of greatness, for his emblems were embossed for posterity to
"admire/That riches can grow" (I. 690) on earth.

In Paradise Lost Milton used the art of the emblem
to portray both reality and fantasy, to give the
baroque sensibility in perspective and as flat art,
to cover the cosmos in linear heights and to plunge
to the depths of the diabolic, to make philosophical
abstractions concrete and psychological man a self-
conqueror, and above all to justify his God to man.

Correlation of Milton's pictures with the existing
emblems is interesting. The emblematists often use
conceits in the metaphysical tradition; in Milton,

14

conceits become symbols of the highest verity. These
symbols can be categorized as concepts in the sub-
strata of man's consciousness, and figurative illustrations of external things. They are designed to convey man's deepest feelings. "The extent to which the
imagery of seventeenth-century poets is visual and
clearly outlined yet at the same time rich with meaning
is proof of the fruitful way in which it penetrated
contemporary habits of thought."[33] In Milton it is
seen as in the techniques of both the early and later
emblem writers. He is objective as well as psychological. He uses traditional symbols and draws on history,
legends and fables, but invents his own images and
develops concepts that transcend the emblems. Taking
as a point of departure Rosemary Freeman's premise
that "it is the narration type which is commonly as-
sumed to constitute the true emblem,"[34] it can be argues that Paradise Lost is an extended series of emblems embodying some of the greatest poetic achievements of the world.

15

FOOTNOTES

[1] Rosemary Freeman, English Emblem Books (New York: Octagon Books, 1970), p. 39.

[2] All references to Paradise Lost are from Merritt Y. Hughes, ed., John Milton: Complete Poems and Major Prose (New York: Odyssey Press, 1957).

[3] Freeman, p. 47.

[4] Freeman, pp. 45, 47, 63, & 116. See also catalogue listing Scolar Press Publications (Yorkshire & London: Scolar Press, 1972), pp. 215-216.

[5] Geoffrey Whitney, A Choice of Emblems 1586, ed. John Horden (facsimile rpt. Menston: Scolar Press, 1973), sig. **4 (n. 5, p. 16).

[6] Harold Osborne, ed. The Oxford Companion to Art (Oxford: Clarendon Press, 1970), p. 369.

[7] Webster's Third New International Dictionary, ed. P. B. Gove (Springfield, Mass.: G. & C. Merriam Co., 1968).

[8] Freeman, p. 48.

[9] Sir Thomas Browne, Religio Medici 1635, Vol. I, ed. G. Keynes, p. 75.

[10] Hughes, ed., p. 631.

[11] Hughes, ed., pp. 784, 815.

[12] The Prose of John Milton, ed. J. M. Patrick (New York: Doubleday, 1967), p. 73.

[13] J. Max Patrick, ed., p. 73.

[14] Helen C. White, The Metaphysical Poets: A Study in Religious Experience (New York and London: Collier-MacMillan, 1962, Sec. ed. 1966), p. 23.

[15] J. Max Patrick, ed. p. 272.

[16] J. Max Patrick, ed., p. 281.

[17] J. Max Patrick, ed., n. p. 294.

16

[18] John Hall, Emblems with Elegant Figures 1658, ed. John Horden (Facsimile. Menston, Yorkshire: Scolar Press, 1970), p. 54.

[19] John Bender, Spenser and Literary Pictorialism (Princeton: Princeton University Press, 1972), p. 152.

[20] George Wither, A Collection of Emblemes, 1635, ed. John Horden (Menston: Scolar Press, 1968), Frontispiece.

[21] Mario Praz, Mnemosyne: the Parallel Between Literature and the Visual Arts (Princeton: Princeton University Press, 1970), p. 6.

[22] William Riley Parker, Milton A Biography (Oxford: Clarendon Press, 1969), p. 146.

[23] Bender, p. 151.

[24] Freeman, pp. viii-ix.

[25] The Revelation of St. John The Divine, Chapter 4, 6, 12, 14, 20, 21.

[26] Freeman, p. 41.

[27] Hall, sig. *2ᵛ (n. 27, p. 17).

[28] Hall, sig. *3ᵛ (n. 28, p. 20).

[29] Forrest G. Robinson, The Shape of Things Known (Cambridge, Mass.: Harvard University Press, 1972), p. 92.

[30] Freeman, n. p. 7.

[31] Earl Miner, Seventeenth Century Imagery (Los Angeles: University of California Press, 1971), pp. 19-20.

[32] Freeman, p. 56.

[33] Freeman, p. 31.

[34] Freeman, p. 34.

17

CHAPTER TWO

MILTON'S LITERARY PICTORIALISM

Written texts have often provided material for artists working on large canvases or walls, in stone or glass; also for those working on miniatures and icons. Artists have translated the words into figures and images, landscapes and attitudes; and have given mobility or statuesque poses to ideas, depending on the artists' understanding of the words, and the social, religious and political milieu in which they work.

The pictorial quality of Milton's work has fired the imagination of artists from its early publication down to the present. According to their fancy they have used elements of the text to express their own interpretation of Milton's verbal pictures. Some have adhered closely to the details of the text, others have used sweeping brush strokes to convey the general idea. Paradise Lost has excited the ingenuity of many an artist, starting with Aldrich and Medina.

Like the emblem writers, the publisher Jacob Tonson knew the fascination of visual interpretation of verbal images. He had the 1688 edition of Paradise Lost illustrated by John Baptista Medina, a Spaniard, born and trained in Brussels and migrant to Scotland and England. Medina's engraver, M. Burghers, captured the beauty of Medina's icons. Medina was a sensitive and well-received artist in the Restoration Period. Among his works were several illustrated volumes; such as the 1701 Oxford Bible, Ovid's Metamorphoses, and probably Tonson's 1713 publication of Paradise Regained. Tonson also had Milton's Works (1720), illustrated, the artist being Louis Cheron, another refugee to England. Cheron's work was elaborate compared to Medina's but lacked Medina's delicate sensitivity and symbolic interpretation. Medina belongs with the illustrators who were faithful to details in Milton's pictures, and tried to delineate the nuances of feelings as of the turns of speech. Medina's pictures of Paradise Lost strike one as intellectual and emotional, cognizant of activity and of pause. In her book, Milton and English Art, Marcia Pointon reminds the reader that the word "illustration" in the seventeeth century meant enlightenment or explanation. Medina takes his work in that light and explains Milton's words and ideas in pictures.

18 a

"The wealth of closely observed and faithfully translated detail in Medina's illustration . . . [show that he was] more familiar with all the intricate detail of Paradise Lost than any other artist . . . His designs as a consequence are a great deal more interesting and vigorous than those of many later artists."[1] Medina lived in the same era as the emblem writers and knew the power and popularity of eye-catching illustrations. Many of his illustrations, like those of the emblematists, are composites of different scenes and episodes and levels of meaning, and appear like dramatically moving pictures frozen in a medallion. His "Satan in the Garden" is one such picture. A satyric Satan and coiled snake dominate the fore-ground of the picture[2] while the temptation scene is shown in five separate vignettes of Adam and Eve in the immediate and distant background of the engraving. The wrath of God figures in a central dark cloud highlighted by a chiaroscuro of clouds and a streak of lightning. The beauty of Medina's illustrations is reminiscent of Georgette de Montenay's device in Emblemes ou Devises Chrestiennes (1571). The juxtaposition of the coiled serpent and the armed figure of death[3] could have suggested the placement of the snake and Satan in Medina's picture. The landscape of both suggest a garden. J. B. Medina's "Adam's Story" is close enough to Montenay's Adam pensoit estre fort bien caché, (Montenay, p. 65). Medina's "Satan Rising from the Flood," is similar to Montenay's Satan a fait & fait tous ses efforts (Montenay, p. 72). Both have caught the spirit of the scriptural text. Medina's icons savour of the baroque and exotic in Milton's art, and come nearest to the pictorial ideas expressed by the emblematists in their devices.

Medina and the emblem writers were as much the progeny of the Renaissance as the literary figures of the period. There is a fusion of mediaeval and classical spirit in their work. Their devices show stock symbols of the mediaeval allegorist and a deep preoccupation with the classical mode. The emblem writers mirror concepts present in Renaissance thought and in Paradise Lost, both in their icons and verses. Their devices carry symbols superimposed, to impress a moral or a philosophical idea. In Paradise Lost Milton often piles on images to drive a point home. His compounded pictures show the traditions of the milieu in which the emblematists existed. In the way Medina brings Milton's verbal pictures to life on

the canvas "The English [Emblem] Books ... touch and illuminate great literature at several points. . . . Emblems were adopted by contemporary poets and dramatists
to serve ends more complex than their own."[4]

Milton's pictures have perennial appeal. In his
poem to Manso Milton hopes he will be celebrated in
marble, crowned with myrtle, and with the immortals
"congratulate himself on ethereal Olympus."[5] Milton
courted both Urania and Clio (seen etched in Marshall's
terrible engraving of the poet, and where he damned
Marshal forever by the Greek lines he made the calligra-
pher write below the portrait). We approach Milton's
icons with his love of beauty and his immortality in
mind.

i. EMBLEMS OF THE CREATOR AND THE ANGELIC WORLD

Milton's universe is theocentric. God is the
focal point of all action: heavenly, earthly, and
even of chaos and hell. He belongs with the supernatural, and his being encompasses the universe.
Milton's heavenly messenger avers in Platonic terms:

> one Almighty is, from whom
> All things proceeds, and up to him return,
> If not deprav'd.
> (V. 469-71)

But Milton's epic deals with the supernatural in human
terms, as though man were creating God, his Son, the
angels and devils in his own image. The characteristics man gives these numinous beings are related to his
own successes and aspirations, failures and defeats.
In God and His Son he sees an ideal, utopian state of
being; in the Devil, the depths to which man can sink.
The psychological polarity makes of man a human tennis
ball, torn between divinity and devilry. Peacham's
emblem, Sic nos Dij aptly depicts man as a ball, bounc-
ing between the celestial hand of God and a marked
terrestrial court:

> The Tennis-ball, when strucken to the
> ground,
>
> With greater force, doth back again rebound,
> His Fate, (though senceles) seeming to
> withstand:

> Yea, at the instant of his torced fall,
> With might redoubled, mounts the highest
>   of all.[6]

Milton, zealously enamored of God, ascends more easily
to his rarified presence; like his angels his "proper
motion" is ascent and his muse soars. But like many
of his predecessor vates, he also journeys to Tartarus. Leland Ryken in The Apocalyptic Vision in Paradise Lost highlights the epic's concern with the unknown and the mysterious, and its pre-historic and
mythic setting. Milton's world, though given in
material terms, is a world of the mind and the spirit.
His faith makes him move between heaven and earth,
not as a pawn or a ball, the plaything of supernatural
creatures, but an observer and visionary to whom the
universe is instinct with unfathomable energy which
is his God; and God is the centre of the epic: "God
in Heav'n / Is Centre, yet extends to all" (IX. 107-8).

        In the Christian Doctrine Milton explains that
God reveals himself only through objects and ideas
that man can comprehend. Man knowing man thus thinks
of God in anthropomorphic terms. To Milton God is
what "The Book of God," the Scriptures, reveal; not
man's thought alone nor the signs or symbols of God
in the "Book of God's Works," nature and the universe.
If man is told to measure heaven by things known:
"measuring things in Heav'n by things on Earth . . .
What might have else to human Race been hid" (VI. 893-
6), he is also given futuristic visions gleaned from
Scriptural events. Michael in the last two books of
the epic makes Adam aware of the extent of God's
mercy, a, trait that supersedes justice, by quoting
incidents from the Bible or showing Adam animate pictures of the incidents. Adam experiences both God's
mercy and justice in full measure at the time of expulsion from Eden.

        In the introduction to Milton's Epic Characters,
John M. Steadman points out that one level of Paradise
Lost is concerned with myth and symbol,[7] a mode current
in the seventeenth century and well illustrated by
the emblematists. The emblematic character of many
verbal pictures in Paradise Lost follows mythical and
symbolic patterns and metaphorically stresses some of
the truths, beliefs and thoughts of the period. Some
of these ideas are obscure to a twentieth-century student, his values being different from Milton's and
Milton's contemporaries. To the twentieth century the

21

denizens of Milton's epic may have little reality, yet
scholars down the ages have found Paradise Lost pulsating
with life. It has titillated the mind since the
seventeenth century, and contemporary scholarship
is just as involved in exploring Milton's thoughts
and beliefs. Many of his ideas, values and figures
are universal and timeless, and have perennial appeal.
One of these is God. The Christian Doctrine, redis-
covered in 1806, establishes the fact of Milton's belief in the supremacy of God, in essence Milton's unitarianism. Like Arian, Milton could not rationally
subscribe to any co-eval with God, not even his Son,
though endowed with all of God's powers. The Son is
posterior to God in time, and requires God's delega-
tion of his authority to be adjudged co-eternal. He
is next to the Father in the great chain of being, for
hierarchy does not admit of any but God, the Father,
at the head. Prior to the fall, the personae of Paradise Lost are preternatural, yet Milton's God displays
more human and humanc characteristics than his awesome
counterpart in Genesis. Though supreme, the God of
Paradise Lost is the prototype of Renaissance man. He
displays the liberality of an intellectual and the
savoir faire of a man of many parts. He does not
force his will on his creatures because he believes in
the sanctity of reason. If he insists on retribution,
it is to espouse justice, yet a justice tempered with
mercy, a concept also seen in emblematist, Quarles'
depiction of God: "I know thy justice is Thyself,
I know, / Just God, thy very self is mcicy too."[8]
Milton's God, "First, Highest, Holiest, Best," (VI.
724), is an absolute monarch, but benevolent. In
himself he has the magnanimity and humility of the
great. He makes no flamboyant speeches like Satan,
nor has he anything specious or vainglorious about
him. He is not the tyrant or adversary Satan and his
cellmates proclaim him in Books I and II of Paradise
Lost. He is omniscient and knows that both good and
evil exist and understands man's frailty. He sends
his angels to fore-warn man, and prepare him to ward
off evil if he so desires. He knows it is not desire, but the choice that is man's.

> Evil into the mind of God or Man
> May come and go, so unapprov'd, and leave
> No spot or blame behind:
>   (V. 117-19)

In the Christian Doctrine Milton tried to clarify his

own stand in connection with seventeenth-century dog-
mas and theology. Many of the positions of the Christian Doctrine are re-emphasized in Paradise Lost with
ornamentation and pictorial conceits. The comprehension of God was a necessity for the seventeeth-century;
a means of salvation was to revaluate God's relationship with man. This could be achieved, within human
limitations, by understanding the nature of God in
juxtaposition with the entirety of life. Like the emblematists Milton knew that comprehension is based on
the mental eye's intake of objects seen, heard, or
felt. The process was an ascent from sense to the intellect. John Hall voices it when trying to delineate God, "Who with a rude yet heedy eye / His maker
finds in every flie," (Hall, p. 30). Man's sense perception was used to formulate pictures, and often the
pictures became composites of many emotions, and the
ideas in them many-faceted. This was the pith of the
baroque in art and the ornamentation in many emblems.
Milton's God is seen in many baroque images, for in
himself he encompasses all the sensibilities.

     Milton's God is himself an emblematist. Milton
says of God, "the Deity has imprinted upon the human
mind so many unquestionable tokens of himself, and so
many traces of him are apparent throughout the whole
of nature, that no one in his senses can remain ignor-
ant of the truth."[9] Milton's belief in God is commensurate with his belief in the palpable and the pictorial; though he accedes that the method is only an
aid to man's partial comprehension of God. In the
Christian Doctrine Milton makes it clear that God has
revealed much of himself in the Scriptures, and conveys it in the language of art, "Our safest way is to
form in our minds such conception of God, as shall
correspond with his own delineation and representation
of himself in the sacred writings. For granting that
both in the literal and figurative descriptions of
God, he is exhibited not as he really is, but in such
a manner as may be within the scope of our own comprehension."[10] Thus the capacity to know God depends
on man's rational interpretation of God's word and
his works. Milton and the emblematists lean heavily
on both.

     The images of Paradise Lost, though part of Mil-
ton's ornate and sophisticated work, are basically
simple. The God of his great works, mentally formulated during 1656-1660, the years of compilation of
the Christian Doctrine, is the essence of simplicity

and frankness and is as forcefully convincing as the
aphoristic and terse emblems. If God is the head of
the ordered universe, he is also a concerned individual, all-knowing yet not interfering in the choices
of his creatures. He is ever conscious that he has
endowed his angels and man with reason. Milton's God
is recreated in pictorial verse. He is a reality imprinted in nature and terrestrial forms, for "There
can be no doubt but that everything in the world . . .
testifies that some supreme efficient Power must have
pre-existed, by which the whole universe was ordained
for a specific end."11 God then is symbolically imprinted in all his works; and in those of artists
like Milton and the emblem writers.

        One of the factors Milton reaffirms in Paradise
Lost is God's eternity. He often uses the adjective
"eternal" as a prefix for attributes of God. He refers to God as "Eternal Providence" (I. 25), "Eternal
eye" (V. 711), "Eternal King Omnipotent" (VI. 227),
"eternal might" (VI. 630), to affirm God's continuity.
Along with the idea of eternity Milton emphasizes
the luminosity of God, and shows it in a striking emblematic picture:

             Hail holy Light, offspring of Heav'n
               first-born,
             Or of th' Eternal Coeternal beam
             May I express thee unblam'd? Since God
               is light,
             And never but in unapproached Light
             Dwelt from Eternity, dwelt thee in
             Bright effluence of bright essence
               increate.
                                 (III. 1-6).

This imprint not only expresses the luminosity surrounding the invisible Deity, but also adds the epigrammatic and theological concept that light, an
attribute of God and an essence which encompasses the
Deity, is the very substance of God. Light and God
are then uncreated, eternal, synonymous. The abstract
and incomprehensible God becomes concrete and realistic with the actuality of light.

        Milton's emblem of light has the "painterly"
instead of "linear" quality of an emblem. The limits
of light are indistinguishable. Physically it sur-
rounds the Deity and can also shine inwards (III. 51).

The imagery is diffuse and creates an illusion of movement in its formlessness. Yet God's light is in focus
at the center of all being and of life itself. The
illusory quality of light is due to God's inaccessibility, but the warmth and power and energy of light
are real and sensate. The imagery stems from the
deep-rooted and often mythical idea of God symbolized
by the sun as the source of all beauty and goodness
and creative energy.

Popular emblems that deal with the concept of God
may not have crossed Milton's mind, yet the traditions
motivating Milton's great works and those of the emblem writers are related and often similar. God's
luminosity and eternity are two concepts loved by
Elizabethans and Milton's contemporaries.

Discussing eternity and light, the essence of
God, Quarles shows the contemplative Anima, against a
backdrop of stars. She is standing on barren, rocky
ground with an anchor resting against her. In the
verses Quarles questions ultimate goodness and its
eternal availability to man. If goodness or God is
eternal, goodness should "neither expire / Nor change;
than which there can be anything high'r: / Such good
must be the utter point of man's desire," and reiterates the thought in a rhetorical question:

> It is the mark, to which all hearts
>   must tend;
> Can be desired for no other end,
> Than for itself, on which all other
>   goods depend.
> What may this excellence be? doth it
>   subsist
> A real essence clouded in the mist
> Of curious art, or clear to ev'ry eye
>   that list?

In the last verse of the emblem Quarles recognizes the
constancy of God; and like Adam reaffirms his trust in
God. As God's goodness and eternity are synonymous,
man can safely rely on God's presence:

> Lord if my hope dare let her anchor fall
> On thee, the chiefest good, no need to call
> For earth's inferior trash; then, thou art
>   in all.

(Quarles, <u>Emblems</u>, p. 327).

And John Hall exhorts man to hold firm to the anchor
or rock, the symbol of eternity:

> Nay grasp whole heaven, though it be
> Without all measure and all end;
> For in her strength and power be
> The greatest things to comprehend.

(Hall, Emblems 1658, p. 86)

Metaphorically, the emotional and ethical compo-
nents of light, beauty and truth, knowledge and inspiration, become the emanations of the eternal God, the
"Fountain of Light" (III. 375). This eternal light is
the progenitor of all that is good; even the good
angels are the "Progenie of Light" (V. 600), and the
brilliance of the heavenly bodies is God's gift to the
celestial globes of his own essence, which permeates
all that is sublime:

> Of Light by far the greater part he took,
> Transplanted from his cloudy Shrine, and
>   plac'd
> In the Sun's Orb, made porous to receive
> And drink the liquid Light,

(VII. 359-62)

Divine Light then becomes essential in God's cosmic
scheme and eternal purpose.

The concept of God as an eternal entity of light
is illustrated by Quarles in several emblems. He,
like Milton, uses the imagery of light to convey his
thoughts on God's refulgence and its ennobling grace:

> Great God, that art the flowing spring
>   of light
> Enrich mine eyes with thy refulgent rays;
> Thou art my path; direct my steps aright;
> I have no other light, no other way:
> I'll trust my God, and him alone pursue;
> His law shall be my path; his heavenly
>   light, my clue.

(Quarles, Emblems, p. 305)

And in verse four of the following emblem, Quarles
comments on the eternal character of God. God in it

26

is the "living fountain of eternal pleasure" and is
the "everlasting treasure" (Quarles, Emblems, p. 306).
The examples serve to illustrate the two themes and
images common to the period.

John Hall in the Praeludium to Emblems with Elegant Figures 1658 (sig. A) invokes God's help to be illuminated: "so shall I find / A greater light possess
my mind." Like Milton, Hall wishes his poetic soul
to be ennobled and uplifted. Milton says, "What in
me is dark / Illumine, what is low raise and support,"
(I. 22-3); and Hall, "Mount up low thoughts and see what
sweet / Reposure Heaven can beget." After Milton has
"drawn Empyreal Air," he requests the heavenly Urania:

> Return me to my Native Element:
> Lest from this flying Steed unrein'd,
> (as once Bellerophon, though from
> a lower Clime)
> Dismounted, on th' Aleian Field I fall
> Erroneous there to wander and forlorn.

(VII. 14-20)

Hall likewise realizes that he cannot maintain that
zenith of mental and spiritual flight for long. His
spirit returns from the exposure to divine light, but
having tasted the essence of God in his light, re-
gretfully says, "Now I'm on Earth again, nor dight /
As formerly in Springing light." But this contact
with the sublime inspires their works and make them
works of contemporary art. Hall shows the power of
this divine light in Emblem 4, Verse I (page 13).
The device has a central ray of light, like a two-
edged sword, poised above a sick, recumbent figure.
An angel tries to revive the figure, while love as
blind cupid hovers near with his bow. In the rear
are the ramparts of a castle and a temple. Earthy
man realizing that without God's light he and all
creation can petrify, invokes God's providence in his
warmth-giving light:

> But since thou let'st thy rays run free,
> And spirit gives
> To all that lives
> Each severall thing continues, but by thee.

(Hall, Emblems 1658, p. 13)

27

And in Emblem 7 (page 25) he emphasizes the energy
and beauty-giving quality of God's light, "Such as
that glorious Prince of light / Whose smiles inamell
every flower." But Hall, like Milton, professes that
God does not reveal his full effulgence; if he did,
like Zeus' Semele, man would be consumed by its glory.
Man can experience partial glory alone: "Since what
we know is but a gleam, / That ow's its lustre to a
beam / Which from that inf'nite spring of light doth
stream" (Hall, p. 30). Hall depicts a related thought
in Emblem 9, where the device shows heavenly rays ig-
niting a winged, human heart. The heart, once lit,
leaves the mundane landscape and mounts upward. Anima
watches its progress:

> Feathered by active fire
> Whereby it mount's and towers up higher
> Then its own grovoling thoughts could reach
> Before that thou didst teach . . .
> . . . I lay
> Without a ray
> Till thou, (great world of light!) broke
> out and then
> My chains did fall.

God's light thus has an emancipating as well as thawing
grace. In Emblem 10 (pages 38-39) Hall proclaims God's
inaccessibility: "Thou center of all light! whom none /
Can look upon: . . . / For Thou art Glory inaccessible."
This argument brings forward the question of God's
inaccessibility. In Paradise Lost God walks and talks
in the Garden of Eden with His Creatures, yet man refers to Him as "Glory inaccessible." In Milton God's
skirts are the nearest view man gets of him. He is a
transcendent God. If He is accessible and visible it
is through his Son and the angels:

> Unspeakable, who sit'st above these
>   Heavens
> To us invisible or dimly seen
> In these thy lowest works, yet these
>   declare
> Thy goodness beyond thought, and Power
>   Divine:
> Speak yee who best can tell, ye Sons
>   of Light,
> Angels, for yee behold him,

(V. 156-61)

Yet the angels also call God "inaccessible" and "invisible" (III. 376 & 375). There is anomaly in God's visible presence in the seventeenth century. The general consensus seems to be that God cannot be seen except in His Son, who is Himself "The radiant image of his Glory" (III. 63).

Imagery in literature often reveals a specific period and culture. Milton's God belongs to Renaissance culture, for his God is symbolic of the values of the period. Experiencing these values can give the same tactile feeling as touching paint and brush and canvas, or tools and marble. There is a three-dimensional quality about the experiences mentioned. The written imagery combines spiritual values and sensuous experience, and conveys a reality in which the spiritual and the physical fuse. The icons of God that appear in Paradise Lost and the emblematists are not aesthetic in the terminology of plastic art, but they are synonymous with beauty of mystery and the "figura." They reflect the images and forms and ideas found in biblical and religious literature, except that in Milton the literary icons and the typological figura take on aesthetic and decorative dimensions. In Milton and his contemporary emblematists, the God of the Old Testament and New Testament is juxtaposed; and many of the pictures of God are composites. If God is martial and demanding, He is also just and compassionate; if transcendent, also immanent.

In the Christian Doctrine Milton classified "the efficiency of God as either internal or external. The internal efficiency of God being . . . independent of all extraneous agency. Such as his decrees." Milton divides the decrees into "general and special," and qualifies the two saying,"General is His own most free and wise and holy purpose" (Hughes p. 911). Among God's general decrees comes the act of creation. God's decree, as Milton states, is the Will of God. The idea of the Will or Decree being one is well illustrated in some emblems of the epic. An emblematic picture of God is conveyed by Belial in his speech in Paradise Lost:

> he, from Heav'n's highth
> All these our motions vain, sees and derides;
> Not more Almighty to resist our might
> Than wise to frustrate all our plots and
> wiles.

29

Shall we then live thus vile, the race of
    Heav'n
Thus trampl'd, thus expell'd to suffer here
Chains and these Torments? better these
    than worse
By my advice; since fate inevitable
Subdues us, and Omnipotent Decree,
The Victor's will.

(II. 190-98)

This emblematic picture corresponds with the qualms
Belial has regarding any wiles they may use to plot
against God, for God's decree is absolute, and his
vigilance constant.

Another example of a theological concept made
into a visual image is the Archangel Uriel who is one
of God's cognisant eyes, constant in surveillance:

Th' Arch-Angel Uriel, one of the sev'n
Who in God's presence, neerest to his Throne
Stand ready at command, and are his Eyes
That run through all the Heav'ns, or down
    to th' Earth
Bear his swift errands over moist and dry,
O'er Sea and Land.

(III. 648-53)

Peacham iterates the same idea regarding traitorous
thoughts. They cannot withstand the searching glory
and will of the all seeing sun; God and the Sun being
one. His device shows the prominent eyes of the full
blazing Sun as they outshine and quench the glowing
embers in a brazier beneath. The verse reads:

The fiery Coales, that in the silent night,

With glowing heate, about did give their...light,
Since glorious Phoebus hath discovered
...
              doe fall to cinders quite.

So traiterous projectes, while they lie
    obscure,
They closely feede the plotter, with their
    light,
Who thinkes within, he hath the matter sure,

30

Not dreaming how, the Truth that shineth
    bright;
Will soone reveale the secrets of his thought;

(Peacham, p. 29)

    The seventeenth century believed in the Decalogue
as the rigid decree of God, and though not related to
God's decree in Paradise Lost, we see its absolutism
in Wither. Illustrating God's decrees, the tablets
of the Ten Commandments appear behind a naked sword
held threateningly in a fist projecting from a cloud,
while bursts of bright lightning illuminate the tablets. Wither significantly writes:

    When God-Almighty first engrav'd in stone
    His holy Law; He did not give the same
    As if some common Act had then beene done;
    For, arm'd with Fires and Thunders, forth it
        came.
    By which, that great Law-maker, might inferre
    What dreadfull Vengeance would on those
        attend,
    Who did against those holy Precepts erre;
    And, that, his Power well-doers could defend.
    Thereto, this Emblem, also doth agree;

(George Wither, A Collec-
tion of Emblems 1635,
p. 3.)

    God's decree or will, is absolute and encompasses
"his eternal counsel and foreknowledge . . . which is
the wisdom of God" (Christian Doctrine, ed. Hughes,
p. 911), but it is not inflicted on his rational creation. It is a matter of choice for man and the angels.
The idea is reiterated when God, speaking to His Son
explicitly explains that His decrees and foreknowledge
of events have nothing to do with man or the angels'
power of reasoning and their will to act in accord
with God's will or against it:

    As if Predestination over-rul'd
    Thir will, dispos'd by absolute Decree
    Or high foreknowledge; they themselves
        decreed
    Thir own revolt, not I: if I foreknew
    Foreknowledge had no influence on their
        fault,

31

Which had no less prov'd certain unforeknown.
So without least impulse or shadow of Fate,
Or aught by me immutably foreseen,
They trespass, Authors to themselves in all
Both what they judge and what they choose;
    for so
I form'd them free, and free they must remain,
Till they enthrall themselves: I else must
    change
Thir nature, and revoke the high Decree
Unchangeable, eternal, which ordain'd,
Thir freedom: they themselves ordain'd
    thir fall.

(III. 114-28)

God's decree is irrevocable and shows God's rigid
absolutism. This is evident when the wisdom and will
of God are one. A good example of it is at the in-
stallation of the Son as Head of all creation and Right
Hand of God, in a dramatically emblematic and heraldic
picture replete with mediaeval pageantry:

            th' Empyreal Host
Of Angels by Imperial summons call'd,
Innumerable before th' Almighty's Throne
Forthwith from all the ends of Heav'n
    appear'd
Under thir Hierarcho in orders bright;
Ten thousand thousand Ensigns high advanc'd,
Standards and Gonfalons, twixt Van and Rear
Stream in the Air, and for distinction serve
Of Hierarchies, of Orders, and Degrees;
Or in thir glittering Tissues bear imblaz'd
Holy Memorials, acts of Zeal and Love
Recorded eminent. Thus when in Orbs
Of circuit inexpressible they stood,
Orb within Orb, the Father infinite,
By whom in bliss imbosom'd sat the Son
Amidst as from a flaming Mount, whose top
Brightness had made invisible, thus spake.
Hear all ye Angels, Progeny of Light,
Thrones, Dominations, Princedoms, Virtues,
    Powers,
Hear my Decree, which unrevok't shall stand.
This day I have begot whom I declare
My only Son, and on this holy Hill
Him have anointed, whom ye now behold
At my right hand; your Head I him appoint;
And by my Self have sworn to him shall bow

32

All knees in Heav'n, and shall confess him
    Lord:. . . him who disobeys
    Mee disobeys, breaks union, and that day
    Cast out from God and blessed vision, falls
    Into utter darkness, deep ingulft, his place
    Ordain'd without redemption, without end.

                    (V. 583-615)

This pronouncement before an assembly is the statement
of an absolute monarch. The decree is arbitrary, a
decree which is bound to provoke a revolt. Among
Satan's angels, only one bold angel, Abdiel, calls
the edict a just decree (V. 814). Being omniscient,
God is conscious of the effect of this order, and Milton equating his omniscience with the all-seeing, constant and vigilant eye, gives another verbal picture.
The picture has its counterpart in many of the emblem
books:

        Meanwhile th' Eternal eye, whose sight
            discerns
        Abstrusest thoughts, from forth his holy
            Mount
        And from within the golden Lamps that burn
        Nightly before him, saw without thir light
        Rebellion rising, saw in whom, how spread
        Among the sons of Morn, what multitudes
        Were banded to oppose his high Decree;

                    (V. 711-17)

    In Paradise Lost God occupies a certain geographic
space yet is omnipresent. In the Christian Doctrine
Milton argues that "Creation is either of things invisible or visible. The things invisible, or which
are at least such to us, are, the highest heaven, which
is the throne or habitation of God, and the heavenly
powers, or angels. ... The first place is due to things
invisible, if not in respect of origin, at least of
dignity. For the highest heaven is as it were the
supreme citadel and habitation of God. . . . Out of
this light it appears that pleasures and glories, and
a kind of perpetual heaven, have emanated and subsist.
[It is here that] God permits himself to be seen by the
angels and saints (as far as they are capable of en-
during his glory)."[12] God in His omniscience and
omnipotence wields his authority and conducts his
"works." The Christian Doctrine emphasizes the fact

                    33

that God is the governor of the entire universe and
that he preserves order in line with his decree and
with "infinite wisdom and holiness."[13]

Aptekar points out that in mediaeval iconology
some of the popular and very ornate and stock icons
are those of God's throne,[14] and the pictures convey
monarchical courts. God's throne is invisible to
mortals, but in Paradise Lost partially visible to
pre-lapsarian man:

> Unspeakable, who sit'st above these Heavens
> To us invisible or dimly seen

> (V. 156-7)

> Angels, . .

> Circle his Throne rejoicing,

> (V. 161-3)

This throne of God, though immaterial, appears in a
magnificent and fascinating emblem:

> Now had th' Almighty Father from above,
> From the pure Empyrean where he sits
> High Thron'd above all highth bent down
>   his eye,
> His own works and their works at once to
>   view:
> About him all the Sanctities of Heaven
> Stood thick as Stars, and from his sight
>   receiv'd
> Beatitude past utterance; on his right
> The radiant image of his Glory sat,
> His only Son;

> (III. 56-64)

Nothing can subvert God's throne or tarnish its rad-
iance, as Belial wittily acknowledges:

> could we break our way
> By force, and at our heels all Hell should
>   rise
> With blackest Insurrection, to confound
> Heav'n's purest Light, yet our great Enemy
> All incorruptible would on his Throne
> Sit unpolluted, (II. 134-9)

34

In the everchanging universe of Paradise Lost the only
steadfast thing is the throne of God; it is the one
constant, the focal point (VI. 832-34; VII. 585-86).
There is a great deal of pageantry about the throne
of God, seen in the circles of angels, the trumpets,
the incense, the orchestra of harps, the songs and
hymns, and the charm of the spectacle, plus in the
spiritual reality which make the throne an emblem of
great beauty. The seat of the Almighty, though metaphoric and allegorical, is also materially engaging.
The allegorical and moral implication of the throne
is that it is a seat of judgment where good and evil
are weighed. Milton's verbal pictures have few equals
in the emblem writers, but their emblematic devices
generally depict God symbolically. Rosemary Freeman
points out that "the abstract symbol" contributes
"significant detail to . . . personification or
anecdote"[15] aptly delineated in the English emblem
books under discussion. Few devices show God in human
lineaments. Generally he is symbolized by a burst of
light at the top of the picture and is shown as an
arc or a segment of a circle emanating rays. Wither
uses the device effectively in his emblems. His seg-
ments often display the Hebrew letters ותח , signifying Yahweh or God, while angels hover close by
(Whither, pp. 65, 77, 91, 166). As "the picture is
not to be interpreted literally but figuratively,"[16]
God is also shown as an eye or a hand emerging from
clouds; the eye being a symbol of his omniscience and
the hand of his creative excellence, power, and sustaining grace (Hall, pp. 6, 28, 32, 40, 64, 76;
Peacham, pp. 1, 12; Quarles, Emblems, p. 137). Whitney does show God as a human figure, but He appears
infinitesimal surrounded by a light-giving orb and
clouds, as though the artist is afraid to give him
human lineaments (Whitney, pp. 32 & 152). A monarchic
court that comes nearest to Milton's verbal imagination appears in Bellarmine's devices, published in
1614. Milton may have known Bellarmine's Catechisme.
It could almost be said that Bellarmine anticipates
William Hogarth's illustration "The Council in Heaven"
by a hundred years.

Two emblematic woodcuts used by St. Robert Bellarmine to illustrate A Shorte Catechisme 1614 juxta-
pose Hell and Heaven,[17] and could well portray Milton's
idea of Heaven and Hell. Hell's billowing fire looks
like the cavernous mouth of a fanged monster dark
within. It shows stunned creatures rolling in the

35

gulf while winged devils oppress them. In the distance
behind the cavern is a spot of intense brightness.
The brightness is carried into the next emblem where
God is seated on a luminous throne resting on clouds
which partially veil him. Rays emanate from his haloed
head, as though they are graphic beatitudes enriching
the bodiless cherubs and saintly councillors around
the oval inset. God as first seen in Paradise Lost
(I. 12) is such an orthodox Deity. He is an enthroned
monarch, unmoved by the raging angels, who battle his
forces with least success and are hurled to the darkness of a fiery gulf. The luminosity around God's
throne grows brighter in contrast with the Hell that
receives the vanquished rebels.

The seventeeth-century God is absolute, and the
prototypes of God on earth are kings, but Milton's
view on the subject changes through the course of
events in England. He had written Eikonoklasts, and
justified the decapitation of Charles I, yet an absolute monarch served his purpose in Paradise Lost. Ruth
Mohl points out that in Milton's Commonplace Book there
are entries, apparently by scribes, made after Milton
became blind in 1652, which quote Machiavelli. Milton
with his own experience in political circles, his
History of England, and his work as the Latin Secretary,
was well aware of the shortcomings of the rulers and
the mighty of the realm. None of them was a prototype
of God. Milton's God was unreachable. The Christian
Doctrine makes it clear that Milton's God was the
epitome of ethical perfection though absolute. His attributes include the highest verities: God is truth, He
is Spirit, He is immense in His infinity, He is Eternal;
He is immutable and incorruptible and is a single unified entity. He is also omnipotent and His vitality
and potency are peerless; and His will is pure and
holy. He is just and glorious though unmitigatedly
militant. These attributes Milton aptly supports from
the Scriptures. Thus in God Milton reads the highest
values and perfection which no king or leader could
emulate. Some of these traits are given to aristo-
crats whom the emblematists adulate, or are seen in
their icons pertaining to kings. Milton does not
claim originality; his treatment of God codifies the
thoughts of the writers, poets and divines of the
seventeenth century, but has a Miltonic aura.

The God of Paradise Lost seems more human than
that of the Christian Doctrine and less distant, though
his abode is heaven. Like Michaelangelo's God of the

Sistine Chapel, he seems less awesome and more visible, often kindly, a concerned patriarch. The Creator in Paradise Lost is more like an Anglo-Saxon Hlaford, human, humane and involved though stern. He sees himself in Adam, "My latest and best creation." Although very human, and aware of good and evil, He never succumbs to evil. He exonerates Himself from any part in the Fall of the Angels or Man. When Wither addresses his Choice of Emblemes to their majesties, King James I and Queen Mary, and makes the rulers appear the epitome of humankind, emblematically he is making them the prototype of the Deity, who conveys in his person the best that man can conceive.

In The Shape of Things Known Forrest G. Robinson has traced the scientific curiosity about God and shown that many of God's attributes stem from Plato's Timaeus and from Aristotle, from the mediaeval patristic literature, and the thinkers of the Renaissance. In his survey Robinson formulates the idea that man's god-like reason made him comprehend God through the visual impression he got of things seen and known. The order in the hierarchical system of the universe was there because each link of the chain of being was endowed with light emanating from the life-giving Sun or God. Thus each part of the chain was an impression or a part of God's totality. The images then as visualized by the seeing eye and the mental eye could build a picture of God by synthesis. Likewise God in his totality could be understood by analyzing the visual impressions perceived. Symbols were incorporated to interpret obscurities. For example, the tree of life, denied to Adam and Eve by God's command, eventually leads to man's salvation in the wooden cross, and is the means of grace to the progeny of the first parents. Water is the hallmark of purification, the dove of the spirit. Each of these verbal symbols maintains in it the pith of narrative. Eternity is the bait for salvation put before Adam in Michael's visionary survey of the future. The "sacra pagina," the sacred page of the scriptures, becomes a means of meditation and comes alive in verbal pictures. These images and illustrations are in constant use in the seventeenth century. With their help the devotee focuses his mind better on the profound, meditational passages of religious literature. The emblematists use symbols for identical purposes, and mostly for meditation.

God of Paradise Lost and of the emblematists is

masculine, but He is also androgynous, and contains
in Himself both the male and female principles evident
in Adam. Adam, created in God's image, is a hermaphrodite. In the pictures of the emblematists where God
appears, He is neither essentially male nor female.
Female icons often are visually indistinguishable from
the male figures except for the clothing. God's wisdom, His Son, is often called "Sancta Sophia" a feminine title. The title is female, yet the devices depict the figure as masculine. God, the King, then,
is the prototype of every man or of Man and Woman. He
is not only the Head of Creation and the Progenitor,
but also a mediator between Man and Himself, an inter-
mediary who is as concerned for His creation as the
Son whom he deputes to act for Him. God represents
the zenith of the potentiality of Man, who at his
optimum is God-Man-Woman, the male-female principle.
Milton being both a verbal and pictorial artist, works
for certain effects like the engraver. His God is
composite, thus androgynous and the source of all entities and concepts of the universe. Everything in
Milton touches God, even evil touches the Will of God,
though it glances off leaving the Almighty unscathed.
The great chain of being connects all the complexities
of life with God.

Being rational, God counterbalances good and evil
in His own mind, but his foreknowledge, His innate
benevolence and creative energy, automatically make
him reject the harmful and the destructive. _Paradise
Lost_ tries to justify God to the seventeenth century
and to posterity via knowledge. It endeavors an intellectual understanding of God: "The end of learning
is to repair the ruins of our first parents by regain-
ing to know God aright."[18] But it is only with the
study of sensuous things, as of icons in nature, that
man can get this understanding of God:

> But because our understanding cannot in
> this body found itself but on sensible
> things, nor arrive so clearly to the
> knowledge of God and things invisible
> as by orderly conning over the visible
> and inferior creature, the same method is
> necessary to be followed in all discreet
> teaching.[19]

In _Of Education_ Milton prescribes a rigorous period of
training for the complete man. The training involves
the development of mind, body and soul. If Milton's

God is the zenith of perfection, man has to fortify his understanding to perfection.

If God's symbol is the circle of perfection, man becomes the equilateral triangle where mind, body and soul need equal development. Man's greatest achievement is right knowledge, whereby he can enter that circle of perfection and touch it. The contact is partial; man falls short of divinity. He has known the bliss of paradise, he has known communion with God and strives to regain Eden and oneness with God:

> the spirit will be restless in our
> dark imprisonment here, and it will
> rove about until the bounds of creation
> itself no longer limit the divine mag-
> nificence of its quest.[20]

The iconography of the emblematists strives to depict the numinous God as the epitome of perfection, a kind of excellence man envies for himself. Milton envisions perfection in his God. Wither tersely puts it down in a couplet:

> For, thou that Wisdome art, (from heav'n
>   descending)
> Which, neither hath beginning, change,
>   nor ending.

> (Wither, p. 145)

In The Reason of Church Government Milton hails man's contact with God, who "sends out his Seraphim with the hallow'd fire of his Altar, to touch and purify the lips of whom he please," and perfect man's rejuvenation. Milton justifies his God, for God's spirit purifies and blesses as it draws man Eden-ward.

FOOTNOTES

[1] Marcia Pointon, Milton & English Art (Toronto: University of Toronto Press, 1970), p. 3.

[2] Pointon, p. 5.

[3] Georgette DeMontenay, Emblemes ou Devises Chrestiennes 1571, ed. J. Horden (Menston: Scolar Press, 1973), p. 40.

[4] Freeman, pp. vii & 1.

[5] Hughes, p. 130.

[6] Henry Peacham, Minerva Britanna 1612, Facsimile (Menston: Scolar Press, 1973), p. 113.

[7] John M. Steadman, *Milton's Epic Characters* (Chapel Hill: Un. of North Carolina, 1968), p. 12.

[8] Francis Quarles, *Quarles' Emblems*, ed. Charles Cowden Clarke (London: Cassell, Petter, Galpin & Co., n.d.), p. 293.

[9] Hughes, ed., p. 904.

[10] Hughes, ed., p. 905.

[11] Hughes, ed., p. 904.

[12] Hughes, ed., pp. 977-78.

[13] Hughes, ed., p. 983.

[14] Jane Aptekar, *Icons of Justice* (New York: Columbia University Press, 1969), p. 21.

[15] Freeman, p. 23.

[16] Freeman, p. 23.

[17] St. Robert Bellarmine, *A Shorte Catechisme* 1614, ed. D.M. Rogers (facsimile, rpt. Menston· Scolar Press, 1973), pp. 114 and 115.

[18] "Of Education," ed. Hughes, p. 630.

[19] Hughes, ed., p. 631.

[20] Hughes, ed., "Seventh Prolusion," p. 625.

THE ANGELIC WORLD

Like God, Milton's angels were immortal. The idea of spirits being eternal came from Plato, who ascribed moving intelligences to the celestial spheres, a belief current until the seventeenth century. His argument was that had the spheres no intelligences there would be no order in their movement, and as the movement of the spheres exhibited no change, the intelligence guiding them was also eternal.[1]

Milton seemed ambivalent about some supernatural beings at the age of twenty when he mentioned "household gods and genii and daemons"[2] in the "Seventh Prolusion" at Cambridge, though it is unlikely he had doubts; he was speaking there in the usual manner of a classical oration. Angels belonged with Christian theology and fitted Milton's poetic design and turns of narration. Any doubts he had about them he conveniently resolved as unnecessary probing into sacred mysteries. This attitude appears in the words of Raphael:

> what thou canst attain, which best
>   may serve
> To glorify thy Maker, and infer
> Thee also happier, shall not be withheld
> Thy hearing, . . .
> Of knowledge within bounds; beyond abstain
> To ask, nor let thine own inventions hope
> Things not reveal'd.

> (VII. 115-22).

The same advice is reiterated by Wither:

> Be wise, in what may to thy good, belong;
> But seeke not Knowledge, to thy
>   neighbour's wrong:
> . . .
> Nor into those forbidden secrets peepe,
> Which God Almighty, to himselfe doth keepe.

> (Wither, p. 147).

Milton was familiar with the existing speculation on Angels, and may have known Burton's Anatomy of Melancholy. Milton mentions Comenius, but not his study of angels. Men who were writing on angels and whom Milton had read were: Bishop Hall, Henry Lawrence, John Dee, William Perkins, Cajetan, Bellarmine, Zanchy, Jean Boden, Thomas Erastus, Ludwig Lavatar, and Jerome Cardan, all angelologists. He was well aware of patristic scholars of angelology: Tertullion, Clement of Alexandria, Origen, Augustine, Aquinas, and Scotus:[3]

> To only one angelologist does Milton show a verbal resemblance strict enough to indicate a direct levy. Two passages of Paradise Lost parallel two in Michael Psellus's Dialogue of Daemons not only in

idea but in the grouping and order of
ideas and even in some of the language; . . . in Paradise Lost I 423-31 and
VI 327-92 they are as pure an angelo-
logical transplantation as a form can
contain. He borrowed the concept that
the substance of the angels was simple,
sexless, alterable, fluid, and sensitive.[4]

Milton's treatment of angels is not all theological,
it is aesthetic. His ageless angels can appear like
Renaissance cherubs, as Satan in his earliest metamorphosis, or like Uriel they can ride a sunbeam.
His angels weep tears, feel physical pain and eat
human food, and their substance mingles in sexual
embraces. Raphael's wings emit a flower-fresh fragrance; and downward flight for angels is anathema.
These are poetic licenses that make Milton's pictures
alluring. His angels have no distinct counterparts in
the emblem books, except that Quarles' angels and
Anima often appear as cherubs, and Wither has a recumbent angel hovering on a cloud, as a king uplifts the
music of his harp to God, God who is signified by a
lighted arc (Wither, p. 65). Hawkins' frontispiece
has cherubs, some bodiless, surrounding the Virgin.
His angels in the "Hortus Conclusus" or pristine Eden,
the prototype of the Virgin, are noted, "Heer whole
Quiers of Angels are accustomed to sing their Alleluyas, at all howers." And after the sin of Adam and
Eve, "an Angel-Porter of the Order of the Cherubins,
with a ficile and two-edged sword," guards the gate
of Eden.[5] Like Quarles many of Hall's angel-figures
appear as Anima, but he has two magnificent woodcuts,
one in which a six-winged angel helps a human soul
to "nimbly flee / Unclog'd with matter" to God (Hall,
pp. 72 and 74); the other a trumpet-blowing angel
standing on top of a globe to usher in God for the
Last Judgment. The angels in these emblems stand for
a whole legion of their kind, the "golden Legions"
(Hall, pp. 108 and 110). In Whitney angels are
shown with bows and arrows, destroying Niobe's children, like the warring angels in Milton (Whitney, p.
13).

    Some of Milton's theological concepts regarding
angels in the Christian Doctrine and Paradise Lost
are reflected in the emblematists, and are part of the
same conventions and traditions that were ingrafted in
Milton's thoughts. The seventeenth century believed,

"Above man are the angelic hierarchies that, because
of their close proximity to God, have an especially
clear insight into the nature of things." Roger Bacon
had written, "the active intellect is primarily God,
and secondarily the angels, who illuminate us."[6]
Reason and intellect were attributes of God, but it
was the angels, the instruments of God, who helped
man to exercise his God-given faculty of reason. God
in mediaeval theology was equated with light and the
sun, the illuminators of the universe and the mind;
and angels, like Uriel of Paradise Lost, were assigned
positions on the stars and the planets. They were
the scriptural emissaries of God to man, and conveyed
to him God's light, precepts, and thoughts. In Paradise Lost the angels project God's ideas pictorially,
so man can see them with his inward eye, where sight
and thought become one. Milton's Adam gets such insights into the mind of God through Raphael and
Michael:

> O Adam, one Almighty is, from whom
> All things proceed, and upto him return,
> If not deprav'd from good, created all
> Such to perfection, . . .
>
> Man's nourishment, by gradual scale
>   sublim'd
> To vital spirits aspires, to animal,
> To intellectual, give both life and sense,
> Fancy and understanding, whence the Soul
> Reason receives, and reason is her being,
> Discursive,or Intuitive; discourse
> Is oftest yours, the latter most is ours,
> Differing but in degree, of kind the same.

> (V. 469-90)

Wither reiterates the creatures' oneness with God;
only in degree is he different:

> I feele
> Soft motions, from that great Eternall
>   Wheele,
> Which mooveth all things, . . .
> And, when to Him, I backe returne,
>   from whom
> At first I came, I shall at Full become.

> (Wither, p. 182)

For, as wee somewhat have of every Creature,
So, wee in us, have somewhat of his Nature:

(Wither, p. 252)

And Whitney adds: "That man is next to God, / Who
squares his speache, in reasons rightfull frame:"
(Whitney, p. 60). Man is nourished to attain God-like
qualities and majesty, and ultimately to become more
like God. Raphael has to print word pictures to show
Adam that man's mind responds to the visual before
capturing the deeper significance of the pictures.
Adam realizes that the figurative is a means to higher
truths:

Well hast thou taught the way that might
     direct
Our knowledge, . . . whereon
In contemplation of created things
By steps we may ascend to God.

(V. 508-12)

Milton's man has rapport with angels, and grasps theological and philosophical truths coming from them.
In Wither a seraphic head illumines an upward-looking
eye placed in a human heart, and the poet writes:

God, gave Mankinde (above all Creatures)
A lovely Forme, and upward-looking Eye,

That he might lift his Countenance on high:
And (having view'd the Beauty, which appeares
Within the outward Sights circumference)
That he might elevate above the Spheres,
The piercing Eye, of his Intelligence:
               . . . till they ascend,
To gaine a glimpse of those eternall Rayes,
To which all undepraved Spirits tend.
For, 'tis the proper nature of the Minde
               . . . upward to arise.
                         (Wither, p. 43)

If Milton's angels in their "proper motion . . . ascend" (II. 75), so does man in trying to comprehend
God:

          but to nobler sights
Michael from Adam's eyes the Film remov'd

44

Which that false Fruit that promis'd clearer
    sight
Had bred; then purg'd with Euphrasy and Rue
The visual Nerve, for he had much to see;
And from the Well of Life three drops in-
    still'd,
So deep the power of these Ingredients
    pierc'd,
Ev'n to the inmost seat of mental sight,

(XI. 411-18)

Michael in revealing the future history of Adam's
progeny through emblematic pictures, becomes his
angelic mentor. The pictures relate the sensation of
sight to thought, and give Adam an instinctive understanding of God's purpose. The didactic impressions
of Paradise Lost are illuminated by insight and
thought, each essential to the other.

Angels act as mediators and catalysts between
divine and human thoughts. In Milton they supply
pictures to illustrate God's intention and make it
explicit. Milton's poetry clarifies the ideas in
verbal icons. Forrest G. Robinson points out, "Emblems and hieroglyphics bridge the gap between thought
and sensation, for they are concepts, in exactly the
same form to both the oculus carnis and the oculus
mentis," for man "cannot think of a character without
thinking of a meaning . . . and cannot conceive of
meaning independently of something visible."[7] Thus
Milton's invisible God is evinced through his angels
to the mental eye. His angels are loyal and willing
emissaries, and are concerned about his new creation.
Placed between God and man in the great chain of being, their words seem reflexive responses to both
God and man: the links that join them are strong.

Quarles refers to the angel hierarchs in an emblem captioned: "And he will give his Angels charge
over thee. Psal. 91." The emblematic device shows
a lit taper with a moth hovering round it. The
chubby profile of an infernal angel-head, probably
that of Satan or Death, is shown trying to blow out
the taper, but another angel from above is bending
over with a guard in his hand to shield the flame
from being extinguished. The picture symbolically
conveys a warning to man, as does Raphael in Paradise
Lost. God's good angels know that evil always lurks
close by, and man can avert it through God's grace

45

and protection. Raphael, the affable angel, takes two and a half books of Paradise Lost to prepare and warn Adam against the calamity that Adam and Eve can avert if they so will. In the emblem Quarles says:

You blessed Angels, you that doe enjoy
The full fruition of eternall Glory,
Will you be pleas'd to fancy such a Toy
As man, and quit your glorious Territory,
And stoop to earth, vouchsafing to imploy
Your cares to guard the dust that lies
    before yee?
Disdaine you not these lumps of dying Clay,
That, for your paines, doe oftentimes
    repay
Neglect, if not disdaine, and send you
    griev'd away?

And will you, Sacred Spirits, please to
    cast
Your care on us, and lend a gracious eye?
How had this slender Inch of Tapour beene
Blasted, and blaz'd, had not this
    heav'nly Screene
Curb'd the provd blast, and timely stept
    betweene!

Referring to God Quarles says:

O Goodness, farre transcending the report
Of lavish tongues! too vast to comprehend!

for it is God who sends down the angels to men. The angels are extolled by the poet as ambassadors of God and are asked to mediate man's good-will to God:

. . . blessed Courtiers of th' eternall
    Court,
Whose full-mouth'd Hallelujahs have no end,
Receive that world of praises that belongs
To your great Sav'raigne; fill your holy
    tongues
With our Hosannas, mixt with your Seraphick
    Songs.

(Quarles, Hieroglyph. pp.
19-20)

Quarles' poems are subjective. His emblems deal with the Soul of man, its never ending queries about good

46

and evil, and its quest for sublimity and God. Quarles
probes the psychological aspects of his poetic thoughts
and pictorial devices. Like Milton's, his angels are
God's courtiers and intermediaries who take up man's
"Hosannas" and offer them to God. As God's messengers,
they shield man from the arch enemy's onslaught, and
are gracious, like Raphael in Paradise Lost sent as a
guardian to Adam and Eve. He tries to protect them.

Peacham in Minerva Britanna also defines the
nature of angels. They are "the Noblest sprightes"
and like the phoenix, the bird of love, their natural
motion (as in Milton) is to mount. They suffer from
no malcontent and no unhappiness:

> Yee Noblest sprightes, that with the bird
>   of love,
> Have learnt to leave, and loath, this
>   baser earth,
> And mount, by your inspired thoughtes above,
> To heaven-ward, home-ward, whence you had
>   your birth:
> Take to you this, that Monarches may envie
> Your heartes content, and high foelicitie.

(Peacham, p. 28)

From heaven's elevation they can observe the cares and
follies of mankind and smile at their foibles.
Peacham's emblem shows a globe, with the phoenix's
head uplifted toward the sun, and outspread wings
striving to mount above the clouds to its natural
home, Heaven.

The Book of Revelation mentions seven angels
standing before the throne of God (8.2). Three are
mentioned by name in The Book of Tobit: Michael, Gabriel, and Raphael. Milton adds Uriel, "the regent
of the sun," as a fourth archangel. Lucifer, the
fallen archangel and adversary of God, is the fifth.
These were God's generals, and next to God's Son, the
most eminent in Heaven. His important behests were
carried out by the archangels. God expected allegiance of all his angels; their service to him was mild
and pleasant. They were his creatures as Satan un-
happily acknowledges: "he deserv'd no such return /
From me, whom he created what I was / In that bright
eminence" (IV. 42-44). Other angels Milton mentions
by name are Abdiel, Ithuriel, Uzziel and Zephon.

47

Milton's angels are not only God's emissaries, they
are beings whose traits approximate to those of God.
Compassion is one of their great qualities. Even
Satan, apostate though he is, displays great tender-
ness toward innocent man, and ironically and paradoxically just before he brings about man's ruin, he says:

> Ah gentle pair, yee little think how nigh
> Your change approaches, when all these
>   delights
> Will vanish and deliver ye to woe,
> More woe, the more your taste is now of joy;
> Happy, but for so happy ill secur'd
> Long to continue, and this high seat your
>   Heav'n
> Ill fenc't for Heav'n to keep out such a foe
> As now is enter'd; yet no purpos'd foe
> To you whom I could pity thus forlorn,

(IV. 366-74)

Quarles mentions the compassion of Angels in Emblems,
"My sins are sev'ral blots; the lookers-on / Are
angels," (Bk. IV No. IV, p. 308). They look at man's
failure with concern and pity, for they are God's
emanations. Milton's angels not only sing their songs
in Heaven, praising God with their seraphic voices,
but their songs, typical of the Platonic belief in
the music of the spheres, ravish whenever they are
heard, be it in Heaven or Hell or Paradise. The
gentler, art-loving angels, though fallen and enmeshed in Milton's vast hell,

> Retreated in a silent valley, sing
> With notes Angelical to many a Harp
>
> Thir song was partial, but the harmony
> (What could be less when Spirits immortal
>   sing?)
> Suspended Hell, and, took with ravishment
> The thronging audience.

(II. 547-55)

Quarles avers that music has the power to beguile any
who are depressed and living in their own hell.
Quarles' Emblem XV of Book IV refers to music as the
Orphic power to charm Hades and equates it with seraphic song. The song of the angel remains unsurpassed,
for Quarles, quoting St. Augustine, points out "thos

48

angelical spirits praise God face to face." Music, as
all else near God, savors of perfection. The Orphic
music in Hades or Hell ("earth's misconstrued Heav'n"),
can charm, and Milton's fallen angels give the pleasure
of full orchestration, though unlike Quarles, they do
not praise God. Quarles writes:

> "How shall we sing the Lord's song in a
> a strange land?" Psalm cxxxvii.4
>
> How can my music relish in your ears,
> That cannot speak for sobs, nor sing for
> tears?
> Ah! if my voice could, Orpheus-like, unspell
> My poor Eurydice, my soul, from hell
> Of earth's misconstrued Heav'n, oh then my
> breast
> Should warble airs, whose rhapsodies should
> feast
> The ears of seraphims, and entertain
> Heav'n's highest Deity with their lofty
> strain:
> A strain well drench'd in the true Thespian
> well,
> Til then, earth's semiquaver, mirth,
> farewell!

The coda at the end of the emblem reads: "O infinitely
happy are those heavenly virtues which are able to
praise thee in holiness and purity with excessive
sweetness, and nonutterable exaltation! From thence
they praise thee, from whence they rejoice. For what
they praise thee: but we, pressed down with this
burden of flesh, far removed from Thy countenance in
this pilgrimage, and blown up with worldly vanities,
cannot worthily praise thee; we praise thee by faith,
not face to face; but those angelical spirits praise
thee face to face, and not by faith. S. August. Med.
Cap. xxxiii." Epig. 15

> Did I refuse to sing? Said I, these times
> Were not for songs, nor music for these
> climes?
> It was my error! are not groans and tears
> Harmonious raptures in th' Almighty's ears?

Was the music of Milton's infernal angels acceptable
to God as Quarles' epigram suggests? Unfortunately
the fallen angels had already been judged.

The evil angels approach man through his senses, while the good angels appeal to his intellect and reason. This is evident in Satan's approach to Eve. His first contact with her is in the form of a toad whispering at her ear. Next he beguiles her with the sight and smell of the delectable fruit of the Tree of Knowledge of good and evil, and urges her to taste the fruit to gain sapience, and be a goddess among gods. Raphael and Michael, the archangels sent to Adam, approach him as peers (XI. 239-40), though Michael's approach is stern and direct (XI. 257). They discuss much of the available knowledge of the seventeenth century, and give Adam a foretaste of the shortcomings and the achievements of his posterity, to the time the second Adam brings men back to the state of grace from which Adam falls. Many of the ideas that Milton incorporates in these concepts of the supernatural are reiterated by the emblematists when good or evil, personified by heavenly or infernal angels, is responsible for man's actions and thoughts, for the angels signify the rationale, the motivation behind man's choices: "God created and illuminated the Angelic Mind, which in turn devolved upon the World Soul, the essence of all rational souls and the principle of form animating material creation. . . . [And God's] divine light manifests itself in different images at each level of the cosmic order: . . . [where] 'sight is twofold, corporeal, and spiritual; the first is that of Sense, the other of the Intellectual faculty, by which we agree with Angels.'"[8]

The nine angelic hierarchies of mediaeval tradition are diffuse in Milton, but his angelic intelligencies move through the vast spatial structure of the epic with flowing ease. The good angels and archangels adore the Deity, being the first of His creation and His emanations. They worship and praise him with words and songs, and recognize His service as perfect freedom. Love, self-discipline and obedience are part of their self-imposed loyalty to God. At His behest they move like romantic meteors, and have the strength of goodness. They are not slow to combat evil, though, not being omniscient, even the keenest-eyed among them can be deceived. Yet their substance is pure, and hypocrisy vanishes like thin veneer if it comes in contact with them:

```
            . . . no falsehood can endure
    Touch of Celestial temper, but returns
    Of force to its own likeness.
```

                    (IV. 811-13)

The "form and nature of the angels . . . proceed incorruptible from God".[9] Their intellect, being of God, is
all comprehensive, except for celestial mysteries
which belong to the Deity alone. And Milton's Adam
reveres God's angels; they come to him in moving
pictures like a benediction, for they are the epitome
of harmony and right reason and God's animating soul:

```
            . . . what glorious shape
    Comes this way moving; seems another Morn
    Ris'n on mid-noon;
```

                    (V. 309-11)

```
                . . . I descry
    From yonder blazing Cloud that veils the
      Hill
    One of the heav'nly Host, and by his Gait
    None of the meanest, some great Potentate
    Or of the Thrones above, such Majesty
    Invests him coming; yet not terrible,
    That I should fear, . . .
    But solemn and sublime, whom not to offend,
    With reverence I must meet,
```

                    (XI. 228-37)

HEAVEN

        Gem-encrusted cities and gardens were not un-
familiar to the ancients. A hero's quest often led
him to such a city. The earliest known human epic,
The Epic of Gilgamesh, envisioned a garden glittering
with gems and it vied with Alcinous' palace in the
Odyssey and the poetic imagination of St. John's "New
Jerusalem:"

```
    There was the garden of the gods; all
    round him stood bushes bearing gems. . . .
    There was Fruit of carnelian with the
    vine hanging from it, beautiful to look at;
    lapiz lazuli leaves hung thick with fruit,
```

sweet to see. For thorns and thistles
there were haematite and rare stones,
agate, and pearls from out of the sea.[10]

The iconography of Milton's heaven is fashioned on
Revelation XXI and sparkles with orient gems, baronial
splendour, symphonic music and ritualistic worship.
Although heaven displays its rivers and trees and
mountains, and all the terrain of nature, it also
bespeaks the glory of a highly developed urban area.

Regarding things supramundane Raphael says to
Adam that the numinous and spiritual can best be explained by analogues and examples from the sensate
world, adding the Platonic concept that the earth may
be an animate and shadowy image of heaven:

                    how shall I relate
        To human sense th' invisible exploits
        . . .
                    how last unfold
        The secrets of another World, . . .

                    . . . what surmounts the reach
        Of human sense, I shall delineate so,
        By lik'ning spiritual to corporal forms,
        As may express them best, though what if
          Earth
        Be but the shadow of Heav'n, and things
          therein
        Each to the other like   more than on Earth
          is thought?
                        (V. 564-76)

And, Milton reiterates, earth is "but the shadow of
Heav'n" (V. 575); "this new-made World, [is] another
Heav'n" (VII. 617-8); it is "like to Heav'n," a
"Terrestrial Heav'n" (IX. 99-103).

Because Heaven was the original of Earth, it had
all the terrestrial features. In the "continent of
spacious Heav'n" (VI. 474) there were "Province[s]"
(VI. 77), "wide Champain[s]" (VI. 2), and urban sophistication: towers and battlements (II. 62 & 1049),
high city walls (II. 343) of crystal (VI. 860), and
gates that used as though the elctronic eye ". . .
self-open'd wide / On golden Hinges turning," (V. 254-
55). Heaven had "bound[s]" (II. 236), was circumscribed
by a wall (II. 353), and had two outposts, both

52

brilliant with heavenly light (II. 538). The "Eternal
Splendor" (I. 610) of "Heaven's Azure" (I. 297) con-
tained a vault (I. 669) and "Starry Cope" (IV. 992),
"Star-pav'd" roads (IV. 976), and pavements of "trodd'n
Gold" (I. 682). Yet heaven was an ecologist's delight
for its expanse was pure (IV. 456).

God sat enthroned in a graphic locality "above the
starry sphere" (III. 416) surrounded by spirits of
celestial mould. Like an earthly king, God carried
a golden sceptre of authority (II. 328). Heaven hon-
ored its angels by high seats of state (IV. 371), pro-
viding them with thrones (I. 360). They in turn served
heaven and enlivened it with angelic, choric songs and
music of golden harps. Their seraphic beauty, crowned
with interwoven gold and fragrant amarant (III. 352),
superseded the glitter of temporal courts. The approach to God's throne was "A broad and ample rode:"
(VII. 517), the galazy, its pavements covered with gold
dust (VII. 576-8). Like palaces on earth, heaven had
its "courts" (V. 650, VI. 889), and pavilions (V. 653),
houses (VII. 576), temples (VI. 890, VII. 148) and
altars (II. 244, XI. 18), and suburbs and purlieus
(II. 833). As of Alcinous' palace, the architect of
Milton's heaven was Mulciber (Hephaistos):

> . . . known
> In Heav'n by many a Tow'red structure high,
> Where Scepter'd Angels held thir residence,
> And sat as Princes, whom the supreme King
> Exalted to such power, and gave to rule,
> Each in his Hierarchy, the Orders bright.

(I. 732-37)

Heaven's architectural excellence was due to Mulciber,
and its baroque opulence was seen in sculptured gold
and precious stones. When Satan went on his voyage of
reconnaissance, he saw heaven as an emblem of ori-
ental splendour:

> Far off th' Empyreal Heav'n, extended wide
> In circuit, undetermin'd square or round
> With Opal Tow'rs and Battlements adorn'd
> Of living Sapphire, once his native Seat;
> And fast by hanging in a golden Chain
> This pendant world, in bigness as a Star
> Of smallest Magnitude close by the Moon.

(II. 1047-53)

                    . . . far distant he descries
          Ascending by degrees magnificent
          Up to the wall of Heaven a Structure high,
          At top whereof, but far more rich appear'd
          The work as of a Kingly Palace Gate
          With Frontispiece of Diamond and Gold
          Imbellisht; thick with sparkling orient
             Gems
          The Portal shone, inimitable on Earth
          By Model, or by shading Pencil drawn.
          The Stairs were such as whereon Jacob saw
          Angels ascending and descending, . . .
          Each Stair mysteriously was meant, nor stood
          There always, but drawn up to Heav'n some-
             times
          Viewless, and underneath a bright Sea
             flow'd
          Of Jasper, or of liquid Pearl, . . .

                         (III. 501-19)

        Geographically the terrain of heaven was not un-
like earth, but its atmospheric component was "fair"
and "purest" light (II. 137), which never receded
beyond twilight, a time of rest for all except the
night watch and the ever vigilant eye of God. Heaven
had both natural flora and formal gardens:

                    in Heav'n the Trees
          Of life ambiosial fruitage bear, and vines
          Yield Nectar, though from off the boughs each
             Morn
          We brush melliflous Dews, and find the
             ground
          Covered with pearly grain:

                         (V. 426-30)

Amarant grew in heaven "shading the Fount of Life"
(III. 357) among "Elysian Flow'rs" and "Amber stream"
(III.359), and flower beds "like a Sea of Jasper shone
/ Impurpl'd with Celestial Roses . . ." (III. 363-4),
and the "river of Bliss" (III. 358) ran through
heaven. In this idyllic paradise, heaven also had an
English wicket gate (III. 484) later manned by St.
Peter.

        The denizens of heaven had their form of govern-
ment, where their emperor was a benevolent dictator.

He believed in councils and consultations, and held assemblies when crucial proclamations were needed and momentous cosmic decisions required.

The on-going life of heaven was not allegorical. The _modus operandi_ of its monarch and the inhabitants was realistic. The inhabitants of heaven knew the joys and _elan_ of gracious living. Their "high feasts" had no Puritanical austerity, neither did their rites of worship:

> Tables are set, and on a sudden pil'd
> With Angels' Food, and rubied Nectar flows:
> In Pearl, in Diamond, and massy Gold,
> Fruit of delicious Vines, the growth of
> Heav'n.
> On flow'rs repos'd, and with fresh flow'rets
> crown'd,
> They eat, they drink, and in communion sweet
> Quaff immortality and joy, secure
> Of surfeit where full measure only bounds
> Excess, before th' all-bounteous King,
> who show'r'd
> With copious hand, rejoicing in thir joy.

(V. 633-41)

But heavenly spirits also knew hunger and the blessings of sustenance by food: "food alike those pure / Intelligential substances require / As doth your Rational:" (V. 407-9), says Raphael, before he and Adam:

> to thir viands fell, . . .
>   with keen dispatch
> Of real hunger.

(V. 434-37)

Heaven was a highly ordered state, and used instruments to maintain discipline, as the scales of justice (IV. 1014), a pair of golden compasses to add new creations (VII. 226), afflicting thunders (II. 166), artillery (II. 715), chariots and horses that thundered through heaven's pavements (VI. 749-51). Its inhabitants could be marshalled into battalions and flying squadrons, and its generals were as well versed in the science of war as of peace and its attendant creativity.

At times Milton's heaven is concrete, and can almost be gauged geometrically" . . . in utmost Longi-
tude, when Heav'n / With Earth and Ocean meets, "(IV.
539-40); at other times its location is diffuse and
can only be assessed imaginatively. It belongs with
all of God's creation, and as Uriel says:

> But what created mind can comprehend
> Thir number, or the wisdom infinite
> That brought them forth, but hid thir
> causes deep.

> (III. 705-7)

The unknown and the mysterious continue to surround
the infinitude and the minutae of the overwhelming
universe. For this abode of God and the angels was
created of God, and was therefore a part of God's
essence.

A new heaven, pendant from the first Heaven, was
lodged in creation within "the hollow Universal Orb"
(VII. 257), and had its "birthday" along with the
earth (VII. 256). The cope of this Heaven had an
axle round which it revolved while it took delight in
the glory of the sun and the moon (VII. 381). But
the Sun was supreme in the physical Heaven, and Dawn
and the Pleiades attended him with dance (VII. 373-75).
There is ambiguity about Milton's Heaven. It stands
for God, for God's abode, the abode of other celestial
beings and bodies, and for a concrete material place,
visible to the naked eye, "the Firmament, expanse of
liquid pure,/Transparent" (VII. 264-65).

Henry Hawkins' treatment of Heaven in his devotional emblems is apparently different in the Partheneia Sacra or The Mysterious and Delicious Garden of
the Sacred Parthenes, Symbolically set forth and enriched With Pious Devises and Emblemes 1633. Unlike
the other emblem writers, he does not express himself
in poetry. Except for a short preamble in the section
entitled, "The Embleme Verse," his medium is poetic
prose. His is a book of meditation, where he expects
his readers to contemplate things spiritual in the
"Garden of their harts"(sig. A2). Like Milton, Hawkins' desire is to express himself in "wayes so new
and strange, and (for ought I know) as yet untraced
or trod of anie" (A2r). Alciati had divided his emblems into three sections the Lemma, Icon, Epigram:

56

Hawkins multiplied the parts to nine: "device," "character," "morals," "the essay," "the discourse," "the emblem," "the poesie," "the theories," and "the apostrophe." Thus his emblem entitled The Heavens is an extended meditation (pages 81-93). The meditation has two pictorial devices, a short poem, and prose passages.

Hawkins' thoughts on Heaven have much in common with the works of his contemporary emblematists and poets, and echo ideas incorporated by Milton. A stylized ribbon on top of his device on Heaven carries the words Capacitatis Immensae. The framed globe below it has a few longitudinal markings, one carrying a strip of alternating large and small stars. There are two more brilliant and larger stars poised below them, and about the centre, placed dramatically opposite to the stars, are the sun and the moon. His is a hieroglyphic mode of conveying excellence beyond par. The Character reads;

> The Heavens are the glorious Pallace of
> the Soveraigne Creatour of all things; the
> purple Canopie of the Earth, powdred over
> and beset with silver-oes; or rather an
> Azure Vault enameld al with diamants, that
> sparckle where they are. And for that there
> is aloft above this seeling, they make a
> paviment likewise for the Intelligences
> and Angelical Spirits, strewed, as become
> such inhabitants, with starres. It is a
> Court, where those blessed Spirits, as
> Pensioners, stand continually assisting
> in the King's presence, with the favour
> to behold him face to face in his greatest
> glorie, while the Starres as Pages attend
> in those spacious Hals and lower roomes.
> If al togeather should make up the bodie
> of an Armie ranged and marshalled in the
> field, the Spirits themselves would make
> the Cavalrie, and the Infanterie the
> Starres, s. Michael General of the one,
> and Phoebus of the other.

Hawkins continues his martial images further by mixing Christian and Greek mythological figures and ideas; and by referring to beasts in heaven, the constellations, and the angels whom he compares with the birds of paradise. He ends the passage on a

57

profound theological belief in the emanations of God:
"And if the upper Region of the Elements be of fire,
the Seraphins are al of amourous fires of Divine love,
and the highest order of the blessed Spirits."

Hawkins refers to God as the Capacitatis Immensae,
for God "truly beholds al Objects, both Intellectual
and Visible; and truly containes them al, being present to al, comprehends al, is Al in Al." Hawkins
elaborates the idea of God and Heaven, but in doing it
he mentions Galileo. Referring to the stars that
"sweetly glide heer and there" and have different
"Motions and Agitations," like Milton, he seems intrigued by Galileo's novas and his optical glass:
"and if perhaps some new Galilaus should devise and
frame us other spectacles or opticons to see with, we
are in danger to find out yet some new Starres and
Heavens never dreamed of before." Hawkins, a Jesuit,
who had been exiled from England in 1618, writing in
1633 was conscious of Galileo and the stir his discovery had made in the Church of Rome. Hawkins'
scholarship and great curiosity enabled him to mention
Galileo dispassionately; perhaps "danger" is the only
word in the script that gives away his leanings.
Hawkins refers to Plato's music of the spheres, and to
the "engraved" Heavens, engraved with constellations
"cut, as with a chisel." His reference to the cosmos
and the movement of the stars is equivocal; it mixes
theology, astronomy, and popular belief, and is capped
with poetic phrases like the heavens "vaulted Arch
enameled al with starres" (Hawkins, pp. 81-85). As
the Partheneia Sacra belongs with literature of the
Marian Secret Societies, the Marian Sodalities, Hawkins continues his meditation on Heaven, but continues to compare heaven with the Virgin Mary. His
heaven, like Milton's is gem bedecked and baroque.

Quarles uses metaphysical conceits in cogitating
about Heaven in Book V Emblem VI of his Emblems:

> To heav'n's high city I direct my journey,
> Whose spangled suburbs entertain my eye;
> Mine eye, by contemplation's great attorney,
> Transcends the crystal pavement of the sky!
> But what is heav'n great God, compared to
>   Thee?

Quarles' flight of fancy veers to the absurd in his
description of Heaven, yet the overtones suggest

Raphael's description of heaven in Paradise Lost. In
Emblem XIV of Book V Quarles uses an illustration with
Anima looking up toward heaven, the motto reads:

"How amiable are thy tabernacles, O lord of hosts!

                    Psalm Ixxxiv.1."

Ancient of days, to whom all times are NOW,
Before whose glory seraphims do bow
Their blushing cheeks, and veil their
    blemish'd faces,
That, uncontain'd, at once dost fill all
    places;
How glorious, oh, how far beyond the height
Of puzzled quills, or the obtuse conceit
Of flesh and blood, or the too flat reports
Of mortal tongues, are thy expressless
    courts!
Whose glory to paint forth with greater art,
Ravish my fancy, and inspire my heart;
Excuse my bold attempt, and pardon me
For showing sense, what faith alone should
    see.
Ten thousand millions, and ten thousand
    more
Of angel-measured leagues, from th'eastern
    shore
Of dungeon-earth, his glorious palace stands,
Before whose pearly gates ten thousand bands
Of armed angels wait to entertain
Those purged souls, for which the lamb was
    slain;
Whose guiltless death, and voluntary yield-
    ing
Of whose giv'n life, gave the brave court
    her building;
The . . . blood . . .
To rubies turn'd, whereof her posts were
    built;
And what dropp'd down in a kind gelid gore,
Did turn rich sapphires, and did pave her
    floor:
The brighter flames, that from his eyeballs
    ray'd
Grew chrysolites, whereof her walls were
    made:
The milder glances, sparkled on the ground,
And groundsill'd ev'ry door with diamond;

But dying, darted upwards, and did fix
A battlement of purest sardonyx.
Her streets with burnish'd gold are
    paved round;
Stars lie like pebbles scatter'd on the
    ground;
Pearl mix'd with onyx, and the jasper stone,
Made gravell'd causeways to be trampled on.
There shines no sun by day, no moon by
    night;
The palace glory is, the palace light:
There is no time to measure motion by,
There time is swallow'd in eternity:

            . . . and death's a stranger there:
But simple love and sempiternal joys,
Whose sweetness never gluts, nor, fulness
    cloys:
Where face to face our ravish'd eye shall
    see,
Great ELOHIM, that glorious One in Three,
And Three in One, and seeing him shall
    bless him,
And blessing, love him, and in love possess
    him.
Here stay, my soul, and ravish'd in relation,
The words being spent, spend now in contem=
    plation.

Francis Quarles explores Heaven in other poems in his
emblem books. Emblem VII in Book IV (page 314) shows
a device, with a palatial house in the rear of a lush
field, and the Son of God leading a human soul by the
hand towards the mansion, the heavenly abode. Quarles
describes the place in the words of the Son:

            Our country mansion (situate on high)
With various objects still renews delight;
Her arched roof's of unstain'd ivory
Her pavement is of hardest porphyry;
Her spacious windows are all glazed with
    bright
And flaming carbuncles; no need require
Titan's faint rays, or Vulcan's feeble fire;
And ev'ry gate's a pearl; and ev'ry pearl
    entire.

Milton's images of the preternatural and the mysterious,

60

like Quarles, are based on Biblical sources and earlier
writings, but Milton's expansive imagination plus his
great learning make him draw these images into elaborate paintings. His metaphors have the same subtle
quality as the nuances in Rembrandt and Titian, and
are also symbolic of deep ethical and religious ideas.
Like all great artists Milton's persuasive powers are
limitless. His images of heaven and its inhabitants
seem plausible, though he is prudent enough to give
Heaven an aura of mystery and ambiguity. His is the
eloquence of silence as well as words. Like hieroglyphics his pictures convey and withhold, and are a
combination of symbols, for no one symbol can do justice to the ornate complexity of heaven. Edgar Wind
writes "the divine ray cannot reach us unless it is
covered with poetic veils."[11] In like manner Milton's
numbers illuminate religious mysteries. Inconography
in the Renaissance was not only an art form, but designed specifically to convey philosophical ideas and
to codify enigmatic concepts. The rays in a picture,
for instance, could mean many things. They were the
emanations of God and conveyed His benevolence, His
forgiveness, His life-infusing essence; on the other
hand Heavenly rays could be malevolent, showing God's
wrath and His destructive power. The richness incorporated in the symbols came not only from Hebraic-
Christian ideas but from the thought patterns of classical and earlier cultures, and symbols became as much
a part of the Church as theological precepts. "The
notorious ease with which the Renaissance transferred
a Christian figure of speech to a pagan subject, or
gave pagan features to a Christian theme, has generally
been interpreted as a sign of the profound seculariza-
tion of Rennaissance Culture."[12] Milton (in himself)
exemplified this idea. Though trained to serve the
church, his classical learning and joy in "all available knowledge," made him too volatile a person to be
stratified in the rigidity and discipline and precepts
of the Anglican Church. He evolved his own religion,
the religion of the thinker, the artist, the cultivated and liberal man, a humanist. Milton could hear
"great 'laughter ... in Heav'n" (XII. 59), and humorously
note that God's throne is at the very pinnacle of
heaven:

            at the holy mount
    Of Heav'n's high-seated top, th' Imperial
       Throne
    Of Godhead, fixt forever firm and sure.
                    (VII. 584-86)

Yet his great devotion to his God is never absent from
his conscious thoughts. God is the centre of Milton's
Heaven.

> And for the Heav'n's wide Circuit, let it speak
> The Maker's high magnificence, who built
> So spacious, and his line stretched out so
>   far;
> That Man may know he dwells not in his own;
> An Edifice too large for him to fill,
> Lodg'd in a small partition, and the rest
> Ordain'd for uses to his Lord best known.

(VIII. 100-6)

Heaven is the epiphany of Paradise Lost. It
bursts into view with dazzling light, and emblematically irradiates the reader, for Milton's heaven is "beyond expression bright" (III. 591), and is the being
of God and the abode of His angels.

Both Milton and the emblematists envision ultimate beauty, joy, peace, magnificence and grandeur in
Heaven. Their point of attention is always God, from
whom flow goodness, love and the very being of created entities.

FOOTNOTES

[1]Robert H. West, Milton and the Angels (Athens:
Univ. of Georgia Press, 1955), p. 7.

[2]Hughes, ed., p. 625.

[3]West, pp. 101-3.

[4]West, pp. 101-3.

[5]Henry Hawkins, Partheneia Sacra 1633, ed. J.
Horden (Menston: Scolar Press, 1971), p. 12.

[6]Forrest G. Robinson, The Shape of Things Known
(Cambridge, Mass.: Harvard University Press, 1972),
pp. 35, 1.

[7]Robinson, p. 213.

[8] Robinson, pp. 54-55.

[9] Hughes, p. 977.

[10] N.K. Sanders, trans. The Epic of Gilgamesh (Baltimore: Penguin, 1968), p. 97.

[11] Edgar Wind, Pagan Mysteries in the Renaissance (London: Faber and Faber, 1968), p. 14.

[12] Wind, p. 24.

ii   EMBLEMS OF THE CREATION

The most profound statement regarding God in
Paradise Lost is given in God's own words to His Son,
and shows the all encompassing nature of "God the
Spirit" and God the substance of the universe, also
of God the free agent, whose Will, though always good,
is not binding on Himself or His creatures:

> Boundless the Deep, because I am who
>   fill
> Infinitude, nor vacuous the space.
> Though I uncircumscrib'd myself retire,
> And put not forth my goodness, which is
>   free
> To act or not,
>
>   (VII. 168-72)

Free will, not "necessity or chance", governs

goodness. The idea is more Miltonic than doctrinal.
God does not dissociate Himself from creation, as
might appear from the lines; but through His similtude,
His Son, He executes His great design of Creation.
The Son is endowed with God's "overshadowing Spirit
and might" (VII. 165) and is competent to do his
Father's behest.

God's will is responsible for His new creation
after the anarchy in Heaven but the Son, the agent
through whom his will is exercised in the chain of being, is delegated to a seat of honour on his right
hand. The Son of God has the secondary position in
Paradise Lost and is lower than God. He has all the
attributes of his Father plus a humility and compassion that emulate the Deity and make the Son uniquely
heroic. The Son is God's vice-regent (V. 609). When
authority is delegated to him he becomes the active
energy of the God-head. In the Christian Doctrine
(Hughes, pp. 958-63) Milton mentions the gifts with
which God endows His Son. Substantiating his premise
from the Scriptures, he enumerates the Son's traits
and attributes. God's Son is endowed with "the power
of conversion, creation, remission of sins, preservation, renovation," and his "mediatorial work" is
"resuscitation from death." He is also committed to
a "future judicial advent" and enjoys "divine honours."
Milton makes it clear that in spite of the Son's lesser
position in the chain of being, he alone in all Creation carries the authentic and complete imprint of
God in himself. Quoting Hebrew V. 3, Milton states
that the Son in himself is "the brightness of His
(God's) glory and the express image of his person."
In Paradise Lost God addresses the son as "Effulgence
of my Glory, Son belov'd,/ Son in whose face invisible
is beheld / Visibly, what by Deity I am, / And in
whose hand what by Decree I do, / Second Omnipotence"
(VI. 680-84).

The Son in Paradise Lost, is deputed by his Father
to drive the warring angels from Heaven, to fashion a
new creation and most important to offer himself as
a scapegoat for man. Each mythology has its sacrifi-
cial lamb,· one who suffers vicariously for others till
the suffering becomes a reality and he physically accepts their distress and the challenge it poses, even
unto death. God foresees Man's lapse and weakness,
but Milton's Son sees the sin of man as an injury to
the Godhead.

64

For should Man finally be lost, should Man
Thy creature late so lov'd, thy yountest Son,
Fall circumvented thus by fraud, though
    join'd
With his own folly? that be from thee far,
That far be from thee, Father, who are Judge
Of all things made, and judgest only right.

                (III. 150-55)

   The Son knows that he has to act as mediator to
save God's new creation from annihilation. Yet not
only as a mediator is he accepted, but as an expiation for Adam's sin.

Behold mee then, mee for him, life for life
I offer, on mee let thine anger fall;
Account mee man; I for his sake will leave
Thy bosom, and this glory next to thee
Freely put off, and for him lastly die
Well pleas'd, on me let Death wreck all
    his rage;

                (III. 236-40)

In an identical spirit, Quarles offers his dramatic
narration. The dialogue is between the Son of God
and the Sinner, the motivating factor is Justice. In
the device a death's head sits atop the fulcrum of a
balance and holds two heavy weights in claw-like paws.
The needle of the balance looks swordsharp and is
pointing to a heart. In the medallion winged Anima,
carrying a cross, seeks to give hope to a sinking
globe, partially entombed in a crater. A symbolic
eye in the globe is directing its glance to the cross,
while the nimbus around Anima's head has lit the globe.[1]
The emblem carries the verse:

"Enter not into judgment with thy
servant; for in thy sight shall no
man living be justified. Psalm
cxliii 2."

The drama conveys the solicitude of Christ for the
Sinner, as of the Son in Paradise Lost.

Drama   Jesus, Justice, Sinner.

   Jes. Bring forth the pris'ner, Justice.

                    65

Just. Thy commands
     Are done, just Judge. See here the
     pris'ner stands.

Jus.. What has the pris'ner done? Say; what's
     the cause
     Of his commitment?

Just. He hath broke the laws Of his too gracious
     God; conspired the death
     Of that great Majesty that gave him breath,
     And heaps transgression, Lord, upon
     transgression.

Jes. How know'st thou this? Just E'en by his
     own confession;
     His sins are crying, and they cry aloud:
     They cried to Heav'n, they cried to Heav'n
     for blood.

Jes. What say'st thou, Sinner? hast thou ought
     to plead
     That sentence should not pass? hold up thy
     head,
     And show thy brazen, thy rebellious face.

Sin. Ah me! I dare not: I'm too vile and base
     To tread upon the earth, much more to lift
     Mine eyes to Heav'n: I need no other shrift
     Than mine own conscience; Lord, I must con-
     fess,
     I am no more than dust, and no whit less
     Than my indictment styles me; ah, if thou
     Search too severe, with too severe a brow,
     What flesh can stand? I have transgress'd
     thy laws;
     My merits plead thy vengeance; not my cause.

Just. Lord, shall I strike the blow: Jes. Hold,
     Justice, stay: Sinner, speak on; what hast
     thou more to say?

Sin. Vile as I am, and of myself abhorr'd,
     I am thy handy-work, thy creature, Lord,
     Stamp'd with thy glorious image, and at
     first
     Most like to thee, though now a poor
     accurst,
     Convicted caitiff, and degen'rous creature,
     Here trembling at thy bar. Jes. Hold,

66

Justice, stay:
Speak, Sinner: hast thou nothing else to say?

Sin. Nothing but mercy, mercy, Lord; my state
Is miserably poor and desperate;
I quite renounce myself, the world, and flee
From Lord to Jesus, from thyself to thee.

Just. Cease thy vain hopes; my angry God has vow'd;
Abused mercy must have blood for blood:
Shall I strike the blow? Jes. Stay, Justice,
hold;
My bowels yearn, my fainting blood grows
cold,
To view the trembling wretch; methinks I
spy
My Father's image in the pris'ner's eye.

Just. I cannot hold. Jes. Then turn thy thirsty
blade
Into my sides, let there the wound be made:
Cheer up, dear soul; redeem thy life with
mine:
My soul shall smart, my heart shall bleed
for thine.

Sin. O groundless deeps! O love beyond degree!
Th' offended dies to set th' offender free.

The Son sees the "Father's image in the prisoner's
eye," for Man is the expression of God; God's projection of Himself and His creativity. In offering to
save Man, the Son paradoxically establishes the invar-
iableness of the Godhead, where being and becoming are
all part of the eternal principle.

The iconography and pictorialism in Milton's
Creation are drawn from several sources, especially
from Ovid's Metamorphoses, DuBartas' Divine Weeks,
Tasso's The Creation of the World (II mondo creato),
Hesiod's Theogony and the first two books of Genesis.

Hesiod's Theogony, considered the oldest account
of the Greek gods and Creation (Hesiod being thought
a contemporary of Homer), was an important source of
many of Milton's pictures and thoughts. Hesiod starts
his work with an eulogy for the Muses, daughters of
Zeus and Mnemosyne, in the epic tradition. He says,
the Muses:

67

                    breathed a sacred voice into my mouth
            With which to celebrate the things to come
            And things which were before.2

Milton before he writes of the things past and the
things to come, invokes Urania, the muse of poetry,
who is also for Milton, God's inspiring spirit. He
asks Urania to inspire him to indite themes unattempt-
ed in prose or rhyme. Hesiod's Muses lived on Par-
nassus and Olympus; Milton envisioned Urania, God's
Holy Spirit and emanation, residing on the highest
mount in Heaven. The mission of Hesiod's goddesses
of the arts, was to watch over "a heaven-favoured"
person from his birth and "pour / Sweet dew upon his
tongue, so that from his lips flow honeyed words."[3]
Milton belonged to that special group of the elect and
knew it.

        Peacham had used Urania in his emblems to inspire
him. In Anagramma Nominis Authoris entitled Hinc super
haec Musa, Peacham addresses Urania:

            Bid now my Muse lighter taske adieu,
            As shaken blossome of a better fruite,
            And with Urania thy Creator view,
            To sing of him, or evermore be mute:
            Let muddy Lake, delight the sensuall thought,
            Loath thou the earth, and lift thy selfe
                aloft.

                        (Peacham, p. 177)

Milton invoked the muse of poetry for his own mellifluous lines as well as to justify God to man. On
invoking the Muses, Hesiod asks to be told of creation
as Adam requests of Raphael. Hesiod learns:

            Chaos was first of all, but next appeared
            Broad-boscmed Earth, sure standing-place
                for all
            The gods who live on snowy Olympus' peak,
            And misty Tartarus, in a recess
            Of broad-pathed earth, . . .

            From Chaos came black Night and Erebos.
            And Night in turn gave birth to Day and
                Space
            Whom she conceived in love to Erebos.

And Earth bore starry Heaven, first, to be
An equal to herself, to cover her
All over, and to be a resting place,
Always secure, for all the blessed gods
Then she brought forth long hills . . .

The mountain clefts . . . .
She bore the barren sea with its swelling
        waves,
Pontus. And then she lay with Heaven, and
        bore
Deep-whirling Oceanus . . .
Last, after these, most terrible of sons,
The crooked-scheming Kronos . . .
Who was his vigorous Father's enemy.

(Hesiod, p. 27)

It was Earth or Gaia who instigated her children to revolt against Ouranos their father, much in the way
Satan conspires with his legionnaires to revolt against
God in Paradise Lost. Kronos like Beelzebub was in
accord with Gaia in her awful plan. Kronos castrated
his father, whose blood in time gave birth to the
Furies and Giants, the nefarious creatures of Tartarus.
From this time forward came all the evils, Night bore
Doom and Ker (a spirit of death), and Death and Sleep
and Dreams. Also by self impregnation Night gave
birth to Blame and Distress, Destinies and ruthless
Fates, Nemesis, Deceit and Love, Age and strong-willed
Strife. Strife in turn gave birth to Work, Forgetfulness, Famine, Pain, Battles, Fights, Murders, Killing,
Quarrels, Lies, Stories, Disputes, Lawlessness with
its self related Ruin, and Oaths, (Hesiods, p. 30).
Milton's Chaos and Old Night contain in themselves and
their vast realm all these misbegotten evils plus the
milling churning elements, cross winds and abstractions.

The emblem writers are not far behind in using
these elements and abstractions for their poems and
illustrations. Perhaps not taking them directly from
Hesiod, but from the mediaeval thinkers, for whom abstractions were stock in trade, they composed their
emblems to be didactic and elevate man ethically. The
emblematists based much of their work on abstractions,
giving them reality in verbal and graphic pictures.
Chaos in Peacham is depicted by an impenetrable forest: "A Shadie Wood, pourtraicted to the sight, / With
uncouth pathes, and hidden waies unknowne: /

69

Resembling Chaos, or the hideous night," (Peacham, p. 182).

In Hesiod all the progeny of Earth and Sky and Ocean are not evil. There is the benevolent Nereus, prototype of justice, truth, honesty, gentility, mercy and law (Hesiod p. 30), and his like-minded daughter, Nemertes (Hesiod p. 31). They are charitable figures.

Ovid gives the story of Creation in Book I of his Metamorphoses. The translation of the Metamorphoses by Mary McInnes is painterly as well as graphic in describing the creation:

> Before there was any earth or sea, before
> the canopy of heaven stretched overhead,
> Nature presented the same aspect the world
> over, that to which men have given the name
> of Chaos. This was a shapeless uncoordinated
> mass, nothing but a weight of lifeless matter,
> whose ill-assorted elements were indiscrimi-
> nately heaped together in one place. . . .
> Although the elements of land and air and
> sea were there, the earth had no firmness,
> the water no fluidity, there was no bright-
> ness in the sky. Nothing had any lasting
> shape, but everything got in the way of
> everything else; for, within that one body,
> cold warred with hot, moist with dry, soft
> with hard, and light with heavy.
>
> This strife was finally resolved by a god,
> a natural force of a higher kind, who
> separated the earth from heaven, and the
> waters from the earth, and set the clear
> air apart from the cloudy atmosphere. When
> he had freed these elements, sorting them
> out . . ., he bound them fast, each in its
> separate place, forming a harmonious union.[4]

Ovid does not tell which god it was that brought this uni-
fying order in allocating the elements their own appointed
areas and limits, but he does say that once the work
was completed, the stars that were covered with a veil
of obscurity began to shine in their respective constellations ("divine forms"), the fish swarmed the
waters, wild beasts covered the earth, as the birds
did the sky and the air, though no creature resembled
the gods or had dominion over the rest of creation.

At this point man came into existence, perhaps emerging from a "divine seed" planted by the creator of all life, or moulded out of earth which still retained the virtue of soaring aether, so lately intermixed with the heavier elements. This earth, still instinct with the divine spark, was fashioned by Prometheus in the image of the gods: "He made man stand erect, bidding him look up to heaven, and lift his head to the stars" (Ovid p. 31).

This man is Milton's Renaissance Hebraic-Christian Adam. The Son of God on creating him gives him dominion over all the rest of the creatures. Whitney takes the same story and moulds it in a fascinating emblem of creation. The device shows the chaotic nature of the elements, with the Greek letters XAOϚ in the center of it. Around the word XAOϚ which is superimposed on a hill, are grouped a sun and its rays, a crescent moon, a star; and impressionistically intertwined rays, clouds, waves of water, and tongues of lightning. A seraphic head, partially visible, is blowing its breath into the chaotic picture and is hardly distinguishable, at first sight, from it. The emblem is entitled <u>Sine justitia, confusio,</u> and is Whitney's rendering of the Ovidian creation which reads:

When Fire and Aire, and Earthe, and Water,
    all weare one:
Before that worke devine was wroughte, which
    nowe wee looke uppon,
There was no forme of thinges, but a con-
    fused masse:
A lumpe, which Chaos men did call: wherein
    no order was.
The Coulde, and Heate, did strive: the
    Heavie thinges, and Lighte.
The Harde, and Softe. the Wette, and Drye.
    for none had shape arighte.
But when they weare dispos'd, eache one into
    his roome:
The Fire, had Heate: the Aire, had Lighte;
    the Earthe, with fruites did bloome.
The Sea, had his increase: which thinges to
    passe thus broughte:
Behoulde, of this unperfecte masse, the
    goodly worlde was wroughte.

(Whitney, pp. 122-23)

71

Like Ovid's this goodly world was perfect, for its
goodness brought it to a golden age of plenty. It
flourished until "pryde, did banishe peace." A time
of bliss after Creation was followed by decline. With
the incursion of crime, the ages declined from the
golden, to silver and then brass, till the degeneration was complete in the quarrelsome, warlike age of
iron, reminiscent of the uncouth war in Milton's
heaven between the loyal and the rebel angels, and
the fall of the erring angels. With the fall entered
the seven deadly sins of the age of iron, so aptly
given by Whitney in the same emblem:

> Then vertues weare defac'd, and dim'd with
>   vices vile,
> Then wronge, did maske in cloke of righte:
>   then bad, did good exile.
> The falsehood, shadowed truthe: and hate,
>   laugh'd love to skorne:
> Then pitie, and compassion died; and blood-
>   shed fowle was borne.   ...
> That nowe, into the worlde an other
>   Chaos came:
> But God, that of the former heape: the
>   heaven and earthe did frame,
> And all thinges plac'd therein, his glorye
>   to declare:
> Sent Justice downe   unto the earthe: such
>   love to man hee bare.
> Who, so survay'd the world, with such an
>   heavenly vewe:
> That quickly vertues shee advanc'd: and
>   vices did subdue
> And, of that worlde did make, a paradise,
>   of blisse.

Whitney ends his poem with an exhortation that Justice
should be courted for the welfare of a country, in his
case England. Milton's grand numbers are devoted
through half of Book V, beginning with line 577 to the
end of Book VII, to the act of Creation and the immediate reason for it. Milton gives a cluster of vignettes, many of them emblematic in character, to justify the classical and the Hebraic creation stories to
his readers. The classical iron age when the seven
deadly sins ("all manner of crime broke out") are ram-
pant, as in the wake of Satan's jealousy and instigation to rebellion part of the heavenly legions, becomes
the reason for the new creation. Chaos seemingly

72

reigns supreme for a while in Milton's Heaven as it
did in the imperial domain of Chaos and old Night.
The new creation is imperative to bring order into the
chaos caused by Satan and his lackeys in God's well-
ordered, peaceful State; ironically in the same state
where God had relegated a high office to Satan. It is
within the Miltonic creation story that the reader
learns afresh of Satan's state in heaven and in Hell;
and he forsees, like God, Satan's worse act of cowardice and degradation; Satan's duping man into disobeying God, thus hurting God vicariously. Chaos, both
internal and external, then, is responsible for the
new creation. In Milton the picture is elaborated
till it becomes a saga of mythical history. Each act
of creation is poetically complete in itself, and is
executed by the Son, the effulgence of God.

An emblematic mode often encountered is the use
of the rhetorical question, where a moralistic adage
at the end of the query emphasizes the emblematic
character of the words. Milton uses it in Adam's
cryptic inquiry of Raphael regarding creation. The
question embraces the whole creation story:

> Deign to descend, now lower, and relate
>
> How first began this Heav'n which we behold
> Distant so high, with moving Fires adorn'd
> Innumerable, and this which yields or fills
> All space, the ambient Air wide interfus'd
> Imbracing round this florid Earth, what
>   cause
> Mov'd the Creator in his holy Rest
> Through all Eternity so late to build
> In Chaos, and work begun, how soon
> Absolv'd, if unforbid thou mayst unfold
> What wee, not to explore the secrets ask
> Of his Eternal Empire, but the more
> To magnify his work, the more we know.

(VII. 84-97)

Raphael makes it amply clear that God's new creation
is to counteract Satan's specious boast. Satan claims
he has depopulated heaven of one third of its denizens.
Milton enshrines in Book VII lines 145-156 God's will
for further creation to deflate Satan's vainglory. The
Son proceeds to the "ever-during gates" of Heaven and
from the brink he and his legions view Chaos with its

73

mingling and dissolving elements. The picture of
Chaos from this new perspective is identical in imagery
to that of Ovid and Whitney and Walt Disney's colorful
Fantasia:

> They view'd the vast immeasurable Abyss
> Outrageous as a Sea, dark, wasteful, wild,
> Up from the bottom turn'd by furious winds
> And surging waves, as Mountains to assault
> Heav'n's highth, and with the Centre mix
>   the Pole.

(VII. 211-15)

The reader had already encountered Chaos in Book II
of <u>Paradise Lost</u>, when its "hoary deep" revealed its
secrets as:

> a dark
> Illimitable Ocean without bound,
> Without dimension, where length, breadth,
>   and highth,
> And time and place are lost; where eldest
>   Night
> And Chaos, Ancestors of Nature, hold
> Eternal Anarchy, amidst the noise
> Of endless wars, and by confusion stand.
> For hot, cold, moist, and dry, four
>   Champions fierce
> Strive here for Maistry, and to Battle bring
> Thir embryon Atoms; they around the flag
> Of each his Faction, in their several Clans,
> Light-arm'd or heavy, sharp, smooth, swift
>   or slow,
> Swarm populous, unnumber'd as the Sands . . .

> The Womb of nature and perhaps her Grave,

(II. 890-903, 911)

The place was not only a confused mass of matter, but
of discontent and strife and discordant noises. It
was a place of no discipline or order. In it was eternal anarchy where matter, sound, and concepts were in
disharmony. It had no shape or form for nothing was
static here; it was a "wild abyss / The womb of nature
and perhaps her grave" (II. 910-11). Its physical
confusion is stressed by the several monosyllabic
staccato spondees in the lines that describe Satan's

74

plight and effort to manoeuvre his way in Book II:

> O'er bog or steep, through strait, rough,
> dense, or rare,
> With head, hands, wings, or feet pursues his
> way,
> And swims or sinks, or wades, or creeps,
> or flies:

(II. 948-50)

Satan's course depends on the elements and crosswinds he meets. The allegorized presence of the monarch of the realm, Chaos, his consort, Night, and their abstract attendants, Orcus, Ades, Rumor, Chance, Tumult, Confusion, Discord, all spell madness.

Charles Grosvenor Osgood points out that the idea of Chaos as King in Milton is from Hesiod, and the Miltonic conception of Night as the consort of Chaos is taken from the Orphic Cosmogony.[5] Night incidentally is the first female figure in evolution, and precedes ordered creation and light. The fantasy of the churning, milling atoms of Chaos intrigued the artist and the writer from early times. Some artists like the emblematists tried to delineate the imaginary mass of matter. Others shared their own comprehension of the region through verbal pictures. The poetic vision offers profounder and deeper thoughts to the student than pictorial truisms. In poetry the landscapes take on the character of human concerns and consciousness. The depths of meaning sensitizes the viewer or reader to the artists' own mood. Milton's mental consciousness not only made him cognisant of the landscapes of Heaven, Paradise and Hell, but made him palpably aware of the primordial abyss, the magnitude of which is staggering and limitless. It is the parent of all things created; of emotions and of conscious and unconscious thoughts. Because it is Chaos that gives substance to God's ordered universe, it has an unique fascination. The landscapes of the epic cannot be seen in isolation, for each is essential to the whole cyclic concept of creation, preservation, destruction and recreation. The pictures are dramatic; some are linear, others impressionistic, but all are closely linked to the author's beliefs and feelings. Aesthetically they convey spiritual and moral concerns, and communicate truths with feelings of melancholy, poignant nostalgia, joy, soaring and uplifting elation, awe

75

and reverence. The landscapes and episodes depict
moral values as they do in many murals and icons and
verbal pictures. The act of Creation is performed at
a time when heaven's hegemony has been shaken. Milton's
"vast profundity obscure" feels the compasses of the
Son carving the universe from its atoms; and the spirit
of God infuses all entity with goodness, harmony and
order. The Creation in Milton is the Hebraic-Christian
Story of Genesis, elaborated and ornamented with Miltonic grace and scholarship. It does not miss any of
the features of the visible universe. From the "Leviathan / Hugest of living Creatures" (VII. 412; so
imaginatively imprinted by Paul Doré in his illustrations of Paradise Lost) to the "Minims of nature," the
ants and the bees, the epic formulates emblems which
carry their motto within them:

> The Parsimonious Emmet, provident
> Of future, in small room large heart enclos'd,
> Pattern of just equality perhaps
> Hereafter,join'd in her popular Tribes
> Of Commonality:

(VII.485-89)

The ant and the bee, which builds her waxen cells and
stores honey, exemplify two of the traits so dear to
the Puritan mind for the good life and success: hard
work and providence.

"The great First Mover's hand . . . wheeled"
(VII. 500) the course of the newly created heavenly
bodies; and earth, personified as a beautiful female,
"in her rich attire / Consummate lovely smiled" (VII.
502). When God thought of his master-work, Man, He
saw him:

> . . . endu'd
> With Sanctity of Reason, might erect
> His Stature, and upright with Front serene
> Govern the rest, self-knowing, and from
> thence
> Magnanimous to correspond with Heav'n.

(VII. 508-11)

a concise and magnificent credo for Renaissance humanity. Milton's spirit indeed soars to the heights when
he puts his soul's aspirations into these four terse
lines and affirms his belief in man. Milton's man is
created glorious.

This then is God's new creation. With the iron age the early Ovidian eras passed leaving chaos open to a new order. Whitney has envisaged it in his emblem of Creation, and Milton's verses sing of Creation after the expulsion of the rebels; for the rebel angels had cultivated in themselves all the degeneracy of Ovid's men of iron. The Son of God is responsible for the grand design of the new creation. In Himself he is endowed with God's might and power and love, and His creation is comsummate perfection. He returns to the seat of God after the creation, and is received in great jubilation by loyal angels thronging the throne of God.

Quarles' Hieroglyphicks, Emblem II (p. 7) has a device showing the hand of God emerging from a cloud and holding flames to light a taper. The background has a river with tree encrusted banks. A tree in the foreground which is enormous, may well be the Tree of Knowledge. A Dantesque head with a woman's profile barely visible behind it Janus-like, is gazing upward as it rests beside a candle urn. The emblem is captioned "And God said, let there be light; and there was light, Gen. 1.3."

In the verse Quarles reiterates the Creation but the emphasis is on man and his concerns:

It was a gracious hand that thus endow'd
This snuffe with flame: But marke this hand
    doth shroud
It selfe from mortall eyes, and folds it in
    a Cloud.

2.

Thus man begins to live; An unknowne flame
Quickens his finisht Organs; now, possest
With motion; and which motion doth pro-
    claime
An active soule, though in a feeble brest:

3.

Was it a parcell of celestiall fire
Infus'd by Heav'n, into this fleshly mould?
. . .

4.

If it be part of that celestiall Flame,
It must be ev'n as pure, as free from spot
As that eternall fountaine whence it came:
. . .

5.

Or, if it were created, tell me, when?
If in the first sixe dayes, where kept till
  now?
. . .

Six dayes expired, all Creation ceast,
All kinds, even from the greatest to the
  least,
Were finisht, and compleat, before the day
  of Rest.

6.

But why should Man, the Lord of Creatures,
  want
That priviledge which Plants and Beasts
  obtaine?
Beasts bring forth Beasts, the Plant a
  perfect Plant;
And every like brings forth her like againe:
Shall fowles, and fishes, beasts and plants
  convey
Life to their issue? And Man lesse than
  they?
Shall these yet living soules? And Man,
  dead lumps of clay?

7.

Must humane soules be generated then?

The poem ends with a stirring motto, taken from Isodor,
"Why doest thou wonder, o man, at the height of the
Starres? or the depth of the Sea? Enter into thine
owne soule, and wonder there. The soule by creating is
infused, by infusion, created." Quarles merely refers
to the creation story in the emblem, but he stresses
some moot ideas of mortality: Adam's despondency after
the fall, his anxiety regarding posterity and God's
providence. The newly infused flame in man, makes
Adam a thinker. He asks himself the theological

78

question, "What is man?" Is he infused with God's
spirit, and a demigod in himself, one who merits the
concern of the Son? Man is the epitome of creation
in most stories of the ancients as in the thoughts of
Milton and his contemporary emblem writers. With man's
creation, the circle of perfection comes to a close.

FOOTNOTES

[1]Francis Quarles, Emblems, ed. Charles Cowden Clarke
(London: Cassell, Peter Galpin, n.d.), p. 34.

[2]Hesiod, Theoginis, trans. D. Wender (Baltimore:
Penguin, 1973), p. 24.

[3]Hesiod, p. 25.

[4]Ovid, Metamorphoses, trans. M. M. Innes (Baltimore:
Penguin, 1953), p. 29.

[5]C. G. Osgood, The Classical Mythology of Milton's
English Poems (New York: Henry Holt, 1900), p. xviii.

Milton rejected the doctrine of the Trinity, yet in classical studies he knew that three was a hermeneutic number. Triads of gods, the graces, the three-visaged deity, the three-headed dog Cerberus, or evil, were part of ancient beliefs. The motifs appeared in Scriptures, and were pictured in emblems and iconography. Some, like the world, the flesh, and the devil, were used for religious instruction. Milton conveys the idea by giving three precise facets to evil: Satan, Sin and Death. He also lists temptations, which approximate the mediaeval world, flesh and devil. In Whitney's rendering of Alciati's emblems three figures often appear, either to depict goodness or evil. Whitney's trinity of evil, equivalent to Milton's Satan, Sin, and Death, is the tripartite Envie, Strife, and Slander. The device shows three women against a backdrop of hills. A Grecian temple nestles in those hills and paths lead to a miniscule town. Each of the women is engaged in a nefarious act. Envy, semi-naked, is holding her heart to her lips as though about to devour it; Slander is pushing a child into a mire with one hand while supporting herself against a tree with the other; Strife, standing on a pair of bellows, is lighting a fire. In addition to these three abstractions, the device carries a nude male figure depicting Time. Time, shown with seraphic wings, carries a long scythe in his uplifted hand. He is bending toward a female figure while attempting to drag her up from a pool. The verses of the emblem portray the ephemeral nature of time allotted to each of the figures. Time will destroy the triad of evil, and as Milton says, itself as well:

> For when as each thing bad thou hast
>   entomb'd,
> And, last of all, thy greedy self consum'd,
> Then long Eternity shall greet our bliss

Triumphing over Death, and Chance, and thee
O Time.[1]

Truth will prevail. In <u>Paradise Lost</u> Milton's triad
of evil is not destroyed, but its end is promised;
indications are that its reign is not for ever:

Death his death's wound shall then receive,
    and stoop
Inglorious, of his mortal sting disarm'd.
I through the ample Air in Triumph high
Shall lead Hell Captive maugre Hell, and
    show
The powers of darkness bound.

(III. 252-55)

Milton indicates that evil will recoil on itself,
evident in the emblematic device and moral as Sin
tells Satan of Death:

Before mine eyes in opposition sits
Grim Death my Son and foe, who sets them on,
And me his Parent would full soon devour
For want of other prey, but that he knows
His end with mine involv'd; and knows that I
Should prove a bitter Morsel, and his bane,
Whenever that shall be; so Fate pronounc'd.
But thou O Father, I forewarn thee, shun
His deadly arrow; neither vainly hope
To be invulnerable in those bright Arms,
Though temper'd heav'nly, for that mortal
    dint
Save he who reigns above, none can resist.

(II. 803-14)

Earlier Sin had enunciated another theological truth
regarding God's wrath and justice: "Justice, bids, /
His wrath which one day will destroy ye both" (II. 733-
34).

Similarly emblem books depended on allegory.
Their stock in trade was the "interrelation between
the arts of poetry and painting"; art was seen as
"a speaking picture"; poems as "dumb poetry"; the two
complementing each other and each integral to the
other. In the emblems above it is difficult to separate the moral from the poetic thoughts and the

81

graphic pictures. If divorced, "the most distinctive
picture of the convention [is] lost."[2]

Steadman refers to Paradise Lost as "an imitation
of a system of ideas."[3] The emblematists too, portray
ideas of their era, and follow Aristotle's precept of
the poet, as being a teacher of ethics and politics.
In the description of his characters Milton not only
paints vignettes but, like the emblematists, attaches
didactic morals to the descriptions. This is evident
in his treatment of His Satanic majesty, who was "of
the first,/ If not the first Arch-Angel" (V. 659-60)
of God. Satan, the most glorious of literary figures,
always reveals himself as immoral. Even in his most
inspiring and grandiloquent speeches, his subtleties
and seemingly humane concerns, some insignificant
quirk gives him away as diabolic. As Satan moves
through the vast panorama of Milton's epic world,
and is seen in relation to things celestial and infernal, paradisaic and earthy and chaotic, he has the
taint of imperfection. As in Paul Doré's illustrations,
one can almost observe pictorially his fall from the
grace of God; his unmatched beauty marred to an extent
that the angelic wings metamorphose into bat's wings,
and each rib, instead of being covered with feathers,
shows a talon at its end; his shapely feet deformed
into cloven hooves; his body, shedding the flowing
robes of Greek philosophers, in nakedness, exposes a
monstrous tail and horns; his visage grown ugly, his
stature bent. In other words his degeneration in
Milton, aptly sketched by Doré, is complete and
scathingly debasing for a magnificent creature who
once could vie with God for the supremacy of Heaven.
In portraying Satan's mental and physical deteriora-
tion Milton is expressing the ideas and beliefs of
his times.

Medina, the first illustrator of Paradise Lost,
draws on earlier pictures of the Devil for Milton's
Satan. Satan seen with Sin and Death is handsome but
diabolic. He has all the tangible marks of the devil
figure. By the time he is seen in Medina's Eden, he
has lost all semblance of seraphic beauty and is truly
hellish.[4] Medina's illustrations were made after
Milton's death, but some of their counterparts are
present in emblematic devices.

The emblematists lack the range of sensibility
and poetic vision as well as the masterly

discipline of Paradise Lost; a discipline which makes
the epic a systematic compendium and storehouse of all
available seventeenth-century knowledge, but in their
own genre, the emblematists touch on Satan and his
diabolic influence on mankind, giving pictures that
can serve as gloss on Milton's Satan. Devices depicting Satan were not rare in art and literature. In
mediaeval and Renaissance iconography Satan was often
ugly, with horns, tail, claws and fleshy wings. Three
of Whitney's Satanic figures are shown trying to undermine truth as found in the Book of God. The principal
figure is muscular and ugly with large ears and horns;
his associates just as menacing. The verse gives their
diabolic designs:

> Thoughe Sathan strive, with all his maine,
>   and mighte,
> To hide the truthe, and dimme the lawe
>   devine.

(Whitney, p. 166)

A counterpart of Satan's is the mischievous god, Pan.
He is jolly, but his pictures resemble Satan (Whitney,
p. 160). In Wither's emblematic devices, the figure
of Vice comes nearest to the images of Satan, except
that Vice is female. She has all the hallmarks of
the devil: horns, tail, claws, fleshy wings, a leering
smile (Wither, p. 22). Bellarmine's devices show
Satan in hell. Along with Satan's expected features, he
carries an uplifted club to torture the fallen creatures (St. Bellarmine, p. 144). In another emblem
of Bellarmine he appears monkey-faced. With a cohort
he comes to fetch the soul of an impenitent man. In
Quarles' Hieroglyphikes, various satanic concepts are
depicted by animal figures, which approximate his
traits. Pride is represented by the "proud neckt
Steed" (p. 40), "Cupid's fire" is depicted by a he-
goat (pp. 42 and 43), a boar symbolizes "Excesse and
Surfet" (pp. 46 and 48), a seated lion, "choler" and
"rage" (pp. 50 and 51), a coiled snake, "envie" and
jealousy (pp. 54 and 56). Hall's symbols for evil
are snakes with devilish faces and a virago trying to
entrap a Soul (p. A3). For Peacham, the crocodile is
the prototype of Satan, "the Ghostly foe, / Who evermore lies watching, to devoure" (p. 154). Although
Milton's portrayal of Satan is developed far beyond
such images, most of them nevertheless, linger in his
poem, to qualify and undercut his more specious and

83

magnificent portraits of evil.

The Christian Doctrine says that man has known
good and evil. He has either believed in God through
some "ocular demonstrations" or believed in "some evil
power whose name was unknown, and who presided over
the affairs of the world."[5] Satan presides over the
affairs of man in several emblems of the seventeenth
century. Whitney has an apt verse showing that Satanic envy is devastating; it is the kind of envy that
lost Satan Heaven. His device is from Aesop's fable,
where a dog loses his bone trying to wrest it from
an image of himself in a pool, of water. The loss is
both of reality and the illusion:

> Whome fortune heare allottes a meane estate
> Yet gives enowghe, oaohc wante ful to
>   suffice;
> That wavering wighte, that hopes for better
>   fate,
> And not content, his cawlinge doth despise,
> Maie vainlie clime, but likelie still to
>   fall,
> And live at lengthe, with losse of maine,
>   and all.
>
>   (Whitney, p. 39)

Milton's Satan aspired higher than he could go, and
lost all that he had; worse, he sank to the lowest
he could fall. Possessing Reason, unlike Aesop's
dog, Satan's loss spurs him to worse acts of devilry.
He undermines God's new creation, especially man, the
"creature late so lov'd," God's "youngest Son" (III.
151). Quarles bewails man's short span of life, as
seemingly the devil is always the victor in his fight
for man:

> Our infancy is consumated in eating
> and sleeping; in all which time what
> differ we from beasts, but by a pos-
> sibility of reason, and a necessity of
> sinne?
>
> O misery of mankind, in whom no
> sooner the Image of God appeares in
> the act of his Reason, but the Devill
> blurres it in the corruption of his will.
>
>   (Quarles, Hieroglyphikes,
>   p. 37)

84

The Satanic figure in Judaeo-Christian mythology
was connected with material wealth and often considered a guardian of treasures. The opulence of Milton's
Pandemonium is an example of the material wealth of
the Devils. In Egyptian mythology the fearsome
Anubis, the jackal-headed god, was the guardian of the
dead. The jackal, one of the most cowardly yet
vicious creatures, whose howl in a pack is enough
to rouse the dead, and who delights in the bones of
the buried, ironically appears in Egyptian hieroglyphics as the guardian of the tomb and their treasures. In Beowulf it is the monster Grendel and his
Mother who hoard treasures in their caves in the
mere; and the fire-dragon of Beowulf's last fatal
battle is a guardian of buried treasures. The emblem
writers stress this aspect of evil. Riches lure man
from goodness.

Questioning man Quarles wonders how he can reach
the ultimate in satisfaction. When he turns his attention to wealth, he finds it diabolic. In the device the contemplative Anima finds it impossible to
imbed her anchor in wealth. The poet on asking himself, "Where shall I . . . fill the gulf of my in-
satiate mind?" answers in counter-questions:

> Lies it in treasure, in full heaps untold?
> Doth gouty Mammon's griping hand infold
> This secret saint in sacred shrines of
>   sov'reign gold?
>
> No, No, she lies not there; wealth often
>   sours
> In keeping; makes us hers in seeming ours
> She slides from Heav'n indeed, but not in
>   Danae's show'rs.
>
> Lives she in honour? No. The royal crown
> Builds up a creature, and then batters down.

(Quarles, Emblems, p. 327)

Wealth then becomes a fetter instead of a boon. Mammon is its custodian, not God, and it leads to Satanic
acts, including fear of discovery. Whitney aptly
shows this fear in Emblemes 1586 where Satan, a thief
of riches, is flying from the wrath of God, God being
seated in the orb of the sun which spotlights Satan
with its terrible rays:

85

The wicked wretche, that mischiefe late hath
    wroughte,
By murder, thefte, or other heynous crimes,
With troubled minde, hee dowtes he shalbe
    caughte,
And leaves the waie, and over hedges climes:
And standes in feare, of everie busshe, and
    brake,
Ye oftentimes, his shaddowe makes him quake.

                              (Whitney, p. 32)

Similarly two of Milton's emblematic pictures under-
line Satan's criminal and guilty nature: first as the
grand thief, leaping the wall of Paradise, then as
a guilty criminal, slinking away from his crime after
the fall of Eve.

One Gate there only was, . . .
        which when th' Arch-felon saw
Due entrance he disdain'd, and in contempt,
At one slight bound high overleap'd all
    bound
Of Hill or highest Wall, and sheer within
Lights on his feet.

                              (IV. 178-83)

but when he saw descend
The Son of God to judge them, terrif'd
Hee fled, . . .
        fearing guilty what his wrath
Might suddenly inflict;

                              (X. 337-41)

Commenting that "guilte mindes, are reack'de with fear-
full fittes:" Whitney adds a motto, similar to Raphael's warning to Adam in Paradise Lost, to beware of
Satan, a thief of the rich human souls (VI. 900-912 &
VIII. 635-643).

Then keepe thee pure, and soile thee not
.   with sinne,
For often guilte, thine inwarde greifes
    beginne.

Evil has the same fascination for man as goodness.
Satanic characters figure in all mythologies, and

often appear as more complex, more versatile than the good. Milton's Satan, the Satan of the Hebraic-Christian tradition, was once the "anointed cherub" of God: a spirit next to God in the hierarchy of His creatures, endowed with brilliance, beauty and power superior to all others save God and His Son in heaven. Of the Prince of Tyrus, the prototype of this great archangel, Ezekiel gives the following vignette in the Old Testament:

> Thou sealest up the sum, full of wisdom,
> and perfect in beauty. Thou has been in
> Eden, the garden of God; every precious
> stone was thy covering, the sardius,
> topas, and the diamond, the beryl, the
> onyx, and the jasper, the sapphire, the
> emerald, and the carbuncle, and gold: the
> workmanship of thy tabrets and of thy pipes
> was prepared in thee in the day that thou
> was created. Thou art the anointed cherub
> that covereth; and I have set thee so:
> thou wast upon the holy mountain of God,
> thou hast walked up and down in the midst of
> the stones of fire. Thou wast perfect in
> thy ways from the day that thou wast
> created till, iniquity was found in thee.
> By the multitude of thy merchandise they
> have filled the midst of thee with vio-
> lence, and thou has sinned: therefore
> I will cast thee as profane out of the
> mountain of God: and I will destroy thee,
> O covering cherub, from the midst of the
> stones of fire. Thine heart was lifted
> up because of thy beauty, thou hast
> corrupted thy wisdom by reason of thy
> brightness: I will cast thee to the
> ground, I will lay thee before kings,
> that they may behold thee. Thou hast de-
> filed thy sanctuaries by the multitude of
> thy iniquities, by the iniquity of thy
> traffick; therefore, will I bring forth a
> fire from the midst of thee, it shall devour
> thee, and I will bring thee to ashes upon the
> earth in the sight of all them that behold thee,
> (Ez. xxviii 12-19). All they that know thee
> among the people shall be astonished at thee: the
> merchants among the people shall hiss at thee:
> thou shalt be a terror, and never shalt thou
> be any more. (Ez. xxvii 36).

This equating Satan with the Prince of Tyrus is not
unusual, for the devil has often been referred to in
the Scriptures as "the prince of the world" (John xii
31; xiv 30; xvi 11), the tycoon of material goods.
Milton's Satan conforms to the Prince of Tyrus, though
Milton's lustrous archangel, has not been matched in
literature. Milton's description of his physical·
beauty and his mental strength and incisiveness place
Satan on a pedestal for most art lovers. His degeneration is subtly planned and complete at the end of
Paradise Lost, but his mind and will remain powerful.
He questions his own acts at times, shows remorse and
is nostalgic for heaven often: is concerned for his
fallen comrades, and at junctures, introspecting,
weighs evil against good. Blake was wrong when he
called Milton "of the Devil's party," but was right
in showing that Milton wrote of Satan with a poet-
creator's sympathy and abandon, elaborating the pithy
statement of Ezekiel for the Prince of Tyrus. Milton's Satan can be compared with the tragic heroes of
the Greek playwrights, but excels them in dignity and
majesty. He is a thinker who does not capitulate even
when he feels that his might cannot match that of his
great Opponent. Other writers such as Caedmon in the
seventh century, Hugo Grotius in Adamus exul (1601),
Jacob Cats in Trou-Ringh (1637), and Vondel in Lucifer
(1654) had also made the Devil an imposing figure;
Milton was not unique. One of the Devil's greatest
fascinations was that he was an advocate of knowledge;
forbidden no doubt, but such that aroused intellectual
curiosity.

Milton's Satan first erred because of jealousy,
which came to the surface at the Son's coronation.
This long-nourished ambition to be equal to God or
to supersede him, had been latent, and God's elevation
of his Son was the moment that triggered Satan's open
revolt. "Satan disturbed the external equilibrium or
harmony of the angels, to form a separate ego, the
origin of dynamic action. . . . The hiatus produced
in Heaven by the secession of the rebel angels caused
the creation."[6]

In Emblems (Book IV No. 1), Francis Quarles gives
a graphic idea of man's mental stress and turmoil:
the illustration shows Anima between personifica-
tions of good and evil. One is pulling her back, the
other inviting her forward. In the verse the Soul
seems buffeted and as much in a quandry as Satan

88

struggling through Chaos, and a logician's mental
somersaults as he weighs the pros and cons of his
situation (IV. 32-110).

> O How my will is hurried to and fro
> And how my unresolved resolves do vary
> I know not where to fix; sometimes I go
> This way, then that, and then the quite
>   contrary:
> I like, dislike; lament for what I could not
> And, at the selfsame instant, will the thing
>   I would not.
>
> Sometimes a sudden flash of sacred heat
> Warms my chill soul, and sets my thoughts
>   in flame.
> But soon that fire is shoulder'd from her
>   seat
> By lustful Cupid's much inferior flame
> I feel two flames, and yet no flame entire;
> Thus are the mongrel thoughts of mix'd de-
>   sire
> Consumed between that heav'nly and this
>   earthly fire.
>
> Sometimes my trash-disdaining thoughts
>   outpass
> The common period of terrene conceit;
> O then methinks I scorn the thing I was
> Whilst I stand ravish'd at my new estate:
> But when th' Icarian wings of my desires
> Feel but the warmth of their own native fire
> O then they melt and plunge within their
>   wonted fire.
>
> I know the nature of my wav'ring mind;
> I know the frailty of my fleshly will!
> My passion's eagle-eyed, my judgment blind;
> I know what's good, and yet make choice
>   of ill.

(Quarles, Emblems, pp.
301-2)

Satan's remorse and perplexity are given by Milton in
comparable emblems as he equates his state in Hell
and chaos and also in Eden, with that in Heaven. Symbolically Satan is tossed around in chaos, buffeted
by different elements, rising with the lighter,

sinking with the heavier and floating in vacuum; all
states of mind in which the fallen archangel is tor-
mented; his natural motion to rise toward God and
Heaven (II. 75) is reversed by his "obstinate pride"
(I. 58) and a mind "not to be changed by place or
time" (I. 253). In pride he ascends, but has reverses
till the elements propel him to Chaos; his mind still
chaotic with conflicting goodness and evil:

> . . . his Sail-broad Vans
> He spreads for flight, and in the surging
>   smoke
> Uplifted spurns, the ground, thence many
>   a League
> As in a cloudy Chair ascending rides
> Audacious, but that seat soon failing, meets
> A vast vacuity: all unawares
> Flutt'ring his pennons vain plumb down
>   he drops
> [Till] . . . some tumultous cloud
> Instinct with Fire and Nitre hurried him
> As many miles aloft:. . .

[While he]

> Swims or sinks, or wades, or creeps, or flies:

(II. 927-50)

In the milling, churning, stormy elements, Satan's
physical journey is as arduous as his mental. His
nostalgia for Heaven, for his gracious Creator (IV.
43) who elevated him to a position next to Himself,
and for "Heav'n's free Love" (IV. 68) abundant and
equal, is searing. He curses his apostacy to evil:

> Nay curs'd be thou; since against his thy
>   will
> Chose freely what it now so justly rues.
> Me miserable! which way shall I fly
> Infinite wrath, and infinite despair?
> Which way I fly is Hell; myself am Hell;
> And in the lowest deep a lower deep
> Still threat'ning to devour me opens wide,
> To which the Hell I suffer seems a Heav'n.
> O then at last relent:

And like Marlowe's Faustus he cries:

                        is there no place
        Left for Repentance, none for Pardon left?
        None left but by submission; and that word
        Disdain forbids me, and my dread of shame
        Among the Spirits beneath, whom I seduc'd
        With other promises and other vaunts
        Than to submit, boasting I could subdue
        Th' Omnipotent. Ay me, they little know
        How dearly I abide that boast so vain
        Under what torments I inwardly groan:
                        . . . only Supreme
        In misery;

                        (IV. 71-92)

Satan's devilry rankles in him several times for he
has sat next to God and retains in himself and in his
person the nobility of the spirits of Heaven. Seeing
the Heaven-like beauty of Eden he revels in it only to
realize his own outcast state; and his mental suffering
becomes as great as his physical in Hell and Chaos:

                        but I in none of these
        Find place or refuge; and the more I see
        Pleasures about me, so much more I feel
        Torment within me, as from the hateful siege
        Of contraries; all good to me becomes
        Bane, and in Heav'n much worse would be my
            state.
        But neither here seek I, no nor in Heav'n
        To dwell . . .
        Nor hope to be myself less miserable
        By what I seek, but others to make such
        As I, though thereby worse to me redound
        For only in destroying I find ease
        To my relentless thoughts.

                        (IX. 118-30)

Satan, created to be good in his eminence, expresses
deep remorse, but like Quarles' sinner is caught in
his own toils and cannot extricate himself; he is a
victim of his own crime.

        Although the lament of Quarles' sinful man re-
sembles that of Milton's Satan, and his remorse, chagrin and despondency are likewise similar, another
parallel is even closer. Quarles depicts hopelessness
by a picture of Anima sitting pensive on the ground,

an hour glass hopelessly opaque by her side. Death
and fantastic figures hover above her, and the caption
to the emblem is:

> My life is spent with grief, and my
> years with sighing. Ps. xxxi.10.

Several lines of Quarles' verses echo Milton's lament
on his physical blindness, but Quarles depicts Satan's
and Adam's spiritual blindness in a way reminiscent
of Milton's Samson: "Day worse than night, night worse
than day appears,"

> Why was I born? Why was I born a man?
> And why proportion'd by as large a span?
> Or why suspended by the common lot,
> And being born to die, why die I not?
> Ah me! Why is my sorrow wasted breath?
> Denied the easy privilege of death?
>
> What sullen star ruled my untimely birth,
> That would not lend my days one hour of
> mirth?
> How oft have these bare knees been bent
> to gain
> The slender alms of one poor smile in vain!
> How often tired with the fastidious light,
> Have my faint lips implored the shades of
> night!
> How often have my nightly torments pray'd
> For ling'ring twilight, glutted with the
> shade!
> Day worse than night, night worse than day
> appears,
> In fears I spend my nights, my days in tears:
> I moan unpitied, groan without relief,
> There is no end or measure of my grief.
> The smiling flow'r salutes the day; it grows
> Untouch'd with care; it neither spins nor
> sows;
> Oh that my tedious life were like this
> flow'r.
> Or freed from grief, or finish'd with an
> hour:
>
> The branded slave, that tugs the weary oar,
> Obtains the sabbath of a welcome shore;
> His ransom'd stripes are heal'd; his
> native soil

Sweetens the mem'ry of his foreign toil:
But, ah! my sorrows are not half so blest;
My labour finds no point, my pains no rest.

(Quarles, Emblems, p.
299)

The remorse of Satan in his soliloquies parallels Emblem XV, Book III and Emblem I, Book IV of Quarles. Satan, a "superman," displays all the emotions of man. His conscience goads him to penitence but pride and shame propel him away from it, almost as though he were torn between centrifugal and centripetal forces. Milton and the emblematist both deal with the conflict of evil and good. In the satanic character the former becomes predominant, but the conflict is ever present; and if not penitence, it often evokes remorse.

Once the Fall is consummated in Paradise Lost, Sin and Death aid Satan gain dominion over the world. They build a causeway or bridge to the new-made world for egress and entry from Hell. The causeway over Chaos perpetuates the Devil's possession of the World, and seals the maxim, "The World, the flesh and the Devil," the diabolic trinity that the early Church had accepted and the seventeenth century was still trying to unravel. This is aptly shown in an emblem of Wither's in which youth (Hercules) has to choose between sobriety and knowledge on the one hand and beauty and lasciviousness on the other. Vice is a naked female figure holding a mask in her right hand to conceal her devilish features and horns and the diabolic wings behind her. Her feet are claws, and a tail is curled beneath her. By her side rests a lute, and behind her is a skull and cross bones. Virtue appears as Moses, with a saintly demeanour, a book, and the caduceus. Behind him grows a sprightly flower. In the verse Wither announces that at eighteen years a youth, lured to the city, brings with him a body and mind fit to be coveted by both vice and virtue, and each tries to win him:

Vice, Pleasures best Contentments promist mee,
And what the wanton flesh desires to have:
Quoth Vertue, I will Wisdome give to thee,
And those brave things, which noblest Mindes
    doe crave,
Serve me said Vice, and thou shalt soone
    acquire

93

All those Atchievements which my Service
    brings:
Serve me said Vertue, and Ile raise thee
    higher,
Then Vices can, and teach thee better things.
Whil'st thus they strove to gaine me, I
    espyde
Grim Death attending Vice; and, that her
    Face
Was but a painted Vizard, which did hide
The foul'st Deformity that ever was.

                                    (Wither, p. 22)

Wither asks for God's grace to eschew Vice and court
Virtue. Material pleasures were considered the
Devil's special realm, and his attendants Sin and Death
were the aftermath of laxity associated with worldly
pleasures.

    In his subjective manner Quarles questions God
regarding the Devil's ascendancy on earth and his
boldness in trying to usurp God's throne. Winged
Anima, arms outstretched, eyes turned heavenward,
reaches for the heart suspended from Heaven, while
the globe of the world, with the Devil's horns growing on top of it, a cloven hoof at the bottom and a
sword in the crank that turns it, looms ominously behind her. Fierce arrowheads are shown emerging from
the devilish globe. Quarles quotes Rev. xii 12, "The
devil is come down unto you, having great wrath, because he knoweth that he had but a short time." He
asks God why he suffers the Devil to operate:

    Lord, canst thou see and suffer? Is
        thy hand
    Still bound to th' peace? Shall earth's
        black monarch take
    A full possession of thy wasted land?
    Oh, will thy slumb'ring vengeance never wake,
    Till full-aged, law-resisting custom shake
    The pillars of thy right by false command?
    Unlock thy clouds great Thund'rer, and
        come down;
    Behold whose temples wear thy sacred crown;
    Redress, redress our ways; revenge, revenge
        thy own.

94

See how the bold usurper mounts the seat
Of royal majesty; how overstrowing
Perils with pleasure, pointing ev'ry threat
With bugbear death, by torments overawing
Thy frighted subjects; or by favours
    drawing
Their tempted hearts to his unjust retreat;
Lord, canst thou be so mild, and he so
    bold?

What do we here? Who would not wish to be
Dissolved from earth, and with Astrea flee
From this blind dungeon to that sunbright
    throne?
Lord, is thy sceptre lost, or laid aside?
Is hell broke loose, and all her fiends
    untied?
Lord, rise, and rouse, and rule, and crush
    their furious pride.

                    (Quarles, _Emblems_, p.
                    234).

These lines give ideas that parallel the war in Milton's heaven. Quarles questions Satan's audacity as
an insurgent, his onslaught on the creatures made in
God's image and his opening the way for Sin, the
devils, and Death. He laments the flight of Astrea
or justice from a world of horrors, and imprecates
God, the Thunderer, to curb "earth's black monarch."
Milton's Thunderer curbed the Satanic revolt through
the agency of His son, but Satan gained ascendancy
over God's creation, because the humane God created
the Will and Reason of both man and angel free. The
theological implication is significant here. Should
God interfere when His creatures err, or should they
not err because they can reason like God and can exert
their will freely? Milton's ideas of liberty are implicit in the argument. In _Paradise Lost_, he is quite
emphatic about man's responsibility to act in justice.
Milton, unlike Quarles, does not bewail the Devil's
freedom of action.

    Quarles ends his emblem with a fatalist's and a
Stoic acceptance of life's offerings in the epigram:

        My soul, sit thou a patient looker on;
        Judge not the play before the play is done:

95

Her plot has many changes: ev'ry day
Speaks a new scene: The last act crowns
the play.

Milton's emblem seems to be in answer to Quarles.
God's sufferance of evil is for a purpose. God is
speaking to his angels as he looks at the marred
world of Sin and sees Death infest the world:

See with what heat these Dogs of Hell
advance
To waste and havoc yonder World, which I
So fair and good created, . . . had not the
folly of Man
Let in these wasteful Furies, who impute
Folly to mee so doth the Prince of Hell
And his Adherents, that with so much ease
I suffer them to enter and possess
A place so heav'nly, and conniving seem
To gratify my scornful Enemies
That laugh, as if transported with some fit
Of Passion, I to them had quitted all,
At random yielded up to their misrule;
And know not that I call'd and drew them
thither
My Hell-hounds, to lick up the draff and
filth
Which man's polluting Sin with taint hath
shed
On what was pure, till cramm'd and gorg'd,
nigh burst
With suckt and glutted offal, at one
sling
Of thy victorious Arm; well-pleasing Son,
Both Sin, and Death, and yawning Grave at
last
Through Chaos hurl'd, obstruct the
mouth of Hell
Forever, and seal up his ravenous Jaws.
Then Heav'n and Earth renew'd shall be
made pure
To sanctity that shall receive no stain:
Till then the Curse pronounc't on both
precedes.

(X. 616-40)

God leaves Satan and Sin and Death to work as scaven-
gers, to clean the world of impurity and pollution,

Milton implies, so that at the last when they are
sealed in Hell, earth will revert to her pristine
glory.

At times Satan, stupified out of his evil designs, dissociates himself from evil and reverts to
his original, heavenly state:

> That space the Evil One abstracted stood
> From his own evil, and for the time remain'd
> Stupidly good, of enmity disarm'd
> Of guile, of hate, of envy, of revenge;

(IX. 463-70)

Milton's Satan represents symbolically the dual
nature of man. He is a composite of good and evil,
the two elements which are perpetually in conflict,
but he gradually takes on all the traits connected
with evil and darkness. His new abode with its
Tartarean fires and its "darkness visible" are psychologically conducive to his courting "works of
darkness." He has glimmerings of light until he
returns to Hell on completing his mission in Eden.
He then becomes consummate Hell. Milton's Hell is
Satan and his abode. It is not only the Hebraic
Gehenna outside the west gates of the wailing wall
of Jerusalem where the refuse of the city is burnt,
making the stench and heat from the fire unbearable,
but the Greek Hades and the Virgilian Tartarus and
Dante's Inferno. Virgil's Tartarus is the prototype
of Milton's hell. It is dark and cavernous and at
great depth, far removed from the light of the gods'
abode. It has the howling hell hounds, and hoary
mountains, and wastelands. It also has all the allegorical and personified evils: terrible shapes,
diseases, old age, loneliness, fear, hunger, evil
counsel, poverty, false dreams, sleep, pain, sin, and
death; also the Furies and Strife. Its hybrid monsters have among them, Scylla, and "Lerna's Beast
with its horrifying hiss," the Chimaera, Gorgons,
Harpies, and the shadow of the "three-bodied Geryon."
Along with these are a multitude of youth. Like Milton's leaves of Vallombrosa the bodies of the young
are "As numerous . . . as the leaves of the forest
which fall at the first chill of autumn and float"
on the Lake of Styx.[7] Tartarus also has its murky,
muddy Acheron; Cocytus with its deep pools, and the
marsh and Lake of Styx. Their waters flow between

"banks of dread," and have "snarling currents." The
burning river of white-hot flames is Phlegethon, and
its shadows are all dark. Milton's picture of Hell
and its new inhabitants stretches over the first two
books of Paradise Lost and subsequent sections of the
epic until Satan is back at Pandemonium in Book X
(419-584); but Milton's compressed and picturesque
derivative of Virgil's hell is best seen in the ex-
plorations of the pioneers and reconnoitrers and dis-
coverers among the hellish angels as they fly in
squadrons:

                    . . . along the Banks
        Of four infernal Rivers that disgorge
        Into the burning Lake thir baleful streams;
        Abhorred Styx the flood of deadly hate,
        Sad Acheron of sorrow, black and deep;
        Cocytus, nam'd of lamentation loud
        Heard on the rueful stream; fierce Phlegaton
        Whose waves of torrent fire inflame with
            rage.
        Far off from these a slow and silent stream,
        Lethe the River of Oblivion rolls
        Her wat'ry Labyrinth, whereof who drinks,
        Forthwith his former state and being forgets,
        Forgets both joy and grief, pleasure and
            pain.
        Beyond this flood a frozen Continent
        Lies dark and wild, beat with perpetual
            storms,
        Of Whirlwind and dire Hail, which on firm
            land
        Thaws not, but gathers heap, and ruin seems
        Of ancient pile; all else deep snow and ice,
        A gulf profound as that Serbonian Bog
        Betwixt Damiata and Mount Casius old,
        Where Armies whole have sunk: the parching
            Air
        Burns frore, and cold performs th' effect
            of Fire.
        Thither by harpy-footed Furies hal'd,
        At certain revolutions all the damn'd
        Are brought: and feel by turns the bitter
            change
        Of fierce extremes, extremes by change
            more fierce,
        From Beds of raging Fire to starve in Ice
        Thir soft Ethereal warmth, and there to
            pine
        Immovable, infixt, and frozen round,

Periods of time, thence hurried back to fire.
They ferry over this Lethean Sound
Both to and fro, thir sorrow to augment,
And wish and struggle, as they pass, to reach
The tempting stream, with one small drop to
    lose
In sweet forgetfulness all pain and woe,
All in one moment, and so near the brink;
But Fate withstands, and to oppose th'attempt
Medusa and Gorgonian terror guards
The Ford, and of itself the water flies
All taste of living wight, as once it fled
The lip of Tantalus.

    . . . through many a dark and dreary Vale
They pass'd, and many a Region dolorous,
O'er many a Frozen, many a Fiery Alp,
Rocks, Caves, Lakes, Fens, Bogs, Dens, and
    shades of death,
A Universe of death, which God by curse
Created evil, for evil only good,
Where all life dies, death lives, and Nature
    breeds,
Perverse, all monstruous, all prodigious
    things,
Abominable, inutterable, and worse
Than Fables yet have feign'd, or fear con-
    ceiv'd,
Gorgons and Hydras, and Chimeras dire.

                    (II. 574-628)

Quarles' Hell is lust, ignited by the feeble and false
love-light of Cupid. It is meant for the "night's un-
Titan'd hemisphere" for "Heaven's scornful flames and
Cupid's can never co-appear", as the latter only "in-
flames desire." "Heaven's bright glory" can quench
at will this fire of Hell. If man chooses Hell's fire
he not only eschews the light of Heaven but quenches
his own heavenly spark;

            Ah, fool! perpetual night
            Shall haunt your souls with Stygian sight.

                    (Quarles, Emblems,
                    p. 235)

There they shall "boil in flames, but flames shall
bring no light." The device shows the cherubic Anima

                    99

bellows in hand, standing against the globe, and trying to divert the fool whose candle is burning low in
the background, while the fool himself is standing on
the brink of an ocean, attempting to quench the light
of the blazing sun with another pair of bellows. The
ocean has monstrous gaping fish-heads ready to swallow
the man. The sexual overtones are evident in the
verses. Erotic love in the seventeenth century was
often associated with stews or brothels and referred
to as hellish and the sure way to a man's physical
and material ruin. Milton's hell has the lewd Belial
(I. 490) and sons of Belial, who swollen with pride
often walked the streets (as in Restoration London)
and joyed

> . . . in the bought smiles,
> Of Harlots, loveless, joyless, unendear'd,
> Casual fruition,

(IV. 765-67)

Milton had no time for "lustful appetence" and the
"sober race of men" who succumbed to the seduction of
the unchaste (XI. 619-24). Milton's hellish Sin and
her offspring, Death and the hell hounds, were the
ultimate in lustful perversion. They were the victims
of their own psychological Hell. Neither did Adam and
Eve's lustful embraces after the Fall bring them nearer
Heaven or give peace of mind. Hell, as in Quarles'
emblem, takes many shapes.

The duplicity of Satan and the World become synonymous in Book II, Emblem V of Quarles. Anima in the
device has been won by the World. Her crown and dress
are more akin to a dunce's than a king's. In front of
her is a crow trying to parade as a peacock with borrowed tail feathers. Anima's attire and vanity complement that of the crow. The verses that follow are
reminiscent of Satan's temptation of Eve, his glozing
lies and promise of a glorious future. Eve succumbs
to his persuasive words, as Anima had fallen a victim
to the world, for Satan's "words replete with guile /
Into her heart too easy entrance won" (IX. 733-34).

Under the caption, "Wilt thou set thine eyes
upon that which is not?" (Prov. xxiii.5), Quarles says
to Satan and the world:

```
       False world, thou ly'st: thou canst not lend
                The least delight:
       Thy favours cannot gain a friend,
                They are so slight:
       Poor are the wants that thou supply'st
       And yet thou vaunt'st, and yet thou vy'st
       With Heaven; fond earth, thou boast'st;
                false world thou ly'st.
```

The next verse embodies Eve's temptation and fall, as
Quarles continues to direct his lines to the Satanic
world:

```
       Thy babbling tongue tells golden tales
                Of endless treasure:
       Thy bounty offers easy sales
                Of lasting pleasure
       Thou ask'st the conscience what she ails,
                And swear'st to ease her;

       Alas! fond world, thou boast'st; false
                world, thou ly'st.
       What well-advised ear regards
                What earth can say?
       Thy words are gold, but thy rewards
                Are painted clay

       Thou art but what thou seem'st; false
                world, thou ly'st

       Thy tinsel bosom seems a mint
                Of new-coin'd treasure
       A paradise, that has no stint
                No change, no measure;
       A painted cask, but nothing in't,
                Nor wealth, nor pleasure
       Vain earth! that falsely thus comply'st
       With man; vain man, that thou rely'st
       On earth: vain man, thou doat'st; vain
                earth, thou ly'st
```

                        (Quarles, Bk. II Emb.
                        V pp. 243-44)

In the following verse, Quarles finds that "The height
of the world's enchanting pleasure is but a flash."
Similarly Eve's euphoria on eating the forbidden fruit
does not last; the morning after the night before, is
a time of recrimination, shame and dismal regrets. The

                        101

effects of Satan's falsity are far reaching for Milton
as for Quarles.

The vicious design of Satan comes full circle in
Quarles Book III, Emblem IX, (p. 285) when the victim
is snared and netted. The imagery of the chase is
appropriate to the device where Anima stands perplexed-
ly enmeshed; the cup that inebriates in one hand, and
a lobbed ball in the other. The images of a hunt symbolically portray the abject state of the soul once
caught in Satan's net. The caption and the verse read:
"The sorrows of hell compassed me about: the snares
of death prevented me. Psalm xviii.5:"

> Is not this type well cut, in ev'ry part
> Full of rich cunning, fill'd with Zeuxian
> art?
> Are not the hunters and their Stygian hounds
> Limn'd full to th' life? didst ever hear
> the sound
> Of music, and the lip-dividing breaths
> Of the strong winded horn, recheats, and
> deaths,
> Done more exact? th' infernal Nimrod's
> halloo?
> The lawless purlieus? and the game they
> follow?
> The hidden engines, and the snares that lie
> So undiscover'd, so obscure to th' eye?
> The new drawn net, and her entangled prey?
> And him that closes it? Beholden, say,
> Is't not well done? seems not an em'lous
> strife
> Betwixt the rare cut picture and the life?
> These purlieu men are devils; and the hounds
> (Those quick-nosed cannibals, that scour
> the grounds)
> Temptations; and the game the fiends pursue,
> Are human souls, which still they have in
> view;
> Whose fury if they chance to 'scape by flying,
> The skilful hunter plants his net close lying
> On th' unsuspected earth, baited with
> treasure,
> Ambitious honour, and self-wasting pleasure:
> Where, if the soul but stoop, death stands
> prepared
> To draw the net, and drown the souls
> ensnared.

Epig. 9

> Be sad, my heart, deep dangers wait thy
>   mirth:
> Thy soul's waylaid by sea, by hell, by
>   earth:
> Hell has her hounds; earth, snares; the sea,
>   a shelf:
> But, most of all, my heart, beware thyself.

(Quarles, Emblems, p.
285)

Eve in Paradise Lost is the first soul caught in the entangling, meshlike designs of the Devil, and has to face the implications. She realizes her own part in the fall, her soul is greatly oppressed and Satan's Hell seems to surround her:

> both have sinn'd, but thou
> Against God only, I against God and thee
>
> . . . sole cause to thee of all this woe,

(X. 931-37)

Emblems of Hell and Satan are synonymous.

Long before Satan seduced Eve, he had bade farewell to all that could lead him back to Heaven: to Hope and Fear and Remorse. He had welcomed Evil to hold "at least / Divided Empire with Heav'ns King. . ." (IV. 110-11), deluding himself, as C. S. Lewis points out that "infernal monarchy has a stability,"[8] and showing a lack of judgment. He remains a prisoner of his own Hell. His seduction of the human pair completes his nefarious mission, yet the evil recoils on him. He leaves "condemn'd,/ Convict by flight, and Rebel to all Law" (X. 82-3). His end though postponed is promised. God's Son will "subdue / My vanquisher, spoil'd of his vaunted spoil" (III. 250-51), and "shall lead Hell captive maugre Hell" (III. 255).

With Quarles it can be said of Satan:

> Ah! treach'rous soul, would not thy
>   pleasures give
> That Lord, which made thee living, leave to
>   live.

103

See what thy sins have done: thy sins have
  made
The Sun of Glory now become thy shade.

                    (Quarles, Emblems,
                       p. 331)

FOOTNOTES

[1]Hughes, ed. "On Time," p. 80.

[2]Freeman, p. 5.

[3]John M. Steadman, Milton's Epic Characters
(Chapel Hill: Un. of North Carolina, 1968), p. 4.

[4]Marcia Pointon, Milton and English Art (Toronto:
University of Toronto Press, 1970), pp. 4 and 5,
Devices 2, 3, & 4.

[5]Hughes, ed., p. 905.

[6]E. H. Visiak, The Portent of Milton (New York:
Humanities Press, 1968), p. 24.

[7]Virgil, Aeneid, trans. W. F. Jackson Knight
(Hammondsworth, England: Penguin, 1968), pp. 151-57.

[8]C. S. Lewis, A Preface to Paradise Lost (London:
Oxford University Press, 1956), p. 96.

Milton did not only borrow part of the creation
story from the Theogony, but his Satan is the prototype of "Typho, terrible and proud / and lawless."
Milton's Sin belongs with Echidna, probably the
daughter of Ceto, granddaughter of Pontus and Earth.

> She [Ceto] bore another monster, terrible,
> In a hollow cave, Echidna, fierce of heart,
> Nothing like any mortal man, unlike
> Any immortal god, for half of her
> Is a fair-cheeked girl with glancing eyes,
>   but half
> Is a huge and frightening speckled snake;
>   she eats
> Raw flesh in a recess of the holy earth.
> Down there she has a cave of hollow rock
> Far from the deathless gods and mortal men;
> There the gods gave a famous home to her,
> And gloomy Echidna keeps her watch down
>   there
> Under the ground, among the Arimoi,
> A nymph immortal, and ageless all her days.[1]

> (Hesiod, "Theogony,"
> pp. 32-33)

Milton's Sin as Spenser's Ignorance is derived from
Echidna.

Typho the Satanic figure loves her and from their
union are born, Orthos a dog of the three headed monster, Geryon; the raw-flesh-eating fifty-headed and
bronze-voiced dog of Hades, Cerberus; the Lernaean
Hydra; and the fire-breathing Chimaera, with a lion's,
a goat's, and a snake's heads. It was Echidna's incest with her first born, the dog Orthos, which gave
birth to the Sphinx and the Nemean lion. Milton's
allegory has created hell hounds that gnaw at their
mother's entrails as they take shelter in her womb,
while her first-born, Death, the father of the hell
hounds, hates and lusts for her at the same time.
Typho then is Satan, Echidna Sin, and Orthos Death.

The emblem writers have taken this motif and
reproduced it in devices that show the bestial side
of human beings in their hypocrisy and heinous mode of

operation. Waist upwards the figures are pleasing; downwards they are either entwining snakes or dragons or fish tails, as shown in this chapter.

Sin is also the counterpart of Virgil's Tisi-phone,[2] guardian of the adamantine and gigantic gates of Tartarus which were impervious to human or divine strength. Tisiphone sat guardian in an iron tower, her robe girt up and bloody. Spenser's emblem of "Errour" is extended into the allegory of Sin by Milton, and both are drawn from Echidna of Hesiod, and from Scylla after her deformity described in Ovid's Metamorphoses[3] as well as Tisiphone; also from Rev. ix 7-10 where locusts with men's faces, women's hair and scorpions' stings and tails are mentioned.

Spenser's Errour is:

> the ugly monster. . .,
> Halfe like a serpent horribly displaide,
> But th' other halfe did womans shape retaine,
> Most lothsom, filthie, foule, and full of
>   vile disdaine.
>
> And as she lay upon the durtie ground,
> Her huge long taile her den overspred,
> Yet was in knots and many boughtes upwound,
> Pointed with mortall sting. Of her there
>   bred
> A thousand young ones, which she dayly fed,
> Sucking upon her poisonous dugs, eachone
> Of sundry shapes, yet all ill favored:
> Soone as that uncouth light upon them shone,
> Into her mouth they crept, and suddaine all
>   were gone.[4]

(The Faerie Queene, I.i.
14-15)

Ignorance when attacked could wind herself round a man and constrict him, so Spenser ends by saying: "God helpe the man so wrapt in Errours endlesse traine"(F.Q. I. i 18). This is a picture given in the emblematic tradition. The visual image precedes the author's own metaphoric and didactic intention explained in a line or two, here it is in the Alexandrine of Spenser's stanza. These serpent-women belong with the Talmudic Lilith and the Roman Lamia; the latter so skilfully used by Keats in his verse narrative.

107

Panofsky in his study of iconology has pointed
out that fraud and hypocrisy are often depicted in
emblems showing a beautiful female with a bestial tail
and ugly claws, such as the Hippocrisia of Cesar Ripa,
with her wolves' feet; Inganno "hiding an ugly face
beneath a beautiful mask and offering water and fire"
alternately; Fraude with two heads, one youthful the
other aged, and two hearts held in the hand nearest
the youthful face, a young mask held in the other.
Fraude also has a dragon's tail and claws for feet.
Panofsky points out that one of the best examples of
fraud is in the Bronzino composition entitled Allegory
in the London National Gallery, where "Fraude" is a
little girl with the body of a scaly fish, lions claws,
and serpent's tail. In her hands she has a honeycomb
and a poisonous creature. The hands are attached to
wrong sides of the body, showing duplicity even in
her offerings of the good and the bad.[5]

A classic example of these are the sirens as
depicted by Whitney in his Emblemes. The device shows
the sirens with musical instruments and coiling
serpentine tails poised on the waves of the ocean,
while Ulysses leashed to the mast is shown being rowed
away. In the background a boat is depicted as foun-
dering. Apparently the same song that was heard by
Ulysses had been the bane of the men in the second
boat, who had upturned their boat to reach the sirens.
Tho verse reads:

> Withe pleasaunte tunes, the Syrenes did allure
> Ulisses wise, to listen theire songe:
> But nothing could his manlie harte procure,
> Hee sailde awaie, and scap'd their charming
>   stronge,
> The face, he lik'de, the nether parte, did
>   loathe:
> For womans shape, and fishes had they bothe.

The second verse warns against fraudulent and
specious beauty; for

> Suche Mairemaides live, that promise onelie
>   joyes:
> But hee that yeldes, at lengthe him selffe
>   distroies.

(Whitney, p. 10)

Peacham, who was considered comparatively inno-
vative and resourceful in his portrayal of his emblematic ideas, gives a powerful vignette of "Deceite"
or fraud, entitled Dolus meaning a trick or cunning.
The device has an elegantly dressed, seemingly pious
man, with hands folded in prayer, but his nether part
trails in two entwined snakes in place of legs. He
is super-imposed on a leopard, whose head is tucked
between his forelegs. The background displays a
church. The border, as the device it frames, has a
baying hound, birds of prey in a cormorant and an
eagle, a serpent-headed dragon, a sinuous snake, a
lecherous monkey, three monstrous heads, and a deer
shown upside down, as if sapped of its bounding energy.
The verses that follow say:

> Of simple looke, with countenance demure,
> In golden coate, lo heere deceite doth
>   stand,
> With eies to heaven upcast, as he were pure,
> Or never yet, in knav'ry had a hand,
> Whose nether partes, resemble to our sight,
> The figure of a fearefull Serpent right.
>
> And by his side, a Panther close you see,
> Who, when he cannot easily catch his pray,
> Doth hide his head, and face,with either knee,
> And shew his back, with spots bespeckled gay
> To other Beastes: which while they gaze upon,
> Are unawares, surprized every one.

(Peacham, p. 47)

Another of Peacham's emblems (page 115) displays
a harpy seated on a pie set on a table, and the verse
recalls the harpies who demolished blind Phineas' food.
In the second verse Peacham compares the harpies to
unscrupulous courtiers, who are slanderers and liars,
or greedy for bribes, or are parasitic, especially if
their overlords are blind to it. In other words
Peacham is decrying political evil and sins that deal
with flattery, extortion and glozing lies, as the title
of the emblem states "Inrepetundos, et adulatores."
Sin, whether depicted at its basest by Milton or as
error by Spenser, or fraud and deceit and extortion
by Whitney and Peacham, is deformed, grasping and
deadly. Ovid's picture of Scylla is similar as seen
in Mary M. Innes' translation of the Metamorphoses.

Scylla has a girdle of fierce dogs round her horrid
waist. She has the face of a girl and, unless all the
poets' tales are false, she was, in fact, a girl once.
Many suitors asked for her hand, but she rejected them.
She used to go to the sea nymphs, who loved her dearly,
and tell them how she had scorned the young men's
love.

On the instigation of Glaucus, who had desired
Scylla and been scorned and rejected by her, and
through Circe's own malicious charms the maid is turned
into a monster with a pack of wild dogs surrounding
her. Ovid explains the deformity of her nether
parts saying there was a little bay that curved
round in a smooth crescent, where Scylla loved to rest,
and retreated there from the midday heat to swim.
Circe poisoned the pool with herbes, resulting in
deadly poison that generated heads of doglike bark-
ing monsters. Her lower extremities were turned into
dogs of all kinds. (Ovid, pp. 312-13).

Wither's emblem entitled Insuperabilis Concordia
(p. 179) gives a picture of Geryon, the monstrous master
of Cerberus. The emblem is taken from Alciati and
represents "une union tres forts." The emblem not
only conveys that concord leads to united strength,
but shows that evil can be strong in itself. The
crowned warrior-king has six arms, each carrying an
instrument of war and destruction. His rich attire
contrasts with his bare feet, and with the lion headed
garter-spats he wears. On one side in the background
is a populous city, on the other barren hills with
a sparse farm. Directly behind him in the valley is
a microscopic emblem of a blind man carrying a lame
man on his shoulders, indicating probably that coop-
eration can help even the handicapped and make them
whole. In the verse Wither apologizes for giving his
own interpretation to the monster. He is interpreting
the strength of unity and not the diabolic character
of aggression, war, and murder displayed by Geryon
in his three armed person. In Alciati and Ripa, in
addition to his six arms, Geryon has six legs and feet.
In Dante Geryon is a monster and the guardian of the
eighth circle of the Inferno, the circle that imprisons
the souls of the fraudulent sinners. Geryon combines
in himself three of Satan's attributes, force, fraud

110

and violence, thus he becomes one of the diabolic
triads. In mythology he was one of the victims of
Hercules, the prototype of the Christ figure. In
Spenser's Faerie Queene Books IV & V, he is a monster,
Geryones. Geryones appears like Geryon and is considered his son and the epitome of evil, force, and
fraud. Eventually his three-fold strength is overcome
by Arthur, another savior figure, and he is slain.

An emblem of Peacham (page 188) entitled, Omnis
a Deo Sapientia, deals with the birth of Pallas Athena.
The emblem shows Jove seated on his eagle while
Hephaestus is near him axe in hand, having cleft Jove's
head. Milton gives a similar birth to Sin from Satan's
head. The difference is that Peacham's maiden is the
sapience of a supreme god, Milton's a thing of sinister
beauty, alluring but frightening. The pagan picture
reflects hope; Milton's Sin spells doom from the time
of her birth, for any wisdom she generates is diabolic.
Sin has also been represented as a female with a
demonic visage. In Wither, as shown in connection with
Satan,[6] sin, as Vice, has horns, claws for hands and
feet, a tail, and fleshly wings. She holds an innocent
visor to conceal her face. Wither exclaims that wooed
both by Vice and Virtue, he experiences the dilemma
of choices, for both are enticing, until death appears behind Vice:

> Vice, Pleasures best Contentments promist
>   mee,
> And what the wanton Flesh desires to have:
> Quoth Vertue, I will Wisdome give thee,
> And those brave things, which noblest
>   Mindes doe crave.
>
> Whil'st thus they strove to gaine me, I
>   espyde
> Grim Death attending Vice; and that her
>   Face
> Was but a painted Vizard, which did hide
> The foul'st Deformity that ever was.

(Wither, Emblemes, p. 22)

Another form that the emblematists used to depict
sin was the icon of a richly attired woman; her wizen-
ed face concealed by a mask, or visor. Wither has
the device on page 229 of his Emblemes XXI. The elder-
ly woman who pretends to be youthful deceives as does

beautiful Sin with her bestial tail. Wither says:

> This is an Emblem, fitly shaddowing those,
> Who making faire, and honest outward showes,
> Are inwardly deform'd;

Like Belial's counsel, their words are couched
in "reason's garb" when his intentions are far from
honorable:

> They chuse their words, and play well-acted
>   parts,
> But, hide most loathsome projects in their
>   hearts;

Wither elaborates the thought to include hypocritical
clergy and their pact with the devil. His words recall Belial further:

> . . . more (yea, most of all) my soule
>   despiseth
> A Heart, that in Religious formes, dis-
>   guiseth
> Prophane intentions; and arrayes in white,
> The coale-blacke conscience of an Hypocrite.
> Take heed of such as these; . . .
> Observe their footsteps, in their private
>   path:
> For these (as 'tis beleev'd, the Devill hath)
> Have cloven feet; that is, two wayes they
>   goe;
> One for their ends, and tother for a show.

He points out that hypocrisy is delusive and self
destructive. His statement brings to mind Belial
again and his shallow arguments:

> Such Fowles as these, are that Gay-plumed-
>   Crew,
> Which (to high place and Fortunes being
>   borne)
> Are men of goodly worth, in outward view;
> And, in themselves, deserve nought els but
>   scorne.
> For, though their Trappings, their high-
>   lifted Eyes,
> Their Lofty Words, and their much-feared
>   Pow'rs,

112

Doe make them seeme Heroicke, Stout, and Wise,
Their Hearts are oft as fond, and faint as
ours.

(Wither, Emblemes, p. 36)

The illustration shows a regal ostrich·with proud extended wings condemned by its corpulence to walk with
the lowly creatures of the earth, while other birds
soar aloft.

Had sin not interfered in their first encounter
Satan would have succumbed to Death. Immortal he considered himself, but her timely warning made him more
sagacious in his dealings with Death as she ejacu-
lated, ". . . neither vainly hope/To be invulnerable
... for that mortal dint,/ Save he who reigns above, none
can resist" (II. 811-14). Her mind functioned like
her father and "Author." She combined in herself the
traits of Satan and his associates: the statesmanship
of Beelzebub, lechery and love of ease of Belial
(II. 867-70), Mammon's lust for riches, Mulciber's
ingenuity and architectonic and engineering powers
(X. 252-61; 285-305); through her son Moloch's blood
lust; and all features of evil in Satan. In the
Hebraic cabala she is Lilith, the bride of Samael
(Satan or the evil angel), where she "is represented
as a naked woman whose body terminates in a serpent's
tail . . . and is drawn from the lili, female demonic
spirits in Mesopotamian demonology."7 As Laila she
is the spirit of darkness. In Persian lore she is a
Peri, a subject of Eblis or Satan and is malevolent
though beautiful. Sin, in Milton, is emblematic. His
sensory perception of the abstraction, makes him ex-
plore the sensuous and sensate in legends and lores,
to give her palpatating strength and energy.

The prescience of Milton's Sin is amazing. Sin
knew success would attend her Sire (X. 239), which
she attributes to the affinity between them, an affinity of evil which, like goodness, transcends time and
distance. But Sin also has her cross; she has to bear
the holocaust of Death. Hateful to each other, the
"odious offspring" (II. 781) and his dam are inseparable "For Death from Sin no power can separate"
(X. 251).

Sin is far from the beautiful "baroque icon"
Paul Doré paints of her, silhouetted in a cavern of

113

hell against an ornate column. She has her bestial
tail, but looks the epitome of innocent beauty. Doré
in the same picture makes Death appear as a faceless
Madonna against the backdrop of carved and imposing
hell-gates. There is nothing bristling or wrathful
about them as Satan views them from a distance. Milton's picture is very different. He gives Sin and
Death Herculean strength, which enables them to build
an incomprehensible though realistic causeway to
earth, and gain ascendancy there. In the allegorical
personification of Sin, Milton has exploited all the
doctrinal thoughts on the World, the Flesh, and the
Devil. Milton's Sin is truly sinister.

FOOTNOTES

[1] Dorothy Wender, trans., "Theogony," Hesiod and Theognis (Harmondsworth: Penguin Books, 1973), p. 33.

[2] Virgil, The Aeneid, trans. W.F.J. Knight (Baltimore: Penguin, 1956), p. 164.

[3] Ovid, Metamorphoses, trans. M. I. Innes (Baltimore: Penguin, 1955), pp. 305-13.

[4] Hugh MacLean, ed. Edmund Spenser's Poetry (New York: W. W. Norton, 1968), pp. 9-15.

[5] Irwin Panofsky, Studies in Iconology (New York: Harper & Row, 1972), pp. 86-90.

[6] Wither, p. 22.

[7] Gustav Davidson, A Dictionary of Angels (New York: Collier-McMillan, 1967), p. 174.

CHAPTER THREE

EMBLEMS OF WAR, MADNESS AND DEGENERATION

The complexity of madness is elusive, for madness
takes many forms, each as unique as the being it effects. To define it in a Lear, an Othello, a Hamlet,
as in Satan or degenerate man is as difficult as pin-
ning it to the romantic, the lover, the poet, the man
of wrath, the melancholic, the paranoid, or the religious fanatic; that is to life at various points of
stress. Madness can be termed psychological aberration, a touch of brilliance, frustration of the untam-
able in a regimented society, yearning for what is not,
the overwhelming onrush and impact of ideas especially
at epiphanies when the mind and body suddenly awake to
the unexpected, or it can be called a physical sickness with mental conditions ensuing from the ailment.
Madness has afflicted man from the beginning of time.
The Bible refers to it in Saul and Nebuchadnezzar, and
"starting from the view of madness that prevailed in
Greek tragedy, in which the gods punished presumptuous
heroes . . . by making them mad, or enraged, philosophers treated madness as a heroic deed."[1] However,
the God of Paradise Lost unlike the Olympians does not
inflict madness on Chaos or Satan or Man. Nor does
the madness of Man and angels seem profoundly philosophical. Circumstances create attitudes leading to
deviations from normalcy and degeneration in once exalted beings. The exception is Chaos in Paradise Lost,
for Chaos is the primeval force of nascent and formless
matter with its component, hot, cold, wet and dry, the
quintessential abstractions of the four elements. The
state of matter in Chaos is imbalanced, intemperate,
and moody, like surging passions. The master mind of
God alone calms its formless confusion and ruffled madness, and structures a highly organized universe from
it. In mythology when the younger gods fight the
older gods, madness takes the form of rebellion, the
rebellion of youth against the old order. In indi-
viduals, like Satan, it often takes the form of pride,
a sin with its attendants the other deadly sins. In
man it is separation from his source of life; an isolation which clouds his reason and brings intense suffering, depression, fear and anxiety, until man re-
asserts his self confidence and oneness with his
Creator.

116

Milton and the emblem writers deal with chaotic
madness in nature, in the angels, in Satan and in Man.

Madness and degeneracy, like their counterparts
goodness and progress, are cyclic in nature. The
state of chaos goes with the former: the state of
order, structure and rule with the latter. For both
the emblematists and Milton, the intellectual pro-
genies of the classics and the Bible, Nature was in
flux and chaos, formless and with unbroken darkness
until the great Architect ordered the four component
elements to stop milling, churning and warring, and
carved the universe from its "vast profundity obscure."
Energy and potential were inseparably present in this
chaotic mass. Generation alone was required. Generation, which is never ex nihilo, could be ordered because of the presence of this conglomeration of elements. Order and structure once achieved became the
hallmark of progress; anarchy and misrule remained
that of madness, furor, and degeneracy.

Milton in Areopagitica[2] concedes that confusion,
disorder, strife can only be assessed in comparison
with order and harmony. The understanding of the two
states is essential for comprehending life's pattern,
for "It was from out the rind of one apple tasted,
that the knowledge of good and evil as two twins
cleaving together leaped forth into the world." The
two states then complement each other as far as man's
behavioral patterns are concerned. This form of madness along with goodness and sanity then becomes an
essential component of life.

Madness and degeneracy are strikingly evident in
the fallen angels. On the burning marl the angels
lie stupefied and strewn as the autumn leaves of
Vallombrosa. Their precipitate fall from heaven had
been of no help to their mental health. Had their
great and diabolic leader not mustered the will to
arouse them from their stupor, they might have remained dormant in that degenerate state perpetually.
Satan still had the "semblance of Heaven" in him, and
so could sue and exhort them to order. In Milton's
epic the chaotic fires of hell yield to the strength
of order, and structures like the magnificent Pandemonium, are exhaled from the molten sea and scorching
plains and frigid hills, symbolically recapturing
an order that returns, to an extent, even among the
infernal spirits. Sparks of heavenly exactitude still

117

have the power to enlighten and uplift the fallen
creatures from total degeneracy. In the infernal
council had they voted for another course of action
than subversion, and had hubris not been such a
powerful motivation in their particular mental state
and attitude, the Miltonic drama might not have been
so potent. Reverting from the nadir of despair and
degeneration they could have re-established their
relationship with their Maker and returned to the
order from which they fell. But the pattern is different; the infernal council opts for perpetuating
evil and thus sustaining abasement. On the new created
earth this decision of theirs will lead to chaos. It
will shatter pristine peace; voices of accusation and
counter-accusation will be heard; harmless animals will
turn predators; seasons will bring about the rigors
of autumn and winter; death and decay will menace
life, and many a time bring back a state of anarchy.
The only assurance of perpetuity is God's throne. Outside creation and removed from the totality of the
universe, it serves the great Architect as a vantage
point from which to view his works dispassionately,
and create and re-create (both literally and metaphorically) from the chaotic flux. Whitney, drawing his
picture from Ovid, describes primeval chaos and the
order brought from it:

> When Fire, and Aire, and Earthe, and Water,
>   all weare one:
> Before that worke devine was wroughte,
>   which nowe wee looke uppon
> There was no forme of thinges, but a
>   confused masse:
> A lumpe, which Chaos men did call: wherin
>   no   order was,
> The Coulde, and Heate, did strive: the
>   Heavie thinges, and Lighte.
> The Harde, and Softe. the Wette, and Drye
>   for none had shape arighte.
> But when they weare dispos'd, eache one
>   into his roome:
> The Fire, had Heate: the Aire, had Lighte:
>   the Earthe, with fruites did bloome.
> The Sea, had his increase: which things,
>   to passe thus broughte:
> Behoulde, of this unperfecte masse, the
>   goodly worlde was wroughte.

> (Whitney, p. 122)

118

Milton's emblematic picture of Chaos draws heavily on
Ovid but he creates a surly unkempt demi-god of his
own, the potentate Chaos who rules the realm of Chaos.
He is a symbol of strife and degeneration. Chaos
ironically is the emperor of misrule, a travesty of
an umpire, whose "decision more imbroils the fray"
(II. 908) of warring elements. And "next him high
Arbiter / Chance governs all" (II. 909-10). Milton
may have had a popular emblem personifying Chance in
mind when he allegorically used the abstraction as a
partner of Chaos. A beautifully striking device personifying Chance in Alciati and in Whitney is also included in Wither's A Collection of Emblemes (p. 4).
In the device a wheel rests on stormy sea-waves, and
a Venus-like figure, a Renaissance nude, poses on it.
Her bare feet are winged, she sports a draped scarf
in one hand and a knife in the other. She is partially bald, but her forelocks which are wild and flying are superimposed on a threatening, clouded sky.
She is Occasion or Chance, and is depicted in Whitney
as fickle but chaste. The verse that follows stresses
these characteristics in a dramatic stichomythia; in
the question and answer mode:

> What creature thou? Occasion I doe showe.
> On whirling wheele declare why doste thou
> stande?
> Bicause, I still am tossed too, and froe.
> Why doest thou houlde a rasor in thy hande?
> That men maie knowe I cut on everie side,
> And when I come, I armies can devide.
>
> But wherefore hast thou winges uppon thy
> feete?
> To showe, how lighte I flie with little
> winde.
> What means longe lockes before? that such as
> meete,
> Maye houlde at firste, when they occasion
> finde.
> Thy head behinde all balde, what telles it
> more?
> That none shoulde houlde, that let me
> slippe before.

> (Whitney, p. 181)

Erratic, maddening ephemeral Chance or Occasion
then is the appropriate symbol to sit arbiter where

119

nothing is constant and the state is degenerate and imbalanced. In Milton's "wild abyss" there is visual
anarchy and audio-cacophony. The region is confusedly
compounded:

> Of neither Sea, nor Shore, nor Air, nor Fire,
> But all these in their pregnant causes mixt
> Confus'dly, and which thus must ever fight,
> Unless th' Almighty Maker them ordain
> His dark materials to create more Worlds,

(II. 912-16)

God alone can generate order and sustain life out of
such utter confusion and disharmony and madness.

Peacham in an emblem thinks of chaos as devastating, and says so in a cryptic tercet:

> Where Chaos and Confusion wee see,
> As well of language, as of differing heartes,
> A bodie severed in a thousand parts.

(Peacham, p. 185)

Peacham's Hell is also chaos, a place of tangled
woods and eerie shades. The device carries a dense
forest with the stars and the moon above it, but as
in The Faerie Queene (I.1. 7) and Comus their rays do
not penetrate the thick foliage;

> A shadie Wood, pourtraicted to the sight,
> With uncouth pathes, and hidden waies
>   unknowne:
> Resembling Chaos, or the hideous night,
> Of those sad Groves, by banke of Acheron
> With banefull Ewe, and Ebon overgrowne:
> Whose thickest boughes, and inmost entries
>   are
> Not pierceable, to power of any starre.

(Peacham, p. 182)

Chaos is the degenerate state of the universe in
Paradise Lost, where inanity and insanity reign supreme. Before God carves the world, chaos runs riot
in space. It has the elements necessary for a structured system and its potential is limitless, but having
no direction, it is a fearful, inconstant and inchoate
whirl of matter. The decisions of its ruler, Chaos,

120

embroil frays further. Its noise as experienced by
Satan, who still has the semblance of Heaven and can
not abide cacophony, is worse than Bellona bellowing
her battle cries. To manoeuvre and negotiate a passage through this state is a feat, where chance not
skill, brings success or defeat. Chaos is "the womb
of nature" and perhaps her grave. It is a state of
uncontrolled fanaticism, hysteria, and discord. Its
"coast of darkness" lies "bordering on light," and
displays the chiaroscuro effects of an "electric cir-
cus," which is blinding and befuddling as madness.

This fearsome and demented state recurs whenever
unhappiness and distress become predominant in the
affairs of man and angels in Paradise Lost. Satan on
touching ground on his nefarious errand, discovers
that the newly created world has its windy wasteland
in the regions which are far removed from the light
of Heaven, both metaphorically and literally, and
adjoin chaos. Adjacent to chaos, this wasteland is
destined to become the limbo of abstractions, where
vanity and frustrated hopes, misplaced zeal, and tran-
sitory fancies look for refuge. It will also be the
home of deviates and the obnoxious; monstrosities
and false deities; but above all of the hypocritical
in the church. Milton's scintillating wit and invective join hands when he refers to "Embryos, and Idiots,
Eremites and Friars / White, Black and Grey, with all
thir trumpery" (III. 474-74) floating in limbo.
Milton illustrates the picture further symbolically
and revels in the degeneration exposed:

> Cowls, Hoods and Habits with thir wearers
>   tost
> And flutter'd into Rags, then Reliques,
>   Beads,
> Indulgences, Dispenses, Pardons, Bulls,
> The sport of Winds: all these upwhirl'd
>   aloft
> Fly o'er the backside of the World far off
> Into a Limbo large and broad, since call'd
> The Paradise of Fools,

> (III. 490-96)

Pandemonium emerging as an exhalation is a highly
structured and magnificent pile, for the spirits of
Heaven, though fallen, order it; but the soil from
which it rises has the awful splendour of death.
Milton's figurative language gives the topography of
Hell peerless potency. Hell is "bottomless perdition"

121

with "penal fire" and "admantine chains"; its burning
sea has rolling billows; it is a wild and dismal wasteland, "a dungeon horrible," where the flames of the
"ever burning sulphur unconsumed" give no light but
make "darkness visible" exposing woe and the wraiths,
and hopeless, unending torture. Chaos reigns there
metaphorically, for transverse winds and flood and
fiery tempests keep making the lot of its denizens
more miserable. For the fallen spirits of Heaven this
"vast and boundless deep" is a pit, a cesspool of
horrors. The plain adjoining its fiery sea is also a
wasteland, "forlorn and wild" and desolate; if lit
it is only with the shadow of the flames. Its gulf
of fire engenders forgetfulness, thus giving a little
reprieve from mental anguish to its unhappy crew. Its
enormous domed vault sports fiery flames, and its
cavernous sides reverberate the voice of its new
ruler. Like chaos Hell too has undiscovered wealth as Mammon well knows, and the potential for an infernal
empire. Thus it is easy for the fallen angels to as-
semble Pandemonium in an hour, and bring about a semblance of order in the wasteland. If Hell suffers
from heat, it also has regions where the frozen ice
burns and sears with intense cold, two degenerate
and dreaded states of Nature, and both conducive to
mental torture.

Satan, the new master of this wasteland, still
possessed a Heavenly charisma to sway his legions,
and they the loyalty to extol him for his leadership
and ingenuity. Unlike Chaos, he is not surrounded by
Orc and Hades, Chance and Night; his counsellors are
the fallen spirits of Heaven, and display many heavenly traits. At the moment of his diabolic triumph they
surround him in a circle of perfection, and emblematically in the fiery, diabolic Hell, along with specious
pageantry, they inject the symbol of wholeness:

> The Stygian Council thus dissolv'd; and
>   forth
> In order came the grand infernal Peers;
> Midst came thir mighty Paramount, and
>   seem'd
> Alone th' Antagonist of Heav'n, nor less
> Than Hell's dread Emperor with pomp Supreme,
> And God-like imitated State; him round
> A Globe of fiery Seraphim inclos'd
> With bright emblazonry, and horrent Arms.

(II. 506-13)

Paul Doré, in Blakeian and cyclic curves, gives graphic
dimension to this gracious emblem, but the setting is
still the awful "hollow abyss" (II. 518); and among
the rank and file, along with the logicians, philosophers and musicians; the pioneer sappers and miners
and raconteurs, the jousting knights and charioteers
and sport lovers, there are also "Hell's Angels", who:

> . . . with vast Typhoean rage more fell
> Rend up both Rocks and Hills, and ride the
> Air
> In whirlwinds; Hell scarce holds the wild
> uproar.

(II. 539-41)

In spite of all the grandeur of Satan triumphant and
his orderly train, all is not well in hell. This
disease reveals itself in the horrifyingly fascinating
picture of Sin and Death; the ultimate in terrifying
hallucination and aberration. Death's amorphous
character has all the terror which still affects the
most sanguine. His propensity to incest, yet hatred
for his mother point out the enormity of Sin. Her
hell hounds and her strength both repel, for as Hall
writes in his emblem of Sin's progeny, they are seen:

> Still gnawing where they first were bred,
> Consuming where they'r nourished,
> Endeavouring still
> Even him to kill
> That gives them life, . . .
> . . . that tyrannick Ill
> So radicated is.

(Hall, Emblem 1658,
vol. 6 p. 101-2)

The triumph of Sin and Death over man is more sinister than that of Satan. Their entry into Paradise
is the beginning of Chaotic misrule and decay on
earth. Death is drawn to earth because of the stench
"of carnage," "the smell / Of mortal change on Earth"
(X 269-73). Chaos returns to Eden; when nature feels
the wound of Eve's disobedience, emphasized by Adam
and his sin:

> Earth felt the wound, and Nature from her
> seat
> Sighing through all her Works gave signs
> of woe.   (IX. 782-83)

123

Earth trembl'd from her entrails, as again
In pangs, and Nature gave a second groan,
Sky low'r'd, and muttering Thunder, some
    sad drops
Wept at completing of the mortal sin
Original.

(IX. 1000-4)

Milton's use of "pathetic fallacy" is grim reality.
It is awesome because the Creator passes his judgment
on Satan and his human collaborators in subversion.
Nature loses its salubrious equilibrium and brings in
the marauders, hardships and catastrophes:

                    At that tasted Fruit
    The Sun, as from Thyestean Banquet, Turn'd
    His course Intended; else how had the World
    Inhabited, though sinless, more than now
    Avoided pinching cold and scorching heat?
    These changes in the Heav'ns, though slow,
        produc'd
    Like change on Sea and Land, sideral blast,
    Vapor, and Mist, and Exhalation hot,
    Corrupt and Pestilent:

    And snow and hail and stormy gust and flaw,

    Beast now with Beast gan war and . . .
    Devour'd each other; nor stood much in awe
    Of Man,

(X. 687-713)

This state of unrest, degeneracy and insanity remains
to stay. In the catalogue of vignettes that Adam is
shown by Michael, chaotic and other forms of madness
keep recurring. Sin and Death bring destruction,
though rays of brightness never quite leave the earth.
If Astrea flees the earth from disillusionment, she
also keeps returning to earth. She has to, for Milton as a Renaissance man and a humanist cannot help
but be optimistic. If degeneracy persists so does
sanity, with her handmaids beauty and knowledge and
kindness. If Eden is shorn of its glory, inundated
and set afloat in Noah's flood, it is also reestab-
lished though as a desolate island in the Persian
Gulf, the Sumerian Dilmun, a spot for sea creatures,
the Seals and Orcs and Whales (XI. 829-35). Yet the

124

rainbow promises a new heaven, its "colours gay, /
Betok'ning peace from God, and Cov'nant new" (XI.
866-67).

Degeneracy and imbalance are characteristic of
Satan and his crew. The war they wage in heaven is
the prime example of aberrations of the mind. For
one insane impulse of jealousy Satan loses his elevated position next to God's throne. In the great
chain of being Milton's Archangel was next to God and
His Son. Satan recalls it as he does his insane ambition:

> lifted up so high
> I sdain'd subjection, and thought one step
> higher
> Would set me highest,

(IV. 49-51)

This mad impulse for supremacy had made Sin spring out
of Satan's head a beautiful but sinister goddess, and
paradoxically from that moment Satan's glory began
to diminish. He could outshine myriads, but the
tarnish of mental imbalance makes him display "dis-
tempers foul" (IV. 118), and he becomes a blot, a
scar, a sun spot on the luminous face of the sun (III.
598-99). The war in heaven is his diabolical enterprise, which enmeshes a third of the angels, and
Heaven, the most peaceful of domains, becomes the
battleground of warring angels. God's anger shown
in smoky clouds and thunder is awesome. The battle
begins systematically with martial music, trumpet
calls and the pageantry of a march, banners and flying squadrons (VI. 71-2). With their battalions
scintillating in shining armour and spears, their
helmets and shields reflecting heaven's light, the
angels move in order and discipline of highly organized armies. Milton gives the civil war and genocide
in Heaven all the picturesque details of the historic
battles of 16th and 17th century England, also the
madness and horror that accompany them. The battle
is conventional though fierce. All the sounds of
battle reverberate through the poem in onomato-
poeic lines, while Satan tries to "turn this Heav'n
itself into Hell" (VI. 291).

The madness is seen in the clash of armour, the
duel of Archangel Michael and Satan, and Satan's

subsequent and first experience of physical pain.
Milton explains the "nectarous humour" of angels'
substance which when injured exudes crimson, but
heals immediately. The imagery of war includes the
two-handed sword of Michael (VI. 251) and the camou-
flaged cannon of Satan, the first inventor of a deadly weapon (VI. 572-619). The cannon is inorganic,
but as sinister as Spencer's Error:

> . . . those deep-throated Engines belcht,
>   whose roar
> Embowell'd with outrageous noise the Air,
> And all her entrails tore, disgorging foul
> Thir devilish glut, chain'd Thunderbolts
>   and Hail
> Of Iron Globes, . . .
>
> By thousands, Angel on Arch-Angel roll'd;

(VI. 586-94)

In his emblem entitled Protegere Regium, Peacham
mentions similar engines of destruction amassed with
identical rancor:

> While deadly foes, their engines have pre-
>   pard,
> With furie fierce, to batter downe the
>   walles,
> My dutie is the Citie gate to guard,
> And to rebate their Rammes, and fierie
>   balls:

(Peacham, p. 31)

After the volley God's angels fare worse. With
satiric rancor Satan comments on their overthrow, and
like a power-hungry maniac incites his troops to
wreak further ill. The strangest moment of madness
comes when the good and bad angels forget all decorum
and discipline of war and resort to the primitive and
pre-historic Titanic mode of fighting in ire. Their
madness results in uprooting hills, replete with all
their physical features, and pelting each other with
those "brick-bat" hills and rocks. The heavenly
promontories become the instruments of pain and suffering with "horrid confusion heapt/Upon confusion"
(VI. 668-69). The angels descend from disciplined
order to barbaric "disorder'd rage let loose" (VI.

126

696). The penultimate madness of both the good and
bad angels is only matched in literature by the
Titans. The emblematic picture is scathingly revealing of the inanity, rage and frustration that destroy
even the most sanguine. The mad rage affects the
good angels as ruthlessly. The last act of battle
loses all semblance of military strategy and planning:

> Thir Arms away they threw, and to the Hills
> . . .
> Light as the Lightning glimpse they ran,
>   they flew,
> From thir foundations loos'ning to and fro
> They pluckt the seated Hills with all
>   th ir load,
> Rocks, Waters, Woods, and by the shaggy tops
> Uplifting bore them in their hands: Amaze,
> Be sure, and terror seiz'd the rebel Host,
> When coming towards them so dread they saw
> The bottom of the Mountains upward turn'd,

                    (VI. 639-49)

In retaliation Satan's crew enact the same scene when
part of the legions are pinioned by the hills, and
chaos and confusion return:

> The rest in imitation to like Arms
> Betook them, and the neighboring Hills
>   uptore;
> So Hills amid the Air encounter'd Hills
> Hurl'd to and fro with jaculation dire,
>
> Infernal noise; War seem'd a civil Game
> To this uproar; horrid confusion heapt
> Upon confusion rose:

                    (VI. 662-69)

Milton's emblem of war is replete with its motto. It
points out that eventually providence interferes and
soothes ruffled insanity and anarchy. God sitting
"Shrin'd in His Sancturary" deplores the savagery,
and sends His son to reestablish order. The supremacy
of God's son becomes paramount for the act. Insanity,
with the erring angels, is relegated to Hell, and
Heaven returns to its pristine harmony (VI. 671-892).

Milton's war in heaven does not only have its root in

the war of the Titans with Zeus as the triumphant god
bringing new order to Olympus, but has counterparts
in the middle-eastern myths. Marduk, the god-hero
fights the evil dragon Tiamat, an original of Satan,
and is proclaimed king on destroying her. Marduk's
"weapons are bow and arrows, mace, lightning, and a
net held at the corners by the four winds; he fills
his body with flame, and creates the seven raging
hurricanes; he mounts his storm-chariot, and advances
against Tiamat and her host."[3] Likewise Phoebe charioted and garbed in her full glory, in Hawkins' emblem
(Partheneia Sacra 1633, p. 111) proceeds to vanquish
the evil of "the Cymmerian night." In Paradise Lost,
emblematically, victory sits as an eagle at the right
hand of God's charioted Son, and a mighty bow and
arrow rest by him. His might and anger, drive the
throng of warring angels through a breach in heav'n's
crystal wall and "Hell saw / Heav'n ruining from
Heav'n" (VI. 868). Satan, his crew, and his insanity
are entombed in "the bottomless pit" (VI. 866). Milton in this magnificent passage expands Christ's words
in Luke 10. 18: "I beheld Satan as lightning fall
from heaven."

     In the Garden of Eden Satan's insane jealousy
and devilish strategy make him enter the serpent. He
never recovers from that image of himself. His
cohorts take on the same guise involuntarily and
represent the bestial malevolence of evil, evil in
any form equated with madness. Milton displays the
same "savage joy of combat"[4] in the battle of the
angels as he had shown previously in his vitriolic
pamphlets attacking his enemies and calling them "hell-
pestering rabble," "the phlegmy clod." His invective
is translated into the insanity of the warring angels.
On a lesser scale, as quoted earlier, Hell's angels
show similar lack of control in the games they play:

          Others with vast Typhoean rage more fell
          Rend up both Rocks and Hills, and ride the
          Air
          In whirlwind; Hell scarce holds the wild
          uproar.

                    (II. 539-41)

The war in heaven and in the destroyed Eden, has the
character of a Civil War; the insanity is fatal.
Whitney shows its devastation in his emblem entitled

"Intestinae Simultates"

> When civill sworde is drawn out of the
> sheathe,
> And bluddie broiles, at home are set a
> broache,
> Then furious Mars with sworde doth rage
> beneathe,
> And to the Toppe, devowring flames incroache,
> None helpes to quenche but rather blowes
> the flame,
> And oile doe adde, and powder to the same.

(Whitney, p. 7)

Insanity reaches its zenith in internecine wars.

Withers refers to the madness of war as subversive
to unity and love. A man raised in the Puritan tradition and suspect by the Royalists, he wrote laudatory
verses to Charles I and Queen Henrietta Mary, praising
the two for having brought the "two Sister-Churches"
together by their marriage. Yet Wither was imprisoned
and, according to Aubrey, it was Sir John Denham who
pleaded for his release on the excuse that if Wither
were executed, he, Denham, would be considered England's
worst poet! Pope commenting on his simplicity called
him "wretched Withers" in the Dunciad, Book I p. 296.
Wither's style of writing is simple and forthright;
but he touches many of the issues that his contemporaries were handling.[5] Milton devoted one and a quarter
books of Paradise Lost to the war in Heaven; Wither
writes of the insanity of war in two short lines
"shew, that, swords, / Flames, Threats, and Furies,
make no true Accords" (A Collection of Emblems, sig.(*)5.
Harmony eschews all signs of strife and threats of
war.

Choler is the form of madness that particularly
belongs to Satan, and helps to reveal his hypocrisy.
Peacham shows the absurdity of mad anger in his emblem entitled Cholera. The device shows a bearded man,
with long bristling hair, naked, except for a loin
cloth, one end of which is angrily flying in the
air, like his hair. He holds a drawn sword and is
striding as though to strike. Incongruously a shield
with a flame in the center lies before him, a lion
looking askance is seated behind and the sky is
lowering, as though these symbols of wrath are

129

questioning the sanity of Man's ire:

> Next Choller standes, resembling most the fire,
> Of swarthie yeallow, and a meager face;
> With Sword a late, unsheathed in his Ire:
> Neere whome, there lies, within a little
>   space,
> A sterne ei'de Lion, and by him a sheild,
> Charg'd with a flame, upon a crimson feild.
>
> We paint him young, to shew that passions
>   raigne,
> The most in heedles, and unstaied youth:
> That lion showes, he seldome can refraine,
> From cruell deede, devoide of gentle ruth:
> Or hath perhaps, this beast to him assign'd,
> As bearing most, the brave and bounteous
>   mind.

(Peacham, p. 128)

Satan too displays a "brave and bounteous" mind when
he wishes to use it thus, but his choler is a conglom-
erate of many types of aberrations of the mind. His
is no just anger. It savors of jealousy, pride, inordinate ambition, sedition, and instigation of the
good to evil. Steadman points out the parallel between
Satan and Homeric heroes, who all fall short of
spiritual virtues, and are recalled more for their
military prowess, anger, or cunning:

> In his destructive wrath, his implaca-
> bility, his pride in his own strength, his
> sense of injured merit, his martial forti-
> tude divorced from right reason and piety,
> Satan offers more than a fortuitous par-
> allel to Achilles. In his eloquence and
> cunning, his tricks, frauds, and lies, his
> professed attempt to save his companions,
> he resembles Ulysses. Like the wily
> Greek, he penetrates an enemy citadel in
> disguise and overthrows it by a simple
> ruse.[6]

Whitney uses Agamemnon. Satan's armor is reminiscent
of Whitney's emblem on Agamemnon, for both symbolically describe the insanity of anger. The caption of
the emblem itself is significant, "Furor &
rabies." The device has a gigantic figure, holding a
shield half his size in one hand and a drawn sword in the

130

other. Flames envelope a rotunda and a domed palace
in the background, while battle tents appear on the
side. Agamemnon's crown is also symbolic, for it
flaunts diabolic horns. The king is a handsome figure,
but his pose is menacing, and the verse is disconcert-
ing:

> The cruell kinges, that are inflam'de with
> ire:
> With fier and sworde, theire furious mindes
> suffise:
> And ofte to showe, what chiefelie they desire,
> Within theire sheildes, they dreadfull shapes
> devise,
> Some Griphins fierce, some gramping Lions
> beare,
>
> . . .
> All which bewraye, theire inwarde bloodie
> thoughte,

>   (Whitney, p. 45)

Similarly Milton uses a device of the Babylonian and
Biblical Nimrod:

>   one shall rise
> Of proud ambitious heart, who not content
> With fair equality, fraternal state,
> Will arrogate Dominion undeserv'd
> Over his brethren, and quite dispossess
> Concord and law of Nature from the Earth;
> Hunting (and Men not Beasts shall be his
> game)
> With War and hostile snare such as refuse
> Subjection to his Empire tyrannous.

>   (XII. 24-32)

All prototypes of Satan, their arrogance is their
insanity. In them violence becomes a state of mind,
and for ulterior motives they work their chagrin and
ire on others. The dux bellorum, like Moloch (another
projection of Satan), is the "strongest and fiercest",
and, in arrogance and anger would "rather than be less /
Car'd not to be at all" (II. 47-8). This is dementia.
Theirs is a lust for power, which loses all proportion.

    In Paradise Lost, appetite plays a more
successful role in psychological warfare.
Neither Satan nor Adam is the incarnate

                      131

Logos, and in both characters passion gains
a decisive victory over reason. Satan's
enterprise aginst man gives the reins to
his own emotions - ire, envy, despair,
hatred, and the same fatal ambition to
reign which has inspired his earlier
revolt.[7]

Inspite of their heroism, the Homeric type heroes
arouse pity and concern. Their counterparts plague
mankind with their imbalance and appetite for ag-
grandizement. Theirs is a madness for war.

Degeneracy does not stop with the external and
visible attitudes, it worms its way to the inner being,
and sears the introspective and contemplative mind.
Satan, "inflamed with rage" is afflicted with his
own error. Proceeding to wreak his ire on unsuspecting
mankind, he has no joy in the prospect, nor peace of
mind. He is in the throes of his own devilry:

> Yet not rejoicing in his speed, though bold,
> Far off and fearless, nor with cause to
> boast,
> Begins his dire attempt, which nigh the
> birth
> Now rolling, boils in his tumultuous breast,
> And like a devilish Engine back recoils
> Upon himself; horror and doubt distract
> His troubl'd thoughts, and from the bottom
> stir
> The Hell within him, for within him Hell
> He brings, and round about him, nor from
> Hell
> One step no more than from himself can fly
> By change of place: Now conscience wakes
> despair
> That slumber'd, wakes the bitter memory
> Of what he was, what is, and what must be
> Worse; of worse deeds worse sufferings
> must ensue.

                    (IV. 13-26)

The turmoil within Satan is chaotic and denotes de-
rangement and frenzy. Quarles' cry for the mind of
fallen man can well apply to the fallen Archangel:

132

Lament, lament; look, look, what thou hast
   done:
Lament the world's, lament thine own estate:
Look, look, by doing, how thou art undone:
Lament thy fall, lament thy change of state:
Thy faith is broken, and thy freedom gone
See, see too soon, what thou lament'st
   too late;

                    (Quarles, Emblems,p. 205)

This chaotic state in the mind of Satan is a projection
of his monstrosity. Isabel Mac Caffrey has pointed
out that dragons (often hallucinations generating fear)
are associated with destruction. Beowulf's Grendel and
his mother live in an unhealthy and terrifying sub-
terranean cavern, as does the devil in Dante's inferno.
Their abode is the "hidden monster ridden world of dark
perplexity."[8] When Satan is first discovered in
Paradise Lost he too lies in mental perplexity prone
on the subterranean floods like a "monstrous leviathan"
cogitating "his own dark designs" (I. 213), an inseparable part of his physical, spiritual and mental degradation and aberration.

   In mediaeval and renaissance art the devil takes
different forms; the most symbolic of them is the composite form though "The earliest known figure of the
devil in Christian art is a third-century fresco in
the catacomb of Saints Peter and Marcellus in Rome;
. . . here the devil appears in his original form as
the serpent coiled around the Tree of Knowledge."[9]
Many of the early pictures depict him as a glorious
man far from unpleasing, but artists start giving
him monstrous shapes, the composite type being the
most horrifying. He is given the physical characteristics of different beasts and birds: fangs, scales,
scorpion tails, claws, beaks, boars' heads, bats'
wings; in other words an admixture of things that harm
and denote a schizophrenic personality. Milton's
Satan metamorphoses himself into aesthetic forms,
degenerating gradually into a viper as in the catacomb mural, but his passions are symbolic of the composite devil, in whom order, symmetry, beauty and
harmony give place to conflict and incongruity, and
a demented state. Because there is no affinity in
beauty and choler, and they lack the attraction of
"Like things to like" (VII. 240), Satan loses his
celestial perfection and becomes a composition of

harmful vices, schizophrenic and imbalanced, so often
evident in his fiery, choleric tantrums. He helps to
destroy what God had created good. One such out-
burst occurs after his visit to the orb of the Sun.

Satan's deception of Uriel brings on a fit of
romantic agony for him. The arch-angel debased himself into the semblance of an inconsequential cherub,
having from "what higheth fallen," from a place next
to God. The masquerade could not last indefinitely.
No sooner does he leave Uriel, chagrin and hatred for
himself and his exalted Foe, make Satan exhibit all
the features of madness. His "inward torments" no
longer contain themselves; the struggle of good and
evil within him could not remain in bounds. He had
weighed all possibilities and had realized that
Heaven had nothing further for him. In bidding fare
well to hope, fiendishly, ho bids farewell to all that
could redeem him. His passion distorts his still
glorious visage, and madness, such as that of many a
tragic hero engulfs him, though his erstwhile nobility
still shields him from stark devilry. Uriel notes the
transformation:

> each passion dimm'd his face,
> Thrice chang'd with pale, ire, envy and
>   despair,
> Which marr'd his borrow'd visage, and
>   betray'd
> Him counterfeit . . .

Uriel sees him disfigured,

> more than could befall
> Spirit of happy sort: his gestures fierce
> He mark'd and mad demeanor,

(IV. 114-29)

This is the unreasonable madness that makes Satan
betray himself before Uriel, the symbol of the all-
seeing eye of God. Satan had given proof of his madness earlier in his insane envy of God's son, his
rebellion, and in his leading astray a third of the
angels; this episode crowns it all. His madness was
reflected in all his followers, and in some of their
arguments at the great conclave in Hell, in the birth
of Sin and in Satan's rapacious and incestuous love
for her. His was the madness of the "angry young

134

men" who demand unlimited liberty and recognition at
any cost. Its first signs had appeared in Satan's
insomnia when he could not sleep like the other denizens of Heaven, at the announcement of God's edict
regarding His Son. The proclamation caused paranoia
and evoked emotions of self persecution in Satan:
Satan thought "himself impaired" (V. 665). His first
act of madness reveals itself in sedition and defi-
ance:

> he resolv'd,
> With all his Legions to dislodge, and leave
> Unworshipt, unobey'd the Throne supreme
> Contemptuous,
>
> (V. 668-71)

From then on his mental state, his great though warped
intelligence, and the maddening hatred of His Creator,
propel him forward to Herculean acts of subversion and
destruction till his imbalance is apparent even to
the "hell and pestering rabble" of the inferno, and
instead of applause, his nefarious exploits are met
with hisses.

Peacham captures Satan's state of mind in an
emblem in which he analyzes in simple terms Satan's
perversion and his desire to succeed at the cost of
harming God's new creation, and especially frail men:

> For many are the stratagems of sinne,
> And Sathan labors still with might and maine,
> Within our soules, a landing place to win:
>
> (Peacham, p. 139)

Satan does find "a landing place" in man, and infuses
him with madness.

Adam passes through phases of madness after Eve
commits the one act prohibited to them; the act of
disobedience. Because she is an extension of Adam,
Eve's sin makes him doubly conscious of guilt in himself. The first impact of madness shows in the meta-
phor of horror. Its effect is both physical and mental.
Adam is stunned into silence.

> On th' other side, Adam soon as he heard
> The fatal Trespass done by Eve, amaz'd,

Astonied stood and Blank, while horror chill
Ran through his veins, and all his joints
   relax'd;
From his slack hand the Garland wreath'd
   for Eve
Down dropp'd, and all the faded Roses shed:

                    (IX. 888-93)

At this point he is the picture of despair and melancholy. Like Peacham's melancholia, Adam, in his
isolation from Eve, momentarily conveys all the features of manic depression. His sudden change in mood,
sorrow and anxiety spell his sense of loss, and silence
him:
         Heere Melancholly musing in his fits,
         Pale visag'd, of complexion cold and drie,
         All solitarie, at his studie sits,
         Within a wood, devoid of companie:

         His mouth, in signe of silence, up is bound,
         For Melancholly loves not many wordes:
         One foote on Cube is fixt upon the ground,
         The which him plodding Constancie affordes:
         A sealed Purse he beares, to show no vice.

                    (Peacham, p. 126)

Milton's Adam at this juncture indeed has no vice in
him and is a model of constancy; it is his perplexity
and astonishment that silence him. Adam breaks the
silence with suave and sophisticated accusations.
His chagrin condemns Eve, but his knightly code of
honor and chivalry makes him offer his life if hers
be taken. As the madness of anxiety and fear silence
him, so the madness of his love for her supersedes
the desire for self-preservation, the two forms of
madness obsess Adam in succession. He addresses Eve:

         O fairest of Creation, last and best
         Of all God's Works, Creature in whom
            excell'd
         Whatever can to sight or thought be form'd,
         Holy, divine, good, amiable, or sweet!
         How art thou lost, how on a sudden lost,

         Rather how hast thou yielded to transgress
                    . . . some cursed fraud

                    136

                 Of Enemy hath beguil'd thee, yet unknown,
                 And mee with thee hath ruin'd, for with thee
                 Certain my resolution is to Die;

                 Should God create another Eve, and I
                 Another Rib afford, yet loss of thee
                 Would never from my heart; no no, I feel
                 The Link of Nature draw me:

                                                    (IX. 896-914)

In spite of all his protestations, the poison of guilt
seeps through his unconscious and conscious mind. His
sleep is "Bred of unkindly fumes, [and is] with conscious
dreams / Encumber'd" and on waking he discovers "How
dark'n'd" (IX. 1050 & 1054) is his mind. The darkness
leads to his abstraction from Eve; and the hysteria
engendered by fear brings accusation and counter accusation. Peacham bewails the married state in his
emblem entitled Matrimonium (p. 132). The device
shows a perplexed man with a yoke on his shoulders
and his feet locked in stocks. The verse exclaims:

                 Who loveth best, to live in Hymens handes,
                 And better likes, the carefull married
                      state,
                 May here behold, how Matrimonie standes,
                 In woodden stocks, repenting him too late:
                 The servile yoake, his neck, and shoulder
                      weares,
                 And in his hand, the fruitfull Quince he
                      beares.

                 The stocks doe shew, his want of libertie,
                 Not as he woont, to wonder where he list:
                 The Yoke's an engine of servilitie:-
                 The fruitefullness, the Quince within his
                      fist,
                 Of wedlock tells, which Satan did present,
                 T' Athenian Brides the day to church they
                      went.

And in the emblem entitled Humanae miseriae he states
"a retchles wife" is man's undoing (p. 119). Peacham
is voicing concerns like Adam's especially in the
post-fall passage where Adam expresses that life would
have been simpler had creation been all male, for man
then would have been saved the agony of enthralment
against his better judgment:

                              137

O why did God,
Creator wise, that peopl'd highest Heav'n
With Spirits Masculine, create at last
This novelty on Earth, this fair defect
Of Nature, and not fill the World at once
With Men as Angels without Feminine,
Or find some other way to generate
Mankind? This mischief had not then befall'n,
And more that shall befall, innumerable
Disturbances on Earth through Female snares,

(X. 888-97)

Adam's mood of recrimination and desire to shift the
blame is a kind of paranoia. In his insanity and
shame he sues for protection of inanimate nature:

Cover me ye Pines,
Ye Cedars, with innumerable boughs
Hide me, where I may never see them more.

(IX. 1088-90)

And "From thus distemper'd breast, / Adam estrang'd
in look and alter'd style" (IX. 1131-32) addresses
Eve in emblematic language, which ends with the
aphorism and adage:

Let none henceforth seek needless cause to
approve
The Faith they owe; when earnestly they seek
Such proof, conclude, they then begin to fail.

(IX. 1140-42)

Henry Peacham's emblem "Icon Peccati" graphically conveys the picture of the demented Adam. Nude and down-
cast he occupies the centre of the picture. He stands
among bare rocks, that sport no foliage except for
menacing weeds. A snake is twined and looped round
his loins and another is entering his bared heart.
The poem captures the madness of man in Adam's fall:

A young man blind, black, naked here is seene,
Ore Mountaine steepe, and Thornie Rock to
passe,
Whose heart a Serpent gnawes with furie teene,
Another's wound about his wast; alas,
Since Adam's fall, such our estate hath bin,

138

The lively picture of our guilt and sinne.

His age denotes youthes follies and amisse,
His blindnes shewes, our want of wisedomes
    sight;
Sinnes deadly waies, those dang'rous stepps
    of his,
His nakednes, of grace deprived quite:
Hell's power the Serpent, which his loines
    doth girt,
A Conscience had, the other eates his heart.

(Peacham, p. 146)

Adam is much more vocal before God in Hall's Emblem 8
than in Paradise Lost after his fall. Hall takes his
caption from Jude 4.15, "The Lord cometh with ten
thousand of his Saints to execute judgement upon all."
The device of the emblem carries a beautiful highlighted angel balancing himself on a sphere and blowing a slender trumpet. Adam (not seen in the picture)
asks in a frenzied lamentation:

        I Heare and tremble! Lord, what shall I doe
        T' avoid thy anger, whether shall I goe?
        What, shall I scale the Mountains? 'las
            they be
        Farre lesse then Atoms if compar'd with thee.
        What, shall I strive to get myselfe a Tombe,
        Within the greedy Oceans swelling Wombe?
        Shall I dive into Rockes? where shall I
            flie
        The sure discovery of thy piercing Eye?
        Alas I know not, though with many a teare
        In Hell they mone thy absence, thou art
            there.
        Thou art on Earth, and well observest all
        The actions acted on this massie Ball;

        Thou hatest sinnes, and if thou once begin
        To cast me in the Scales, I all am sinne.

(Hall, p. 109)

And in some striking metaphysical statements and conceits Hall continues to probe man's mind and give ob-
servations on man's nonentity, akin to Adam's nadir of
despair in Paradise Lost:

139

So perfect nothings, such light blasts are
   we,
That ere w'are ought at all, we cease to be.

And while we sleep, what do we else but die?

This gapes for Marriage, yet his fickle head
Knows not what cares waite on a marriage-bed.

Ascend the higher, [yet who] shall more
   wretched fall. . . .
This thirsts for knowledge: yet how is it
   bought
With many a sleeplesse night and racking
   thought?

How slippery are thy pathes, how sure thy
   fall?
How art thou nothing when th' art most
   of all?

                              (Hall, pp. 105-6)

Yet Hall concedes that man is the epitome of all the
universe; the microcosm of the macrocosm:

      Discover what thou art within;
      That spirit which imprison'd lies
      What a vast essence will be seen?

      This globe ha's somewhat in't of every star
      Mans soul of each thing some small charac-
         ter,
      How els could a pure intellect be seen
      To turn at anytime, to any thing?

                              (Hall, pp. 86-7)

Adam's sense of guilt in Milton imbalances both his
mind and his body. When God commands him to appear
before him he cries out that his beautiful body is
tainted by its nakedness and he has to hide from God.
He fears "both sin and punishment" (X. 133) and God's
omniscience in gauging the wrong. Accusations of
Eve come easily to the lips of this once heroic creature. But God gives him the acutest cut of all saying,
"Thou didst resign thy Manhood," (X. p. 148), for
Adam had forgotten the classic precept of knowing himself. He is told "hadst thou known thyself aright"
(X. 156) he might not have joined Eve in her sin.

                          140

Adam's anger and dejection echo the timeworn question
of the sorely anguished soul:

> Did I request thee, Maker, from my Clay
> To mold me Man, did I solicit thee
> From darkness to promote me,
>
> (X. 743-45)

He questions God's justice in being held responsible
for "The good he sought not" (X. 752). Adam's disturbed spirit argues the pros and cons of the whole
episode. Milton's training in disputation and debate
comes to the fore, as Adam tries to comprehend both
the justice and injustice involved. He can argue both
sides of the issue equally well, but he cries like the
disturbed:

> How gladly would I meet
> Mortality my sentence, and be Earth
> Insensible, how glad would lay me down
> As in my Mother's lap!
>
> (X. 775-78)

His torment is more for his sentient soul than his
body. Still unsure, in the words of Adam, Milton
voices his own doubts as to the existence of the
spirit after physical mortality. The torment stems
from a theological conjecture that there is no death
for the soul until the day of judgment.

> Lest that pure breath of Life, the Spirit
>   of Man
> Which God inspir'd, cannot together perish
> With this corporeal Clod; then in the Grave,
> Or in some other dismal place, who knows
> But I shall die a living Death? O thought
> Horrid, if true! Yet why? it was but
>   breath
> Of Life that sinn'd; what dies but what
>   had life
> And sin? the Body properly hath neither.
> All of me then shall die: let this appease
> The doubt, since human reach no further
>   knows.
>
> (X. 784-91)

Other doubts assail Adam's guilt-ridden and troubled
thoughts. Like the bad angels, his mind is "in wan-
d'ring mazes lost" (II. 562). The idea that death
may be a recurring misery sears his spirit, and rever-
berates through his sick mind like thunder:

> Ay me, that fear
> Comes thund'ring back with dreadful
>   revolution
> On my defenseless head; both Death and I
> Am found Eternal, and incorporate both,
> Nor I on my part single, in me all
> Posterity stands curst: Fair Patrimony

(X. 813-18)

His mind is still befuddled, but he realizes that God
is not to blame for his shortcoming; he alone is responsible for his abject mental state and degeneration:

> Him after all Disputes
> Forc't I absolve: all my evasions vain,
> And reasonings, though through Mazes, lead
>   me still
> But to my own conviction; first and last
> On mee, mee only, as the source and spring
> Of all corruption, all the blame lights due;

(X. 828-33)

At this stage Adam's madness, his despair and hopelessness are at their nadir. He laments aloud, his is the
seventeenth-century black melancholy, which keeps him
awake through the night, and everything appears to him
in hallucinations, as "double terror" (X. 850). Like
the demented, he rolls on the ground, curses his creation, and sues for extinction. His are the symptoms
of mental ailment suffered under tremendous stress.
Like Othello he is "perplexed in the extreme." His
attitude toward Eve is far from his earlier concern.
The suave sophistication is lost in acrimony, besti-
ality, and stinging insults:

> Out of my sight, thou Serpent, that name best
> Befits thee with him leagu'd, thyself as
>   false
> And hateful;

And like the emblematists depicting fraud he points
out:

                    nothing wants, but that thy shape
        Like his, and color Serpentine may show
        Thy inward fraud, to warn all Creatures from
        thee

                        (X. 867-71)

And as God had attacked his manliness, he hurts her by
attacking her individuality and womanhood; calls her a
"supernumerary" "all but a Rib / Crooked by nature,
bent" (X. 884-87). Adam's insane anger knows no
bounds at this juncture. All his cowardly invective
is directed at his mate, whom a little earlier he had
extolled as a goddess. Such is the balance between
sanity and insanity; generation and degeneration.

        Two of Whitney's emblems graphically express
Adam's dilemma. The first, entitled <u>Dominus Viuit et
Videt</u>, shows Adam kneeling and hiding his face against
the trunk of a tree and the eye of God (asking <u>ubi es</u>) is shining
in dreadful glory behind. The second, captioned <u>Ex
maximo minimum</u>, shows a sadly grinning skull with a
femur in front of it and broken pebbles on the side.
A full-grown lily and a shrub behind the skull denote
the continuity of life in spite of death. The verses
give Adam's state of mind after the fall, while the
devices illustrate passages from the epic and convey
Adam's agonized thoughts:

        Behinde a figtree great, him selfe did Adam
            hide:
        And thought from God hee there might lurke,
            and should not bee espide.
        Oh foole, no corners seeke, thoughe thou a
            sinner bee;
        For none but God can thee forgive, who all
            thy waies doth see.

        Where lively once, Gods image was expreste,
        Wherein, sometime was sacred reason plac'de,
        The head, I meane, that is so ritchly
            bleste,
        With sighte, with smell, with hearinge,
            and with taste.
        Lo, nowe a skull, both rotten, bare,and drye,
        A relike meete in charnell house to lye,

                    (Whitney, p. 229)

                    143

Milton's Adam is fore-shown similar consequences of
his sin, which will redound on his posterity. He is
moved to tears and questions how God can destroy his
own image:

> Can thus
> Th' Image of God in man created once
> So goodly and erect, though faulty since,
> To such unsightly sufferings be debas't
> Under inhuman pains? Why should not Man,
> Retaining still Divine similitude
> In part, from such deformities be free

(XI. 507-13)

Milton's Adam does not experience death and its de-
nuding power, but he suffers from the sickness of
guilt which was "roten, bare, and drye," draining him
of all the joy and well-being he had known hitherto
in Eden. At the nadir of his despair he is indeed in
the abyss of the "charnell house." Insanity's most
abject condition is seen in Adam's vision of the
future. The mountain-top experience is exhilarating
for Adam, but also heart-rending; he sees degeneration
and madness in man. He sees Cain, his child, kill
his brother, because of inordinate jealousy:

> Whereat hee inly rag'd, and as they talk'd,
> Smote him into the Midriff with a stone
> That beat out life; he fell, and deadly pale
> Groan'd out his Soul with gushing blood
> effus'd.

(XI. 444-47)

Among the patients at the Lazar-house Adam has a pre-
view of "all maladies / Of ghastly Spasm, or racking
torture, qualms / Of Heart-sick Agony, all feverous
kinds," and among those symptoms of mental abrasions
"Convulsions, Epilepsies . . . Daemoniac Frenzy,
moping Melancholy / And Moonstruck madness, pining
Atrophy," accompanied by their tortuous and physical
symptoms, for "Dire was the tossing, deep the groans,
despair / Tended the sick busiest from Couch to Couch"
(XI. 480-90). Adam weeps at the sight and questions
how man, created in "Divine similitude" could so suffer. Michael's answer is similar to that of many an
emblem:

144

               Thir Maker's Image . . .
               Forsook them, when themselves they vilifi'd
               To serve ungovern'd appetite, and took
               His Image whom they served, . . .
               Disfiguring not God's likeness, but thir own,

                                            (XI. 514-21)

Michael concludes with the adage, "Nor love thy life,
nor hate; but what thou liv'st / Live well, how long
or short permit to Heav'n" (XI. 553-54).

     Then Adam experiences another form of madness,
which Milton satirically terms heroic virtue:

               For in those days Might only shall be
                  admir'd,
               And Valor and Heroic Virtue call'd;
               To overcome in Battle, and subdue
               Nations, and bring home spoils with infinite
               Man-slaughter, shall be held the highest
                  pitch
               Of human Glory, and for Glory done
               Of triumph, to be styl'd great Conquerors,
               Patrons of Mankind, Gods, and Sons of Gods,

                                            (XI. 689-96)

The passage exemplifies the madness of power and
material lust, and its result aggrandisement at any
cost, be it rapine, slaughter or robbery. This
imbalance is the aftermath of forgetting the classic
precept, "The rule of not too much, by temperance
taught" (XI. 531). Adam forgets that he is "Created,
. . . to nobler end / Holy and pure, conformitie
divine" (XI. 605-6). Conscious and willing degeneration become the negation of all potential. Milton
and the emblem writers portray madness in its multi-
farious forms, and show that man can overcome it by
asserting his divinity. Adam's insanity is not long
lived. Michael, as a mentor, gives him a sense of
balance and self confidence. After Adam has communed
with Michael he regains the peace he had lost, and can
depart "Greatly in peace of thought" (XII. 558).
Hawkins, like Michael, gives a panoramic view of the
earth, which enables him to affirm his belief in
Heaven:

                          145

Mountains are some of the gallantst
things in Nature, especially if we regard
the Prospect they afford, to deliciat the
eyes with; when taking a stand upon some
good advantage, you behold from thence a
goodlie river underneath; which in token of
homage, as it were, runnes kissing the foot
therof, along as it goes. But the most
delicious it is, whē you see on the other
side, a vast playne suspended before you,
and diversifyed with little risings, hills,
and mountains, heer and there, which bounding not the view too short, suffers the
eyes with freedome to extend themselves
into the immensitie of Heaven,

(Hawkins, p. 226)

Adam had once again seen and experienced the immensity
of Heaven and Earth, and had "calm of mind all passion
spent." He could project his mind into the timeless
magnitude of eternity, which Peacham conveys by a
female figure encompassed by a girdle of stars:
Peacham's Eternitas.

A Virgin faire, purtraicted as you see,
With haire dispred, in comelie wise behind:
Within whose handes, two golden balls there
    be:
But from the brest, the nether parts are
    twin'd
Within a starrie circle, do expresse,
Eternitie, or Everlastingnes.

Eternitie is young, and never old:
The circle wantes beginning and the end:
And uncorrupt for ever lies the gold:

(Peacham, p. 141)

Adam's mind at rest, he becomes part of eternity and
less concerned about the aftermath of his sin; he can
address the angel in unforgettable words that belie
all time and space, and assure man that knowledge is
a limb of eternity, and like Peacham's emblem can
claim Heaven's ever during light:

How soon hath thy prediction, Seer blest,
Measur'd this transient World, the Race
    of time,

146

Till time stand fixt: beyond is all abyss,
Eternity, whose end no eye can reach.
Greatly instructed I shall hence depart
Greatly in peace of thought, and have my fill
Of knowledge, what this Vessel can contain;

(XII. 553-59)

Adam, while still in the throes of his deranged suffering has gained wisdom. Like Bacchus and Ceres and
Christ he can empathize with those who suffer and
emerge phoenix-like more glorified. He has "attain'd
the sum / Of wisdom? (XII. 575), and will "possess /
A paradise within thee, happier far" (XII. 587).
Peacham's emblem recaptures the scene. The device
shows a mountain peak shot above the clouds and bright
with the rays of the sun above it, its base part of
the earthy landscape. The lit peak is the troubled
mind that has found its peace and bliss:

> The godly mind, that hath so oft assaid,
> The perils that our frailtie here amate,
> Though heavenly wisdome, is no more afraid
> Of Fortunes frowne, and bitter blastes
>   of Fate:
> For though in vale of woes, her dwelling be,
> Her nobler part's above untouch't and free.

(Peacham, p. 163)

Hall reaffirms his faith in man's capacity by asking
leading questions. He says, if man suffers mental
abrasions he is also the epitome of creation:

> Lord! what is man?
> A mass of wonders cluster'd in a span:
> . . . who can find
> The uncontrouled swiftness of his mind?

(Hall, p. 49)

Yet Hall signifies that man is an enigma though the
masterpiece of God's work. This enigmatic characteristic of man is due to his unfathomable mind and soul,
and the balance or imbalance of his spirit and his
thoughts:

> Enjoying what wild fancie can invent:
> Pray! can you say you are content?

147

Do not your labouring thoughts inlarge and
    still
Grow far more empty as they fill

Vast soul of man! wno cannot find in thee
A circumscrib'd infinitie. . .
But ramble still, and feed thy fury, groan,
. . .
Thou doest but multiply thy cares and toss
Like men amazed at a loss.
Or like a crazy vessell which doth lie
On th' drunken tyranny
Of each insulting wave, whilst every blast
Jussell's and threaten's that her last.

                    (Hall, pp. 65-6)

Decked in God's "own similitude," Adam's acts and
decisions are more onerous than if he were one of the
other creatures. If he can joy in things, he also
experiences sorrow. His very existence is enigmatic
and paradoxical, and his greatness and his deviations
make him an entire entity, a small universe, a microcosm in the cosmos. Milton's Adam outshines myriads
of his sons and daughters, even though men like
Quarles bewail man's ignorance and darkness. The
device shows an unlit, sable candle and candlestick
resting on a coffin:

        Was it for this, the breadth of Heav'n
            was blowne
        Into the nostrils of this Heav'nly Creature?
        Was it for this, that sacred Three in One
        Conspir'd to make this Quintessence of
            Nature?
        Did heav'nly Providence intend
        So rare a Fabrick for so poore an end?

        Was Man, the highest master-piece of Nature,
        The curious Abstract of the whole Creation,
        Whose soule was copied from his great
            Creator,
        Made to give Light, and set for Observation,
        Ordain'd for this? To spend his Light
        In a dark-Lanthorne? Cloystred up in night?

                    (Quarles, Hieroglyphikes,
                    p. 31)

                    148

Similarly Milton expresses Adam's qualms and doubts
"Why is life giv'n / To be thus wrested from us?"
(XI. 502-3); "Why hast thou added / The sense of end-
less woes? inexplicable / Thy justice seems" (X.
753-55); "Why am I mockt with death, and length'n'd
out / To deathless pain?" (X. 774-75). But Milton's
Adam is not benighted for long. With his mind at rest
and faith in himself and his Maker's providence, he
wends his way out of Eden.

Madness as depicted in Eve appears in an emblem
of Harvey where she is offering her heart, the symbol
of human will and affection, to the snake in the
Garden. Giving her heart away to the serpent signifies detaching herself from God-likeness, the heart
being the seat of goodness and divine love. Once the
heart is in the keeping of the snake, Eve's state is
that of darkness, and she succumbs to "covetousness,
vanity, hardness, and insatiability" (Harvey, Schola
Cordis, London 1647, Ode II). Eve is seen standing
under the Tree of Knowledge of Good and Evil flirting
with the serpent.[10] In Quarles, the serpent has
already possessed the heart and is coiled round it
(Emblem I, pp. 203-205); Eve's separation from God is
complete. Milton's Eve on tasting the fruit suffers
all the maddening effects of the euphoria it brings
her. The temptation is great and she succumbs to it
by plucking the fruit and eating it. The heady fruit
makes her lose all sense of proportion, (IX. 780 ff.)
Her first impulse constrains her to worship the tree,
and in inebriate words, promise it her allegiance.
She imagines she is worshipping the repository of
sapience which will make her an all-knowing goddess.
Then appears her insatiable greed in gorging herself
beyond hunger with the fruit. Her jocundity leads
to wily cogitation, as often observed in the demented.
She hopes that God has overlooked that lapse of hers;
and wonders how to approach Adam and break the tragic
news to him. Using his uxuriousness as the bait,
she schemes to make him subservient to her and acknowledge her his superior:

> Shall I to him make known
> As yet my change, and give him to partake
> Full happiness with mee, or rather not.
> But keep the odds of Knowledge in my power
> Without Copartner? so to add what wants
> In Female Sex, the more to draw his Love,

                    And render me more equal, and perhaps,
                    A thing not undesirable, sometime
                    Superior;

                              (IX. 817-25)

Eve's failure is sensate, so irresponsible. But her
tempting of Adam is premeditated like the wily insane.
Each move is calculated, though Adam is not fooled.
The goodness of her heart has departed from Eve,
leaving the madness of Evil. In its wake appear
jealousy and thoughts of murder. Her insanity appears
in all her acts, her worship of the tree, her boldness
in bearing a branch full of the fruit to Adam (IX.
851). She speaks to him in specious words full of
circumlocution as her mind somersaults through cunning
and deceit often observed in the unbalanced. Here
is the heart seen in the emblems that strays from God
and needs to be returned. Eve has undergone the
turbulence of separation, and it is not until her
repentance (X. 914 ff.) that she regains sanity.

        The garland that slips from Adam's fingers be-
comes the first symbol of death and decay in Eden.
His sorrow at sight of her is like a sigh of dismay:

              How art thou lost, how on a sudden lost,
              Defac't, deflow'r'd, and now to Death devote?

                              (IX. 900-01)

The eating of the fruit on Adam's part spells the
decay of chivalry and decorum and the graciousness of
love. Adam errs intellectually. The first symptom
of their mutual madness is inordinate lust and the
heat of desire. The aftermath of consummated lust
is no joy to either Adam or to Eve. It disturbs the
brain:

              Soon as the force of that fallacious Fruit

              About thir spirits had play'd, and inmost
                 powers
              Made err, was now exhal'd, and grosser sleep
              Bred of unkindly fumes, with conscious
                 dreams
              Encumber'd, now had left them, up they rose

                              150

As from unrest, and each the other viewing,
Soon found thir Eyes how op'n'd, and thir
   minds
How dark'n'd;

(IX. 1046-54)

   For Wither, all forbidden knowledge was part of
Adam and Eve's sin. Carnal appetites were perpetrated
by original sin, the sin of Milton's Adam as he lusted
for Eve after tasting the fruit. Wither says of
those who visit the nefarious stews:

   They venture for their Knowledge, Adam-like;
   And, such as his, will their Atchievements
      bee.

(Wither, p. 27)

This unknown appetite, the sexual drive is bewildering
in their hitherto state of innocence, and coupled
with their guilt benights Adam and Eve further. The
result is self pity and remorse and deep depression.
Enraged Adam loses all self-control and blames Eve:

   Is this the Love, is this the recompense
   Of mine to thee, ingrateful Eve, express't
   Immutable when thou wert lost, not I,
   Who might have liv'd and joy'd immortal bliss,
   Yet willingly chose rather Death with thee:
   And am I now upbraided, as the cause
   Of thy transgressing?

   I also err'd in overmuch admiring
   What seem'd in thee so perfect, that I
      thought
   No evil durst attempt thee, but I rue
   That error now, which is become my crime,

(IX. 1162-81)

   As in the emblems, the motto follows this speech
of remorse. Adam voices thoughts applicable to all
men in similar states of mind.

         Thus it shall befall
   Him who to worth in Woman overtrusting
   Lets her Will rule; restraint she will not
      brook,

151

And left to herself, if evil thence ensue,
Shee first his weak indulgence will accuse.

(XI. 1182-86)

Their sin of disobedience to God's will becomes the
rambling serpent within them. They bicker and quarrel
and lose all composure and sanity.

One gets the same sense of accusation as far as
women are concerned in a dramatic emblem of Peacham's,
Philautia, in which a daughter of Eve stands with a
looking glass in one hand and a serpent coiled round
the other:

> A Virgins face with Robes of light aray,
>   Why hath (Selfe-love) our Poets thee
>   assign'd?
> Philaut: Love should be young, and fresh as
>   merry May,
>   Such clothing best agreeth with my mind.
> What meanes that poisonous serpent in thy
>   hand?
> Philaut: My bane I breed, by this you
>   understand.
> I' th other hand say why that looking glasse?
> Since in thee no deformitie I find,
> Philaut: Know how in Pride Self-love doth
>   most surpasse,
>   And still is in her Imperfections
>   blind:
>   And save her owne devices doth
>   condemne
>   All others labours, in respect of
>   them.

(Peacham, p. 5)

Peacham's preceding emblem in the book shows a milk-
white doe running toward a thicket where her antlers
get entangled and enmeshed. She is the target of the
hunters' arrows, which stick in her flanks. The
verse carries a verbal picture of the wounded deer
and moralizes as though with Milton's Adam and Eve in
mind:

> So oft we see the man whome Conscience bad
> Doth inwardly with deadly torture wound,
> From place to place to range with Furie mad,

152

And seeke his ease by shifting of his ground
The meane neglecting which might heale the
        sinne,
That howerly ranckles more and more within.

                    (Peacham, p. 4)

    Chaos, Sin, and Death all become paramount once
Eve is tempted, deceived and succumbs to evil. Her
disobedience completes man's degeneration and that of
his world. No sooner Satan offers sapience of the gods
to the mortals, the natural equilibrium of the great
chain of being is subverted. Man's overreach takes
away his rationality and limits him in time and space--
frustrations that man has never outlived. Nature, being one substance with man, feels the aberration and
knows "all [is] lost" (IX. 784). The degeneration is
universal. Its psychological effects are seen in all
the reactions of Eve and Adam. In her euphoria Eve
believes herself a goddess. Her venerated, "Sovran,"
voiceless tree becomes her "Best guide" (IX. 808).
It teaches her guile, and even spurs her to think
of becoming the first murderess (IX. 830-33). Adam
transgresses chivalrously and knowingly. The result
of their sin is more scars on Nature, a night of inordinate passion (not Milton's chaste, conjugal love),
and an aftermath of confusion, chagrin, fear, blame
and counterblame, a sordid state of mental disruption:

                    They destitute and bare
        Of all thir virtue: silent, and in face
        Confounded long they sat, as struck'n mute,

                    (IX. 1061-63)

                    not at rest or ease of Mind,
        They sat them down to weep, nor only Tears
        Rain'd at their Eyes, but high Winds worse
            within
        Began to rise, high Passions, Anger, Hate,
        Mistrust, Suspicion, Discord, and shook sore
        Thir inward State of Mind, calm Region once
        And full of Peace, now tosst and turbulent:
        For Understanding rul'd not, and the Will
        Heard not her lore, both in subjection now
        To sensual Appetite.

                    (IX. 1120-28)

                    153

It is to this Adam that Quarles continues to say in
bewailing man's great loss:

> O thou that wert so many men, nay, all
> Abridged in one, how has thy desp'rate fall
> Destroy'd thy unborn seed, destroy'd thyself
>   withal!
>
> Uxurious Adam, whom thy Maker made
>   Equal to angels that excel in pow'r
> What has thou done? O why hast thou obey'd
>   Thine own destruction? Like a newcrept
>   flow'r,
> How does the glory of thy beauty fade!
>   How are thy fortunes blasted in an hour!
>   How art thou cow'd that hadst the power to
>   quell
>   The spite of new fall'n angels, baffle hell
> And vie with those that stood, and vanquish
>   those that fall!
> See how the world (whose chaste and pregnant
>   womb
>   Of late conceived, and brought forth
>   nothing ill)
> Is now degenerated, and become
>   A base adultress, whose false births do fill
> The earth with monsters, monsters that do
>   roam
>   And rage about, and make a trade to kill:
> Now glutt'ny paunches; lust begins to spawn;
>   Wrath takes revenge, and avarice a pawn;
> Pale envy pines, pride swells, and sloth
>   begins to yawn.

And using the Ovidian imagery of the North Wind prior
to the destruction of man in the <u>Metamorphoses</u>, Quarles
says:

> The air that whisper'd now begins to roar
>   And blust'ring Boreas blows the boiling
>   tide;
> The white-mouth'd water now usurps the shore,
>   And scorns the pow'r of her trident guide;
> The fire now burns, that did but warm before,
>   And rules her ruler with resistless pride:
> Fire, water, earth, and air, that first
>   were made
> To be subdued, see how they now invade;
> Thy rule whom once they served, command
>   where once obey'd.

154

Behold that nakedness, that late bewray'd
Thy glory, now's become thy shame, thy
                              wonder;
Behold those trees whose various fruits were
                              made
For food, now turn'd a shade to shroud thee
                              under;
Behold, that voice (which thou hast disobey'd)
That late was music, now affrights like
                              thunder.
Poor man! are not thy joints grown faint
                    with shaking,
To view th' effect of thy bold undertaking,
That in one hour didst mar what Heaven six
          days was making?

                    (Quarles Emblems, Bk I,
                    No. II pp. 205-7)

Quarles has aptly described the trauma of the whole situation. The blemish of disobedience affected the once
perfect principals as well as Nature in its pristine
beauty. Degeneration resulted from the madness. The
seven deadly sins came in the wake of the original sin,
and Death's ravenous appetite bound man in time and
space. Madness became a progeny of dissolution; dissolution caused by Satan, Sin and Death.

    Another form of insanity which ensued is seen in
the behaviour of the animals. Woodcuts of the early
publications of Paradise Lost show that the lion and
the lamb sat beside Adam, unmindful of differences in
their species and habits. There was accord in heaven,
but there was also perfect amity in Eden. The fall
changed the picture. The predators became vicious.
Man's sin effected the whole creation. Insane violence invaded the serenity of Paradise.

          Beast now with Beast gan war, and Fowl with
              Fowl,
          And Fish with Fish; to graze the Herb all
              leaving,
          Devour'd each other; nor stood much in awe
          Of Man, but fled him, or with count'nance
              grim
          Glar'd on him passing:

                    (X. 710-14)

155

Though still the terrestrial head of life in Eden, man
is not secure after the fall. He is buffeted by incle-
ment weather and the hostility of the beasts, as well
as his own mental unrest.

Art had not been remiss in painting pictures of
the dreaded Hell. The Judeo-Christian hell had little
charm of Hades, but ever since man conceived irregu-
larity and illogical actions as sinful, Hell had fired
the artistic imagination. Evil in Paradise Lost leads
to madness and degeneration; and Evil's usurpation of
the "goodly earth" culminates in Hell. Evil finally
condenses in a picture of a horrible Snake Pit in
hell. Satan's return and triumph are received with
hisses of shame and anger by his compeers, they themselves having metamorphosed to vipers. The grove
that miraculously springs up in the pit, flaunts
tempting fruit before the reptile. Their "scalding
thirst and hunger fierce" goad them to reach for the
fruit.

> But on they roll'd in heaps, and up the Trees
> Climbing, sat thicker than the snaky locks
> That curl'd Megaera: greedily they pluck'd
> The Fruitage fair to sight, like that which
> grew
> Near that bituminous Lake where Sodom flam'd;
> This more delusive, not the touch, but taste
> Deceiv'd; they fondly thinking to allay
> Thir appetite with gust, instead of Fruit
> hew'd bitter Ashes, . . .
> Thus were they plagu'd
> And worn with Famine long, and ceaselss hiss.

(X. 558-74)

Their torment exceeds that of Tantalus:

> Heare Tantalus, as Poettes doe devine,
> This guerdon hathe, for his offence in hell:
> The pleasante fruite, dothe to his lippe
> decline,
> A river faire unto his chinne dothe swell:
> Yet, twixt these two, for foode the wretche
> doth sterve,
> For bothe doe flee, when they his neede
> shoulde serve.

(Whitney, p. 74)

Paradise Lost gives all the torments of mental and
physical aberrations. Milton's imagination was painting pictures of madness, degeneracy, chaos and hell
like his contemporary artists and literati. Sculptures,
cathedral frescoes and murals, large and small canvases, woodcuts and lithographs, poems and sermons
and illuminated works of the Renaissance had dealt
with sinister creatures, gargoyles and monsters depicting the motif of madness. Preoccupation with the
after life and horror of hell were responsible for
this plethora of output. In Milton the theme and the
pictures bring this popular fancy to Baroque perfection.

        Quarles in like manner warns the unwary of death
and the horror of hell, which promise nothing more than
chaos and mental frustration:

            Look, look, what horrid furies do await
            Thy flatt'ring slumbers! If thy drowsy head
            But chance to Nod, thou fall'st into a bed
            Of sulph'rous flames, whose torments want
                a date.

            Mark, how the ready hands of death prepare;
            His bow is bent, and he hath notch'd his
                dart;
            He aims, he levels at thy slumb'ring heart;
            The wound is posting, O be wise, beware.

            What! has the voice of danger lost the art
            To raise the spirit of neglected care?

                        gull thy soul no more
            With earth's false pleasure, and the world's
                delight,
            Whose fruit is fair and pleasing to the
                sight;
            But sour in taste, fake as the putrid core

            Her words protest a heav'n; her works
                produce a hell.

The emblem ends on the note:

                        death that flings at all,
            Stands arm'd to strike thee down, where
                flames attend thy fall.

                        (Quarles, Emblems, pp. 210-17)

                        157

Quarles' hell has its "pale-faced" jailer who makes
arrests and the dungeon is:

> the jail
> Of Stygian darkness, bound in red-hot chains,
> And griped with tortures worse that Tityan
> pains.

(Quarles, Emblems,
p. 260)

It is a place "where light ne'er shot his golden ray,
That hides your actions in Cimmerian shades."

(Quarles, Emblems,
p. 253)

Milton gives full rein to madness in Paradise Lost.
It appears in wilted nature, in animal hostility, in
Adam and Eve's guilt, frustration and rancour, in the
uncouth war of the angels, in the sickness of the once
glorious archangel Satan, in the metaphorical and literal ugliness of Sin and the frightening, amorphous
Death, in the searing flames and ice of Hell, the
tortuous hell that Satan carries within himself, and
in chaos, where there is perpetual unrest. Milton
probes madness and degeneration like a psychologist,
except he gives the maladies a grandeur unequaled in
literature or science.

FOOTNOTES

[1]Bridget Gellert Lyons, _Voices of Melancholy_ (New York: W. W. Norton, 1975), p. 3.

[2]Hughes, ed., p. 738.

[3]S. H. Hook, _Middle Eastern Mythology_ (Baltimore: Pelican, 1963), p. 44.

[4]James Holly Hanford, _A Milton Handbook_ (New York: Appleton-Century-Crofts, 1954), p. 71

[5]Rosemary Freeman, pp. 140-41.

[6]John M. Steadman, _Milton and the Renaissance Hero_ (Oxford: Clarendon Press, 1967), p. 18.

[7]Steadman, _Milton and the Renaissance Hero_, p. 74.

[8]Isabel MacCaffrey, _Paradise Lost as Myth_ (Cambridge: Harvard U. Press, 1967), p. 109.

[9]Robert Hughes, _Heaven and Hell in Western Art_ (New York: Stein & Day, 1968), p. 243.

[10]Rosemary Freeman, p. 134.

CHAPTER FOUR

PICTORIAL CONCEPT OF MAN

i   Man and His prelapsarian Habitat

In Paradise Lost the Son, God's Word, obeys
God's mandate to circumscribe heaven and earth (VII.
163-65) and out of chaos create new worlds (VII. 209).
Mathematically he uses a pair of golden compasses to
carve a globe of perfection out of chaos' "vast profundity obscure" (VII. 229). In this conglobed matter
he places Eden, the Utopian garden of bliss, recalling
gardens in art and literature from early times; such
as the biblical garden of Genesis 2.8, and Alcinous'
garden in Scheria, to the highly stylized, formal
enclosed garden, the hortus conclusus of medieval art.
The earth around the garden God makes verdant, and
fills with lush foliage; both with common English
plants and exotic herbage:

> Then Herbs of every leaf, that sudden
>   flow'r'd
> Op'ning thir various colors, and made gay
> Her bosom smelling sweet:

                    (VII. 317-20)

Among the plants are vines laden with grapes,
swelling gourds, "corny reeds," shrubs and bushes,
and stately, dancing trees flush with fruit and
flowers. Densely wooded hills and valleys, fountains
and pools, and tree-embanked rivers complete the
picture, making Earth an extension of Heaven, a place
fit for gods. The garden has provision for the
trees to be ever-fresh; celestial dews rising from
the earth water them (VII. 310-39). This beautiful
picture of God's garden on earth corresponds to the
landscapes of the emblem writers, who like Milton
derive many images from contemporary English gardens
and mediaeval illustrations and verses.

The amply supplied, though formalized, Eden is
an enclosed plateau atop a hill. It has dense, tree-
covered sides like bastions that allow neither entry
nor exit:

160

                              so thick entwin'd
     As one continu'd brake, the undergrowth
     Of shrubs and tangling bushes had perplext
     All path of Man or Beast that pass'd that
     way.

                    (IV. 174-77)

The verbal image is as dense as the scene it describes,
and one can picture Satan, baulked by the lush growth,
overleaping the wall. In this garden God places the
first man. Like the hortus conclusus the garden is
self-contained: a Paradise, a circular, emerald encrusted crown (IV. 132-33 & 303-8). The picture is
not peculiar to Milton, for the enclosed circular
garden was the stock in trade of the mediaeval sym-
bolist. It had been equated with the Virgin; the enclosure signifying her perfection and purity as sealed
in the garden of her womb. The circular frame of the
enclosure highlights the central object in the picture.
In Paradise Lost the center of action is the Garden
of Eden, though the panorama of the epic encompasses
the universe.

     The Jesuit, Henry Hawkins, uses the device of the
enclosed garden in his emblem book Partheneia Sacra
(1633),[1] and studies it from many angles and in detail. His work belongs with the Marian literature,
extolling the Virgin for her perfection, and using
each detail of the portrayed symbols of her person
for contemplation and meditation.

     Hawkins' prose Partheneia Sacra, unlike the
works of other emblematists, is original and fascinating. Hawkins uses short verse stanzas with his devices and emblems, but they do not attain the richness
and lyricism of his prose. As Rosemary Freeman has
pointed out Hawkins is ornate and rhetorical but also
colloquial in his prose style. His could be termed
the style of an aristocrat of letters. It comes
nearest, among the emblematists, to the Miltonic mode
and cadence. He apparently enjoys ideas, and the
imagery he uses to express the ideas seems to enthrall
him. Yet he never loses sight of his mission, the
promotion, through emblems, of meditation on Mary.
In his hortus conclusus he has images reminiscent of
Milton:

                         161

a little drop of Deaw falling from the
heavens, . . . on the Flowerdeluce, would
seeme perhaps to you but a little round
point of water, and a meer graine of
Cristal, but if the Sun do but shine upon
it, Ah! what a miracle of beautie it is?
while of the one side it wil looke like
an Orient-pearl, and being turned some
other way, becomes a glowing Carbuncle,
then a Saphir, and after an Emerald, and
so an Amethist.

(<u>Partheneia Sacra</u> pp. 65-6)

It recalls the foliage in Heaven and has "all the
powers of sensuous evocation."[2]

in Heav'n the Trees
Of life ambrosial fruitage bear, and vines
Yield Nectar, though from off the boughs
each Morn
We brush mellifluous Dews, and find the
ground
Cover'd with pearly grain:

(V. 426-30)

Both artists convey sensuous details and their mental
awareness of things felt and seen in texture, form,
and color. Both deal with heavenly perfection.

Hawkins' garden provides twenty-four emblematic
pictures to help meditation. He expounds each emblem,
comparing its details to the physical and spiritual
beauty of the Madonna. Among the many flowers he mentions, he expressly emphasizes the quality and beauty
of the rose, the lily, the violet, and the sunflower
or heliotrope.

Milton's heaven is emblematically "Impurpled with
celestial roses" (III. 364), and as earth is but the
shadow of heaven, roses appear in earthly Eden, along
with other delightful blooms. The flowers are profusely inlaid in Adam and Eve's love grotto, their
bower of bliss:

the roof
Of thickest covert was inwoven shade

Laurel and Myrtle, and what higher grew
Of firm and fragrant leaf; on either side
Acanthus, and each odorous bushy shrub
Fenc'd up the verdant wall; each beauteous
    flow'r,
Iris all hues, Roses, and Jessamin
Rear'd high thir flourisht heads between,
    and wrought
Mosaic; underfoot the Violet,
Crocus, and Hyacinth with rich inlay
Broider'd the ground,

                                    (IV. 692-702)

Milton's description of the love grotto brings to mind
the frontispiece of Partheneia Sacra. Hawkins' composite device of the hortus conclusus carries all the
emblems he expounds, and there indeed the flowers
"rear high their flourished heads," while the sun and
a star and the rainbow and God's grace, seen in con-
centric arcs, seem to bless the walled garden. Hawkins describes each of his flowers for its beauty and
celestial significance, but his verbal painting of
the tulip recalls Keats:

        Here are sweetpeas, on tip-toe for a flight:
        With wings of gentle flush o'er delicate
            white.
        And taper fingers catching at all things,
        To bind them all about with tiny rings.[3]

The tulip for Hawkins is an artist's masterpiece; it
evokes similar romantic thoughts and emotions in
the poet:

            looke and observe it wel. How were
        it possible, one would think, so thin a
        leaf, bred and nourished in the same ayre,
        and proceeding from the same stem, should
        be golden in the bottome, violet without,
        saffron within, bordered on the edge with
        fine gold, and the prickle of the point
        blew as a goodlie Saphir?

                            (Partheneia Sacra, p. 10)

Hawkins' garden has the "bashful Rose, the candid
Lillie" both symbols of pristine purity, "the purple
violet of humility and goodlie Heliotropian" their

colours befitting a queen and containing the gory germ
which presages sorrow. The garden is a part of her
perfection, as signified by the iris, a symbol of
majesty as well as of the graveyard (her sorrow).
These objects of nature, Hawkins continues, are "enclosed round, and compassed-in with a wall." The
garden also displays the peaceful olive, resounds
with the harmony of Philomel, and sports the stately
palm. Hawkins' garden is replete with a crystal
fountain of plenty and the innocence of the dove. Like
Milton's before the fall, it has no seasons. Only
Post-lapsarian gardens experience

> . . . change
> Of Seasons to each Clime; else had the Spring
> Perpetual smil'd on Earth with vernant
>   Flow'rs,

(X. 677-79)

[Its] Allies [are] streight and even, strewed
al with sands, that is, a streight, vertuous,
and Angelical life, yet strewed with the
sands and dust of . . . proper Humilitie;
where are Arbours to shadow her from the
heats of concupiscence, flowrie Beds to
repose in, with heavenlie Contemplations;
Mounts to ascend to, with the studie of
Perfections: where the hearbs, and Simples,
soveraigne medicines of al spiritual
maladies, where (I say) are the Flowers of
al Vertues: The Lillie of spotles and im-
maculate Chastitie, the Rose of Shamfastnes
and bashful Modestie, the Violet of
Humilitie, and Gilloflower of Patience, the
Marygold of Charitie, the Hiacinth of Hope,
the Sun-flower of Contemplatio, the Tulip
of Beautie and gracefulnes. In this Garden
Enclosed are certain risings to be seen of
Hils in elevations of mind, . . . Vines of
spiritual gladness, and Groves of a retired
solitude. . . . Heer spring the limpid fountains of all Graces; whence streame the
little rils and brooks watering the Paradice on al sides, . . . [Here] whole Quiers
of Angels are accustomed to sing their
Alleluyas, at al howers, . . . [and pools
teem with] harmles fry of her innocent
thoughts, . . . and there are certain

labyrinths [mazes of formal gardens] formed
in the hearbs of Her endles perfections.

(Partheneia Sacra, pp.
11 & 12)

No romantic could have described the beauty of
Eden as Milton does in scenes of idyllic charm. Milton
has a sub-terranean stream bubbling out as a spring
and then joining the main stream that branches into
four rivulets flowing in different directions. The
water of the fountain is sapphire in colour and flows
in "many a rill" and "crisped brooks," through "mazy
error under pendant shades." The garden rejoices in
hills and dales and plains; groves, lawns and downs;
roses and flowers of every hue; waterfalls and lakes;
choirs of birds; and revels in pastoral and classical
images (IV. 223-86).

Hawkins' Partheneia Sacra revels in its birds.
They vary from the dove, the swan, the hen and night-
ingale to the phoenix. His trees include the symbolic
palm, the prototype of the upright, and the peace-
showering olive. Like Milton, Hawkins' garden has
"formally trimmed bushes, trees often fragrant and
aromatic, a fountain, a mount, pools and walks."[4]

Milton's garden is landscaped to satisfy the most
discriminating connoisseur of art, yet each of the
images could signify a deeper truth; most obviously
water with its potency for cleansing, purifying and
rejuvenating. Hawkins suggests that the devotee,
for the sake of edification, should concentrate on
the symbols portrayed and enumerated in the devices
and verbal pictures:

And this method would I have thee keepe in
al. . . . [So that] with the wings of Contemplation [ye] may . . . secretly view, reflect,
review, survey, delight, contemplate, and
enjoy the hidden and sublime perfections
therein,

(Partheneia Sacra p. 4)

Milton's garden, though apparently less symbolic,
stems from the same allegorical tradition, and probably expects a similar response from its readers.
It too portrays nature in its prelapsarian

and pristine glory. It has "Cedar, and Pine, and Fir,
and branching Palm,. . . a woody Theatre / Of state-
liest view." Its "circling row" of fruit-laden trees
and enameled blossoms are enriched by the Sun as it
emblematically impresses its beams on them. The sky
shows "fair Evening Cloud, or humid Bow," and to Milton "lovely seem'd / That Lantskip." It "to the
heart inspires / Vernal delight and joy, able to
drive / All sadness but despair" (IV. 139-55). Hawkins' garden is not only pure but has sensuous beauty.
He too uses theater imagery. It

> is a goodlie Amphitheatre of flowers, upon
> whose leaves, delicious beauties stand, as
> on a stage, to be gazed on, and to play
> their parts, not to see so much, as to be
> seen; and like Wantons to allure with their
> looks, or enchant with their words, the
> civets and perfumes they weare about them.
> It is even the pride of Nature,

(Partheneia Sacra, p. 5)

Milton's garden follows the pattern. In Milton the
heady fragrance of fruit and flower recall the per-
fumes of Saba and Arabia:

> now gentle gales
> Fanning thir odoriferous wings dispense
> Native perfumes, and whisper whence they
> stole
> Those balmy spoils.

(IV.156-63)

Milton's Eden appeals to the senses, and embodies in
itself all aspects of perfection including abstract
ideas, such as divine and human love, joy, and man's
desire for God's providence and protective grace.
Milton spares neither elaborate verbal pictures nor
delicate details to convey his ideas.

The difference between the emblematist's garden
and Milton's is that Hawkins' garden retains its
original and sacramental innocence while Milton's is
marred by Sin:

> I speake not of Eden, the Earthly Paradice,
> nor of the Garden of Gethsemany, watred

166

with Bloud flowing from our Saviour's
precious bodie: But I speake of Thee,
that Garden so knowne by the name of
Hortus Conclusus; wherein are al
things mysteriously and spiritually to
be found, . . .

for that the Garden of <u>Eden</u>, a Terrestrial
Paradice, was not so exempt from Sinne, but
the place where Sinne began; and was not so
free from the Serpent, but that he could
get-in and work the mischief; so as for
avoyding more ensuing dangers, it was nec-
essarie to place at the gates therof for
ever after, an Angel-Porter of the Order
of the Cherubins, with a fierie and two-
edged sword, to guard the same.

(<u>Partheneia Sacra</u>, pp. 11-12)

Both gardens mirror theological truths. The crystal
and sacred waters of the pool and fountains reflect
spiritual light such as "Siloa's Brook that flow'd /
Fast by the Oracle of God" (I. 11-12). Garden images
often signify characters and situations in the Scriptures. In secular literature the garden connotes pro-
fane love, as in sacred literature it does divine love.
The Canticles use garden images profusely, and the
seclusion of the garden is often associated with
man's proximity to God. The paradisal is interpreted
both literally and allegorically as man's desire for
perfection. Hawkins is explicit about its significance.

E. M. of <u>Ashrea</u> also deals with garden imagery.
He uses the word "Ashrea" for his symbolic writing,
as its Hebraic counterpart signifies a wood or grove
and also to make blessed. The tree imagery of <u>Ashrea</u>
symbolizes blessings, and each of the eight trees
mentioned in the book stands for one of the beatitudes. The emblems, E. M. avers, are but a device to
aid memory in recalling blessings; they are part of
<u>Ars Memorativa</u>, the Art of Memory, but he also points
out, in the very beginning, that his grove is sacred,
for

Here no Sylvanus haunts our Grove,
Here no prophane wild Satyrs rove,
Nor in our glades,

167

```
                     And blissful shades,
              Diana and her Nymphs resort

                       (Ashrea, "An Invitation")
```

Among the eight trees he uses, five are better known:
the myrrhe, the woodbine, the vine, the cornel, and
the fig tree. The other three are more exotic: the
clove, the Adam's Apple tree, and the Indian Banyan
or, as termed in seventeenth-century diction, the
Indian Fig tree. Interestingly Milton also mentions
the Banyan, and calls it "the fig tree." Adam and Eve
seek its shelter when oppressed by their nakedness:

```
                  and both together went
           Into the thickest Wood, there soon they chose
           The Fig-tree, not that kind for Fruit
              renown'd,
           But such as at this day to Indians known
           In Malabar or Decan spreads her Arms
           Branching so broad and long, that in the
              ground
           The bended Twigs take root, and Daughters
              grow
           About the Mother Tree, a Pillar'd shade
           High overarch't, and echoing Walks between;

                       (IX. 1099-1107)
```

To E. M. the Indian fig tree signifies humility. In
verse and prose he justifies the tree's properties as
humble:

```
        So do the Meek, to fix their Roots,
        Humbly let down as many Shoots,
        As good Desires, which spring from Love,
        Take root in Heaven, the Land above.
```

This Tree, above all others, may be said to
be possessed of, or to inherit the Earth:
For the Branches of it bending downwards
to the ground, no sooner touch it, but
they immediately take root, and grow up
into other Trees, which afterwards produce
others; so that in time they spread over all
the ground they meet with; . . . Another
thing commonly observ'd of these Trees is,
that they afford a secure retreat,

                       (Ashrea, pp. 15-16)

                 168

Milton's Garden of Eden is a microcosm of the
macrocosmic earth and Heaven, for it has:

> In narrow room Nature's whole wealth, yet
>   more,
> Of Heav'n on Earth:
>   (IV. 207-8)

Eden, which contains the garden, has a definite geographical location; it spreads "From Auran eastward
to the royal tow'rs / Of great Seleucia . . . / Or
. . . Telassar" (IV. 211-14).

But as the Hortus Conclusus is Hawkins' "Garden
shut up from the very beginning,"[5] so is Eden first
created. According to Jean Duvignaud these gardens
are the prototype of the secret gardens of the privi-
leged; sacred to their own society and inviolate. Because of its exclusiveness, ironically, "the secret
garden is a prison, a ghetto which shelters a way of
life unsure of its own continuation, which it can
only preserve by persuading itself that the world
resembles it and that it is unique in the world."[6]
This is what makes Shakespeare's Antony and Cleopatra
wish to "all alone / . . . wander through the streets"[7]
of Alexandria and mix with the inconsequential of
Egypt, breaking bonds that make them a hero and a
goddess. It is inevitable in the unique but enclosed
Eden that rational beings like Adam and Eve should
rebel against the one restraint put on them and be
constrained to leave their utopia. Being sentient,
their quest for knowledge could not be contained by
a hortus conclusus, however perfect.

FOOTNOTES

[1]Henry Hawkins, Partheneia Sacra 1633, Facsimile
(Menston: Scolar Press, 1971).

[2]Freeman, p. 174.

[3]John Keats, Poetical Works (London: Collins, n.d.),
p. 10.

[4]Freeman, p. 179.   [5]Freeman, p. 181.

[6]Jean Duvignaud, The Sociology of Art, trans.
Timothy Wilson (New York: Harper & Row, 1967), p. 76.

[7]Shakespeare, Antony and Cleopatra, Act I, Sc. i,
lls. 52-3.

169

Matrimonii Typus. Barthélemy Aneau, *Picta Poesis* (Lyon, 1552), p. 14.

ii ADAM, THE GOODLIEST OF MEN, UNPARADIS'D

Like Hawkins' Madonna, mankind was expected to attain perfection in communion with God, and maintain an unscathed innocence. Thus God places Man in this wonderful garden of perfection as though in the womb of the Hortus Conclusus. Conversely the man that God places there has to be perfect. God's behest to his Son is, "Let us make now Man in our Image, Man / In our similtude." And creating Adam from the "Dust of the ground" God breathes His divinity into him. Adam is repeatedly told that God: "in his own Image hee/ Created thee, in the Image of God / Express,

170

and thou becam'st a living Soul" (VII. 519-28). When
Adam recalls his advent into this garden of bliss, his
first conscious thought is of Heaven, and his first
motion is to spring toward the life from which he had
sprung. The axis of approach Milton shows is vertical.
In it is conveyed God's outreach to man and man reaching upward to God. The thought has often been expressed
by theorists and theologians that Man carries in himself godhead as he is of God. God being the universe,
man then becomes the prototype of the universe in miniature. Infused with the principles that inform the
universe, he is a hermaphrodite, until God at his re-
quest fashions his female counterpart from him, the
two complementing each other to perfection. In Indian
philosophy the universe is collectively God, and each
natural object is a projection or emanation of God.
In Christian thought Man is an Expression of God, on
whom is seen God's emblematic impress.

Peacham's emblem entitled "Homo Microcosmus"
elaborates the idea. The device depicts the universe
as a globe, with the sun and moon placed diagonally
opposite and the stars all around. Man, dominating
the scene is in the center of the picture. One arm
points upward, the eyes following it; the other
stretches downward, as though to bless the universe.
In the verse Peacham anatomizes man, after he asks
the question, "Heare what's the reason why a man we
call a little world?" Then he compares the parts of
man's body to the elements. He epitomizes his theory
in two lines at the end of the second verse of the
emblem showing that man is a microcosm, because in
him he contains the elements that constitute all
matter:

> Of Earth, Fire, Water, Man thus framed is,
> Of Elements the threefold Qualities.

> (Peacham, p. 190)

In spite of the reassurance that Man is the image of
God and in himself a little world, Milton's Adam
questions his identity as did the Renaissance man,
and as man has always done:

> But who I was, or where, or from what cause,
> Knew not;

> (VIII. 270-1)

171

His intellectual curiosity makes him examine and question animate and inanimate objects in the garden to be enlightened on the issue:

> Thou Sun, . . . fair Light,
> And thou enlight'n'd Earth, so fresh and gay,
> Ye Hills and Dales, ye Rivers, Woods, and
>   Plains
> And ye that live and move, fair Creatures
>   tell,
> Tell, if ye saw, how came I thus, how here?
> Not of myself; by some great Maker then
> In goodness; and in power pre-eminent;
> Tell me, how may I know him, how adore,
> From whom I have that thus I move and live,
> And feel that I am happier than I know.

(VIII. 273-82)

Man finds his answer in a dream and in reality, for God communes with him and pronounces Adam lord of Eden and of all the earth (IV. 339-41).

The question arises concerning Man as this idol favoured of God: is he the protagonist of Milton's great epic? The answer is ambivalent. For Milton, a Renaissance artist, the maxim that the greatest study of mankind is man, is of considerable significance in Paradise Lost. Man had created God in his image, and could not isolate himself from the concept of Perfection that he ideally fashioned and desired for himself. Nor could man isolate himself from the cosmic scheme and order of which he made God the supreme and the all encompassing entity. Before the fall, Adam of Paradise Lost is the prototype of the cosmic order. In his prelapsarian perfection, he is God projected on earth. God and man, being in perfect accord at this stage, reflect one another, and the dominant character of the epic is God-man or man-God. If the Son of God is the protagonist, Adam is the tragic hero of the epic, and the magnificent Satan just the antagonist. Adam's frailty alone costs him oneness with God but makes him wonderfully human.

Quarles reemphasizes the idea of man complementing God in the first Emblem of Hieroglyphikes:

172

Man is mans ABC: There is none that can
Reade God aright, unless he first spell Man:
Man is the Stayres, whereby his knowledge
    climes
To his Creator;

> (Quarles, Hieroglyphikes,
> p. 3)

The study of God thus becomes the study of man. Without knowledge of man, God is meaningless: "Ye have
known me thus ye know my Father, whom now ye have
known and seen" says the God-man (John XIV 7). If
Quarles' man is the stairs, and "These stairs be the
wayes to Heav'n," Man has to be lit by the "divine
fire" of heaven's perfection. Man's immortal soul is
lit by God's inspiring light:

> Whose humane soule-enlightning sunbeames
>   dart
> Through the bright Crannies of th' immortall
>   part.

> (Quarles, Hieroglyphikes,
> I. p. 3)

If God and man are one, then man becomes immortal, im-
perishable and can reach the ultimate in wholeness.
Milton's Creator is synonymous with man's quest and
aspiration for the highest and the best. In Milton's
hymn to light he invokes God's light-giving spirit,
which can infuse Man's mind to soar "above the Aonian
mount" to God-like heights, such as Milton reaches
himself. Quarles in like tradition invokes God's
light for his inspiration:

> And here, thou great Originall of Light,
> Whose error-chaceing Beames do unbenight
> The very soule of Darkness, and untwist
> The Clouds of Ignorance; do thou assist
> My feeble Quill; Reflect thy sacred Rayes
> Upon these lines, that they may light the
>   wayes
> That lead to thee; So guide my heart, my
>   hand,
> That I may doe, what others understand:

> (Quarles, Hieroglyph, I
> p. 3)

173

Man creates God, but he fails to live up to his
conception of God, and so looks up to God with awe.
This conception of God is informed with man's highest
aims and goals, and involves man's mind and spirit.
With it are tied man's attainments and achievements.
The ideally eminent man who achieves a measure of
perfection becomes a Creator, the symbol from whom
good proceeds. Hence for man, God as the ultimate in
perfection is the be-all and end-all of all knowledge,
all power, and the fashioner of human life and destiny.
In Genesis i:27 God creates "man in his own image,
in the image of God created he him; male and female
created he them." In the emblems as in Paradise Lost
the idea of man's fallibility against God's perfection becomes the issue. Man sees himself far removed
from the infallible, omniscient, omni-present Deity
he would like to emulate. Thus it becomes imperative
for the poets that the Creator should light and infuse
their souls with his own Spirit. The general poetic
and theological belief is that if God is in "Heav'ns
high Court" he is also in the heart of man, and He
instructs as He rules. Quarles says:

> This golden Precept, Know thy selfe,
>   came downe
> From heav'ns high Court; It was an Art
>   unknowne
> To flesh and blood.

and pointing to the lit candle in his emblem, Quarles
ruminates on man's life:

> Ev'n such was Man (before his soule gave
>   light
> To his vile substance) a meere Child of night;
>
> Thus liveless, lightless, worthless first
>   began
> That glorious, that presumptuous thing,
>   call'd Man.

> (Quarles, Hieroglyph I
> p. 4)

At the zenith of His creation, God made glorious man.
Such is the creation of man in Paradise Lost. Quarles
still ruminating in another emblem continues the
thought; though he questions the taint in man. His
contention is that if man is indeed infused with God's

174

spirit of perfection, and carries it within him he
has no failings in him:

> Thus man begins to live; An unknowne flame
> Quickens his finisht Organs; now possest
> With motion;
> If it be part of that celestiall Flame
> It must be ev'n as pure, as free from spot
> As that eternall fountaine whence it came.

> (Quarles, Emblems, V.
> 2. p. 77)

God, it is argued, could have prevented the
temptation of man, in spite of giving man free will
and reason, but Milton's God is the creation of
Renaissance man. He does not believe in man's
"cloistered virtue." "For . . . all Vertue consisteth
in Action, . . . for hardly they are to be admitted
for Noble who . . . consume their light, as in a darke
Lanthorne in contemplation and a Stoical retiredness."[1]
Man has to assay all manner of things, before he can
prove himself virtuous. God does not deter Satan from
tempting and proving man. If man fails he is unable
to maintain that perfection which he envisioned for
himself in the person of God.

Man was not only given free will but a conscience
and judgment. In Paradise Lost God explicitly states:

> And I will place within them as a guide
> My Umpire Conscience, whom if they will
> hear,
> Light after light well us'd they shall
> attain,

> (III. 194-6)

Adam's uxoriousness and inordinate love for his wife
make him lose all sense of proportion. Endowed with
Reason, "Reason also [being] choice," (III. 108), Man
knows the uniqueness and the preeminence of reason:
"in the Soul / Are many lesser Faculties that serve /
Reason as chief" (V. 100-3). He also knows that man
alone was singled out to possess this divine quality:
"a Creature . . . not prone / And Brute as other
Creatures, but endu'd / With Sanctity of Reason . . . /
. . . self-knowing" (VII. 506-10). Yet when he most
requires the faculty of reason, his emotional drives

175

supersede his reason and come to the fore, and he forgets to obey God's sole command. He tastes death.
But soon he realizes that lust is momentary and its
aftermath distasteful. In disobeying God he knows
that he has unconditionally severed his relationship
with God and that he will henceforward deal with a
transcendent God. Man's greatest woe is that he is
debarred Paradise; it is a greater sorrow than being
rusticated from a University, and Milton knows its
sting. The emblem writers' favorite and stock theme
is man's guilt, the acknowledgment and confession of
his error. Adam is a prime and moot example of one
who did not use his God-given faculty of reason and so
suffered. Adam's lament in Paradise Lost displays the
acknowledgement of his guilt and his folly. It is
evident in his physical and psychological distress:

> O miserable of happy! . . .
> Of this new glorious World, and mee so late
> The Glory of that Glory, who now become
> Accurst of blessed, hide me from the face
> Of God, whom to behold was then my highth
> Of happiness: yet well, if here would end
> The misery, I deserv'd it . . .
>   O fleeting joys
> Of Paradise, dear bought with lasting woes!

(X. 720-42)

The lament is tortured and poignant. This soul-sear-
ing mode of expression was common and a penitent's
way of self-mortification. It occurs in religious
verse, and the emblematists find it the right medium
for their expression of remorse and repentance. In
the fall of Adam, the trio Satan, Sin and Death, gain
ascendancy and become mankind's arch enemies. In
Quarles' Emblem II, Book I, they appear fighting for
Man's soul. Quarles' poem illustrates this dilemma
in the life of prehistoric Adam; as does Milton's
fascinating and repelling allegory of Sin and Death
and the terrorizing fact of the two abstractions for
Adam. Quarles' illustration shows Adam looking down
on a Globe, through which Beasts heads, the Vices,
protrude. "Then, when lust hath conceived, it
bringeth forth death.--James i. 15," quotes Quarles.
And the motto adds: "They are justly punished that
abuse lawful things, but they are most justly-
punished that use unlawful things: thus Lucifer fell
from heaven: thus Adam lost his paradise--Hugo de
Anima."

176

EMBLEME CHRESTIEN

VBI ES.

In the device the monstruous heads jutting out of
the globe symbolize the vices. From top left they are
a peacock (vanity), a rooster (boastfulness), a wolf
(viciousness), a fox (slyness), a hawk (predacity), a
pig (sloth). The central head is the devil's. An
apple lies at the side of the picture, and the background has flames on one end and Boreas blowing fur-
iously on the other, making the sea around the globe
boisterous and unruly. Boreas has a clenched fist
faintly etched to indicate anger. Adam's sin of
disobedience let loose the other six deadly sins and
put man in mortal danger, as indicated by the device.
Quarles is obsessed by Adam's sin, and its aftermath,
disorder and corruption.

Adam suffers but his lament in Milton, as in the
emblematists, shows the injustice of the situation;
and voices the oft-repeated query:

> Did I request thee, Maker, from my Clay
> To mould me Man, did I solicit thee
> From darkness to promote me, or here place
> In this delicious Garden? As my Will
> Concurr'd not to my being, it were but right
> And equal to reduce me to my dust,
> Desirous to resign, and render back
> All I receiv'd, unable to perform
> Thy terms too hard, by which I was to hold
> The good I sought not.

(X. 743-52)

Like Milton's Adam Quarles in Emblems Book II, Emblem
No. VIII voices great despondency at Man's state. His
words are full of self-pity and chagrin:

> A man was born: alas! and what's a man?
> A scuttle full of dust, a measured span
> Of flitting time; a furnish'd pack, whose
>   wares
> Are sullen griefe, and soul-tormenting cares:
> A vale of tears, a vessel tunn'd with breath,
> By sickness broach'd, to be drawn out by
>   death:
> A hapless, helpless thing, that, born, does
>   cry
> To feed, and feeds to live, that lives to
>   die.

177

But when Quarles invokes the God-man, "Theanthropos"
to assist him with his songs, and recalls his state of
non-being, he affirms his faith in God's all-prevenient
grace for recovery:

> Thou great Theanthropos, that giv'st and
>   ground'st
> Thy gifts in dust, and from our dunghill
>   crown'st
> Reflecting honour, taking by retail
> What thou hast given in gross, from lapsed,
>   frail
> And sinful man: that drink'st full draughts
>   wherein
> Thy children's lep'rous fingers, scurf'd
>   with sin,
> Have paddled; cleanse, oh cleanse my
>   crafty soul
> From secret crimes, and let my thoughts
>   control
> My thoughts: oh teach me stoutly to deny
> Myself, that I may be no longer I:
> Enrich my fancy, clarify my thoughts,
> Refine my dross; oh wink at human faults.

The context of the two statements is different, Adam
is questioning God's justice in punishing unsuspecting
and frail man. Quarles is asking God to assist him
in his frailty to rise and write inspired songs, yet
their imagery has much in common.

Milton using the Ovidian idea of the Fall as
Quarles had done in the emblem discussed above, re-
lates the change in seasons in Adam's once salubrious
Eden: a natural consequence of the Fall. Adam laments
his state. The pre-lapsarian Eden becomes a land of
raging storms, as does the breast of Adam:

> At that tasted fruit
> The Sun, as from Thyestean Banquet, turn'd
> His course intended;

> Now from the North . . .
> Bursting thir brazen Dungeon, arm'd with ice
> And snow and hail and stormy gust and flaw,
> Boreas and Caecias and Argestes loud
> And Thrascias rend the Woods and Seas up-
>   turn;

                    Thus began
Outrage from lifeless things; but Discord
    first
Daughter of Sin, among th' irrational,
Death introduc'd through fierce antipathy:

                . . . these were from without
The growing miseries, which Adam saw
Already in part, though hid in gloomiest
    shade,
To sorrow abandon'd, but worse felt within,
And in a troubl'd Sea of passion tost,
Thus to disburden sought with sad complaint.
O miserable of happy! Is this the end
Of this new glorious World, and me so late
The Glory of that Glory, who now, become
Accurst of blessed, hide me from the face
Of God, whom to behold was then my highth
Of happiness: . . .

                    O voice once heard
Delightfully, Increase and multiply,
Now death to hear! for what can I increase
Or multiply, but curses on my head?

                    O fleeting joys
Of Paradise, dear bought with lasting woes!

                . . . fear
Comes thund'ring back with dreadful revolu-
    tion
On my defenseless head; . . .
Nor I on my part single, in mee all
Posterity stands cursed;

                (X. 687-818)

     Quarles reiterates Adam's doubts but he also
asserts man's will for recovery, which is part of man's
innate and God-given potential. Man cannot accept
anything pernicious without trying to change it. This
places him between the animals and the angels and
makes him uniquely homo sapiens. His intellectual
journey cannot end in despondency; he demands recovery and proceeds to get it for he, like his Creator, is an inventor, and cannot accept defeat.
Quarles examines the idea of regression and progres-
sion in Book III, Emblem No. V of Emblems.

                    179

In the illustration, Anima is shown fashioning the
image of Man on a Potter's Wheel, and the caption
reads: "Remember, I beseech thee, that thou hast
made me as the clay; and wilt thou bring me unto
dust again? Job X. 9."

> Thus from the bosom of the new-made earth
> Poor man was delved, and had his unborn
>   birth;
> The same the stuff, the self-same hand
>   doth trim
> The plant that fades, the beast that dies,
>   and him.

Quarles then states that all life, plant and animal
and man, is one. The first two are man's older kin,
and the plants are in "more fairer robes array'd,"
"the beast in sense exceeds" man and in strength, and
"the three-aged oak doth thrice exceed them both."
Quarles asks:

> Why look'st thou then as big, thou little
>   span
> Of earth? what art thou more in being man?
> Ah, but my great Creator did inspire
> My chosen earth, with the divine fire
> Of reason; gave me judgment and a will;
> That, to know good; this, to choose good
>   from ill:
> He puts the reins of pow'r in my free hand
> A jurisdiction over sea and land,
> He gave me art to lengthen out my span
> Of life, and made me all, in being man.
> Ay, but thy passion has committed treason
> Against the sacred person of thy reason:
> Thy judgment is corrupt, perverse thy will
> That knows no good, and this makes choice of
>   ill:
> The greater height sends down the deeper
>   fall,
> And good declined, turns bad, turns worst
>   of all.
> Say then, proud inch of living earth, what
>   can
> Thy greatness claim the more in being man?
> Oh! but my soul transcends the pitch of
>   nature,
> Borne up by th' image of her high Creator.
> My heart's a living temple t' entertain,
> The King of Glory and his glorious train:

Eternal Potter, whose blest hands did lay
My coarse foundation from a sod of clay,
Thou know'st my brittle temper's prone to
    break;
Are my bones brazil, or my flesh of oak?
Oh, mend what thou hast made, what I have
    broke:
Look, look with gentle eyes, and, in thy day
Of vengeance, Lord, remember I am clay.

                    (Quarles' Emblems. Bk. III,
                     No. V, pp. 277-8)

   Man in Quarles sues for God's light once again,
and for recovery. What Milton gave in a continuous
narrative, Quarles gives in separate, repetitious vignettes. Once man has made a commitment to a new life,
he petitions for means to achieve it. The illustration shows "One seeking to remove an Angel's hand,
which is hiding the Angel's face." The biblical verse
accompanying the emblem is: "Wherefore hidest thou
thy face, and holdest me for thine enemy? -Job xiii.
24."

       Why dost thou shade thy lovely face? Oh why
       Does that eclipsing hand so long deny
       The sunshine of thy soul enliv'ning eye?

       Without that light, what light remains in me?
       Thou art my life, my way, my light; in thee
       I live, I move, and by thy beams I see.

       Thou art my life; if thou but turn away,
       My life's a thousand deaths: thou art my way;
       Without thee, Lord, I travel not, but stray.

       My light thou art; without thy glorious sight,
       Mine eyes are darken'd with perpetual night.
       My God, thou art my way, my life, my light.

       Mine eyes are blind and dark, I cannot see;
       To whom, or whither should my darkness flee,
       But to the light? and who's that light but
           thee?

       My path is lost, my wand'ring steps do stray;
       I cannot safely go, nor safely stay;
       Whom should I seek but thee, my path, my
           way?

181

Oh I am dead: to whom shall I, poor I,
Repair? to whom shall my sad ashes fly
For life? and where is life but in thine eye?

And yet thou turn'st away thy face, and
    fly'st me;
And yet I sue for grace, and thou deny'st me!
Speak, art thou angry, Lord, or only try'st
    me?

Unscreen those heav'nly lamps, or tell me
    why
Thou shad'st thy face? Perhaps thou think'st
    no eye
Can view those flames, and not drop down and
    die.

Disclose thy sunbeams, close thy wings and
    stay;
See, see how I am blind and dead, and stray,
O thou that art my light, my life, my way.

(Quarles' <u>Emblems</u> Bk. III
No. vii, p. 281-3)

The recovery of man leads to reassertion of his
dignity. Quarles gives Adam's insatiable thirst for
knowledge and his quest for the ultimate in understanding as a Renaissance man. Fallen man is not
daunted. He rises and is soon attuned to an appropriate way of life. As in all his emblems Quarles
begins with a biblical text: "There is no end of all
this labour; neither is his eye satisfied with riches.
Eccles. iv:8"

Oh, how our widen'd arms can over-stretch
Their own dimensions! How our hands can reach
Beyond their distance! How our yielding
    breast
Can shrink to be more full and full possest
Of this inferior earth! How earth refined
Can cling to sordid earth!

Man is constantly planning and organizing his life, and
his imagination helps the journey forward:

the busy mint
Of our laborious thoughts is ever going,
And coining new desires, desires not knowing
Where next to pitch; but, like the boundless
    ocean,

Gain, and gain ground, and grow more strong
    by motion.

    so the vulture of insatiate minds
Still wants, and wanting seeks, and seeking
    finds
New fuel to increase her rav'nous fire.

We cross the seas, and midst her waves we
    burn,
Transporting lives, perchance that ne'er
    return;
We sack, we ransack to the utmost sands
Of native kingdoms, and of foreign lands;
We travel sea and soil, we pry, we prowl,
We progress, and we prog from pole to pole;
We spend our midday sweat, our midnight oil,
We make art servile, and the trade gentile,
(Yet both corrupted with ingenious guile.)
To compress earth, and with her empty store
To fill our arm, and grasp one handful more
Thus seeking rest, our labours never cease,
But, as our years, our hot desires increase:
Thus we, poor little worlds! with blood and
    sweat,
In vain attempt to comprehend the great;
Thus, in our gain, become we gainful losers,
And what's inclosed, incloses the inclosers.

The motto to the poem is an advice to the readers:

Be wisely worldly, be not worldly wise;
Let not thy nobler thoughts be always raking
The world's base dunghill; vermin's took by
    taking;
Take heed thou trust not the deceitful lap
Of wanton Delilah; the world's a trap.

                    (Quarles, Emblems. Bk. II
                    pp. 237-8)

    Whitney emphasizes the idea that man's reason
can prevent a Fall. In the emblem entitled Temeritas
he shows a two-horse-drawn chariot: the horses are
rushing forward uncontrolled though the man in the
chariot, whip and bridle in hand, is trying to calm
them. The sky has louring clouds, the ground is rough
and pebbly. The adage reads:

                    183

That man, whoe hath affections fowle untam'de,
And forwarde runnes neglecting reasons race,
Deserves by right, of all men to bee blam'de,
And headlonge falles at lengthe to his deface,
Then bridle will, and reason make thy guide,
So maiste thow stande, when others doune doe
    slide.

                        (Whitney, Emblemes, 1586,
                         p. 6)

Adam's uxoriousness did not allow him to use his reason,
hence came the fall. Whitney stresses the urgency of
reason in other emblems. Recalling the great names
of antiquity in the emblem Silentium (page 60) he says:
"That man is next to God / Whoe squares his speache,
in reasons rightfull frame," and "in whome doth sacred
reason reste". Milton's Adam was a rational creature
till Eve tempted him and the madness of guilt obsessed
him. His lament is long, is both rational and irrational and shows a soul sorely oppressed, but recovery
soon comes, with a reaffirmation of faith in life and
an anticipation of progress. Recalling God's goodness
and providence Adam has, "new hope to spring / Out of
despair" (XI. 138-9) and words such as the following
show his confidence in the future and himself:

        Hee will instruct us praying, and of Grace
        Beseeching him, so as we need not fear
        To pass commodiously this life, sustain'd
        By him with many comforts,

                   (X. 1081-4)

        Eve, now expect great tidings, which perhaps
        Of us will soon determine, or impose
        New Laws to be observ'd;

                   (XI. 226-28)

        So many grateful Altars I would rear
        Of grassy Turf, and pile up every Stone
        Of lustre from the brook, in memory,
        Or monument to Ages, and thereon
        Offer sweet smelling Gumms and Fruits and
           Flow'rs :

                   (XI. 323-27)

                        184

M. *Say novv the Aue Maria.*

S. Haile MARIE full of grace; Our Lord is vvith
thee; blessed art thou amongst vvomen,
And blessed is the fruite of thy vvombe IE-
SVS.

C 5   Holy

Adam's reawakened rationality makes him utter words of
timeless and universal sapience: "Man over men / He
made not Lord; such title to himself / Reserving, human
left from human free" (XII. 70-72). Adam has enjoyed
paradisaical bliss, has suffered, has been instructed,
and can reassert his dignity in a cyclic motion that
returns him nearly to his original sanity and sapience,
and faith in his God-given intellect:

> I shall hence depart,
> Greatly in peace of thought, and have my fill
> Of knowledge, what this Vessel can contain;

(XII. 557-59)

FOOTNOTES

[1] Freeman, "Peacham's The Compleat Gentleman, 1634,
p. 2," p. 72.

186

iii EVE, THE PICTORIAL SNARE

The fascination of Eve is perennial. Her tale
is the stock in trade of man and his thoughts. In her
prelapsarian stage she appears a goddess. After her
act of disobedience in Paradise Lost she takes on all
the versatility of a goddess cum woman. Milton sees
her as a mortal, long before she unwittingly courts
Death, for even in her prelapsarian stage she has tho
foibles of many of her capricious daughters. Eve
has the vanity of Narcissus, preferring her own image
in a pool to the godman, Adam. She believes in her
own individuality and dexterity, when she demands that
Adam and she work separately (for she believes in the
Puritan ethic of work before play.) Asserting her
will, against his better judgment, she leaves Adam to
accomplish what she feels is her own particular assign-
ment in the lush garden of Eden. Her intellect is no
less keen than Adam's, and all her discussions with
him have the pith of reason and understanding. She
is well acquainted with liberty, for her poet creator,
Milton, had sung of liberty since his youth, and con-
ceded it to woman as well as man. She knows the ruses
to win Adam's amorous attention. She prefers not to
listen to Raphael when he expounds the theories of
astronomy, and narrates the war in heaven; because
she desires the account from Adam:

> Her Husband the Relater she preferr'd
> . . . hee, she knew, would intermix
> Grateful digressions, and solve high
>   dispute

With conjugal Caresses, from his Lip
Not Words alone pleas'd her.

(VIII. 52-57)

She is mistress of her own board, and when advised by
Adam to prepare a lavish meal, she admonishes him and
advocates frugality:

Adam, earth's hallow'd mould,
Of God inspir'd, small store will serve,

(V. 321-22)

though later she herself is lavish in her hospitality.
Eve has all the "infinite variety" of the eternal
woman before and after the fall: and it makes her the
joy of Milton's literary composition. The emblem
writers use many vignettes of Eve, as the ideal and
provident female, the Madonna-mother, the Ceres figure,
the femme fatale, the Circe, the Siren, and the emblem
of Sin. Emblems of Eve that parallel Milton's mother
of mankind are fascinating and plentiful. Eve appears in all the guises that Milton uses for her in
Paradise Lost. Her tale is too familiar not to be
repeated in words and pictures by emblem writers to
point a moral. But for Adam she is "Heav'n's last
best gift, my ever new delight" (V. 19).

Whitney, describing the creation, states the
seventeenth-century belief that each created thing ex-
celled in ways unique to it. Accordingly he describes
woman as a creature of grace and excellence in Miltonic terms:

When creatures first weare form'd, they had
by natures lawes;
The bulles, their hornes: the horses, hoofes:
the lions, teeth, and pawes.
To hares, shee swiftenes gave: to fishes,
finnes assign'de:
To birdes, their winges: so no defence was
lefte for woman kinde.
But, to supplie that wante, shee gave her
suche a face:
Which makes the boulde, the fierce, the
swifte, to stoope, and pleade
for grace.

(Whitney, p. 182)

188

In the icon Whitney does not give graphic details of
the woman's physical features. But the device that
goes with the poem is like a baroque tapestry in miniature. In an idyllic garden scene, the horse and
hare and lion gambol around a female figure, while a
fish goes floating by in the stream and an angel wings
its way above.

And Milton's "fairest of her Daughters Eve" (IV.
324) appears as fetchingly beautiful when she first
is seen by Satan and the reader. She and Adam are in
"this [fictitious] Assyrian Garden" among "all kind /
Of living Creatures new to sight and strange" (IV. 286-
287), and the two human figures have their Maker's
stamp on them. Eve's particular gift is in her "grace."
Milton describes her physical beauty in rippling out-
lines of hair and torso. It is not until Adam tells
the story of her birth from his side, with God's
fashioning her into shape like a great Sculptor, that
we see Eve's ("lovely fair") beauty. This is a
beauty that "infus'd Sweetness" into Adam and love into
all creation. All the beauty and goodness of the world
in Adam's view are "summ'd up" in her. Such is Eve's
pristine magnetism (VIII. 465-77).

Before the actual temptation and fall Milton's
Eve is seen in a romantic picture tending the lush
garden, busy and unwary of the creatures around. It
appears, that for Milton at this stage, Eve, though
untainted, conjures images of Circe among her bestial
entourage. Soon after, Eve does become a Circe figure
when she proffers the nectarous apple to Adam. In
this metamorphosis Satan is a collaborator. He has,
as a magnificent serpent, lured her with the bait of
supernal sapience. He stealthily draws near to
Eve, displaying his splendour in:

> many a wanton wreath . . .
> To lure her Eye; shee busied heard the sound
> Of rustling Leaves,but minded not, as us'd
> To such disport before her through the Field,
> From every Beast, more duteous at her call,
> Than at Circean call the Herd disguis'd.

> (IX. 517-22)

Whitney's device (p. 82) dealing with a Circean figure,
her animals and garden, has the same baroque splendour.
Circe, partially clothed, wand in hand, surveys the

animals which she has just transformed. Whitney warns
men to beware of Circe's "cuppes." He points out that
Circe's magic does not work on her victims' physical
form alone, but on their spirit. Once transformed,
her prey opt to remain brutish rather than regain
their humanity. Milton's allusion to Circe is two
fold in reference to Eve and Satan. Satan has skilfully manoeuvred Eve into eating the forbidden fruit.
Euphoria from it makes her a double prey to Sin and a
snare for others. The tainted Eve stimulates the
lower appetites in Adam; while Satan has already
metamorphosed to the most venomous of creatures to
approach and lure her. The effect of the heady fruit
is bestial.

       Peacham in a curious emblem (p. 51) entitled
Sic opibus mentes tells of a common Italian tree, the
Hyosciame, whose flowers carry weeds that are coveted
by birds. The seeds are intoxicating and as soon as
the birds eat them, "griddle downe they fall / And
have no power, to flie away at all," thus becoming
prey to the fowlers. Eve's eating of the fruit of the
Tree of Knowledge has an identical effect, and she
becomes the prey of her ambitions and desires, the
bait that propels Adam to his bane and mortality.

       Yet Eve's traits in Paradise Lost paradoxically
meet all the requirements of a good and ideal wife
of the seventeenth century. In his emblem entitled
"Uxoriae virtutes," Whitney conveys the qualities
upheld in a spouse. The ideal wife in the emblem
significantly appears against the backdrop of a
lush garden. She has one hand on her lips, to convey reticence, and a bunch of keys in the other to
show providence and thrift. She looks demure,
especially as she stands atop a slow-moving tortoise.

       Whitney says:

              This representes the vertues of a wife,
              Her finger, staies her tonge to runne at
                   large.
              The modest lookes, doe shewe her honest life
              The keys, declare shee hathe a care, and
                   chardge,
              Of husbandes goodes: let him goe where
                   he please.
              The Tortoyse warnes, at home to spend her
                   daies.
                                        (Whitney, p. 93)

                        190

Milton's Eve has the good taste and the art of listening to others speak, though when she wishes she uses cogent arguments to impress her own views. Her innocence and modesty are one before she errs, and she has nothing to hide from Adam till Satan's venom starts spinning prevarications and guile in her. She is careful of God's gift of food to her and Adam, and classically argues that plenitude does not suggest excess. Unlike Whitney's ideal wife, she is lithe and winning in her movements and more mobile than Adam. She has all that is required of a "worthy" woman, but she also has the lure of the Siren. Quarles gives the picture of a Siren in Emblemes Book II Emblem No. III, where Anima is shown enmeshed in a net, and the caption, taken from Job xviii.8, reads "He is cast into a net by his own feet and walketh upon a snare." The verse conveys Adam's dilemma and capitulation:

> Alas! thy sweet perfidious voice betrays.
> His wanton ears with thy Sirenian baits:
> Thou wrapp'st his eyes in mists, then
>   boldly lays
> Thy lethal gins before their crystal gates;
> Thou lock'st up ev'ry sense with thy false
>   keys,
> All willing pris'ners to thy close deceits:
> His ear Most nimble, where it deaf should
>   be;
> His eye most blind, where most it ought to
>   see;
> And when his heart's most bound, then thinks
>   himself most free.

Quarles elaborates the image of deceptions further in Emblem VI of Book II, though it is double-edged, referring to the new science as well as womankind:

> Believe her not her glass diffuses
> False portraitures: thou canst espy
> No true reflection: she abuses
> Her misinform'd; beholder's eye;
> Her crystal's falsely steel'd; it scatters
> Deceitful beams; believe her not, she
>   flatters.
> This flaring mirror represents
> No right proportion, view or feature:
> Her very looks are compliments;
> They make thee fairer, godlier, greater;

191

> The skilful gloss of her reflection
> But paints the context of thy coarse com-
>   plexion
>
> The soul that seeks the noon of grace
> Shrinks in, but swells if grace retreat
> As Heav'n lifts up or veils his face
> Our self-esteems grow less or great.

Here Anima carries "a false and multiplying glass," a glass such as the verbal spell Milton's Satan casts over the unsuspecting Eve, which Eve, in turn, casts over the all-too-knowing but all-too-loving Adam. His uxoriousness takes precedence over his yearning for God's grace, and catapults his downfall. Adam's capitulation is not entirely volitional, for Eve has taken on the Circean characteristics and woven her insidious charm around him with specious words; had Adam not succumbed to her wiles, his humanity would have been in doubt. Eve has very plausible reasons for luring Adam. She has no designs to let him live without her. After the euphoria of the fall Eve takes on the characteristics of the femme fatale. Among the multiform evils in Pandora's box is the sin of envy. Eve envies Adam's innocence, his un-marred heritage of immortality, and a fancied Eve who may replace her if Death ensues from her act of disobedience. Her envy is such that the first human desire to murder is born in her breast. If she is to be destroyed, she wishes Adam destroyed with her. It is in the spirit of envy that she offers Adam the fatal fruit:

> Confirm'd then I resolve,
> Adam shall share with me in bliss or woe:
> So dear I love him, that with him all
>   deaths
> I could endure, without him live no life.

                (IX. 830-34)

Dissembling she speaks spurious, deceitful words to Adam:

> For bliss, as thou hast part, to me is bliss,
> Tedious, unshar'd with thee, and odious soon.
> Thou therefore also taste, that equal Lot
> May join us, equal Joy, as equal Love;
> Lest thou not tasting, different degree

                        192

Disjoin us, and I then too late renounce
Deity for thee, when Fate will not permit.
(IX. 879-85)

The psychological impact of envy is seen in Whitney's device. He personifies envy as a surly old woman, holding a coiled snake between her teeth, a staff in one hand and wrenching her bared heart with the other. The verses state:

What hideous hagge with visage sterne
    appeares?
Whose feeble limmes, can scarce the bodie
    staie:
This, Envie is: lean, pale, and full of
    yeares,
Who with the blisse of other plnes awaie.
And what declares, her eating vipers broode?
Thal poysoned thoughtes, bee evermore her
    foode.

What meanes her eies? so bleared, sore,
    and redd:
Her mourninge still, to see an others gaine.
And what is mente by snakes upon her head?
The fruite that springes, of such a
    venomed braine.
But whie, her harte shee rentes within
    her brest?
It shewes her selfe, doth worke her owne
    unrest.

Whie lookes shee wronge? bicause shee woulde
    not see,
An happie wight, which is to her a hell:
What other partes within this furie bee?
Her harte, with gall: her tonge, with
    stinges doth swell.
And laste of all, her staffe with prickes
    aboundes:
Which showes her wordes, wherewith the
    good shee woundes.

(Whitney, p. 94)

Eve's mental state is exactly that of Whitney's Envy once Eve has gorged herself of the fruit and has started to picture the impact of the act on her future. In Milton's highly stylized language she

193

goes through all the cogitations and reactions of
Whitney's Envy as she ruminates her relationship with
Adam.

Milton mulls over good and evil, and writes
about it, like the emblematists, in his early works.
Comus debates it, and Areopogitica explains its
complementary character in an emblematic picture in
1644:

> Good and evil we know in the field of this
> world grew up together almost inseparably;
> . . . It was from out the rind of one
> apple tasted, that the knowledge of good
> and evil, as two twins cleaving together,
> leaped forth into the world. And perhaps
> this is that doom which Adam fell into
> of knowing good and evil, that is to say of
> knowing good by evil.

(Hughes, p. 728)

Good is only known by evil, and so, paradoxically, by
her act Eve opens the way to choices. Higher reason
for Milton is the logical result of right choice.
Man has to go through the "dust and heat" of choices,
for thinkers like Milton, cannot hide a fugitive and
cloistered virtue; they advocate trial and experi-
mentation. The twins who sprung from the apple
at one birth, like Cain and Abel, coexist in the
emblem writers also. They are depicted in many forms,
especially that of the wheat and the tares. Whitney's
emblem shows an upright lily surrounded and almost
smothered by tares. His verses proclaim:

> Where as the good, do live amongst the bad:
> And vertue growes, where seede of vices
>   springes;
> The wicked sorte to wounde the good are
>   glad:
> And vices thrust at vertue, all their
>   stinges:
> The like, where witte, and learning doe
>   remaine,
> Where follie rules, and ignorance doth
>   raigne.

Yet as wee see, the lillie freshlie bloomes,
Though thornes, and briers, enclose it
  round aboute:
So with the good, thoughe wicked have thir
  roomes,
They are preserv'd, in spite of all their
  route:
And learning lives, and vertue still doth
  shine,
When follie dies, and ignorance doth pine.

                    (Whitney, p. 221)

In eating the fruit Eve had evoked both good and evil.
Thus the knowledge of evil dearly bought by Eve in
her understanding of good, made her emerge chastened
and noble. Even before her fall Adam had recognized
in her a keen intellect. He had said of her: "All
higher knowledge in her presence falls / Degraded,
Wisdom in discourse with her / Loses discount'nanc't"
(VIII 551-53). He gave her precedence over God and
the image of God in himself. Raphael attributed
this statement of Adam to his uxoriousness. Yet
there is a spirituality, an inward beauty in Eve
that has the power to soothe even the malignant
malice of Satan. Her presence has the balm of making Satan involuntarily extricate himself from his
gnawing anger:

          That space the Evil one abstracted stood
          From his own evil, and for that time
            remain'd
          Stupidly good, of enmity disarm'd,
          Of guile, of hate, of envy, of revenge;

                    (IX. 463-66)

But the disarming grace of this goddess is fallible.
It fails aginst glozing lies and pleasing flattery:

          Wonder not, sovran Mistress, if perhaps
          Thou canst, who are sole Wonder, much less
            arm
          Thy looks, the Heav'n of mildness with
            disdain,
          Displeas'd that I approach thee thus, and
            gaze
          Insatiate, I thus single, nor have fear'd

                    195

Thy awful brow, more awful thus retir'd.
Fairest resemblance of thy Maker fair,

(IX. 532-38)

Whitney in two emblems warns of flatterers and syco-
phants. The title of the first emblem is <u>Interiora</u>
<u>vide</u>. It is a warning to be more circumspect, which
Eve was not, when the iridescent serpent approached
her in the garden.

Though outwarde thinges, doe trimme, and
    brave appeare,
And sightes at firste, doe answere this
    desire,
Yet, inwarde partes, if that they shine
    not cleare,
Suspecte the same, and backe in time
    retire:
For inwardlie, such deadlie foes maie lurke,
As when wee trust, maie our destruction
    worke.
    . . .
Though Natures giftes, and fortunes doe
    excell:
Yet, if the minde, with heinous crimes
    abounde,
And nothing good with in the same doe dwell:
Regarde it not, but shonne the outward
    showe,
Untill, thou doe the inwarde vertues knowe.

Since fauninge lookes, and sugred speache
    prevaile,
Take heede betime: and line thee not with
    theise.
The gallant clokes, doe hollowe hartes
    conceile,
And goodlie showes, are mistes before our
    eies:
A face deform'de, a visor faire dothe hide,
That none can see his uglie shape within,
To Ipocrites, the same maie bee applide,
With outward showes, who all their credit
    winne:
Yet give no heate, but like a painted fire;
And all the zeale, is: as the times require.

(Whitney, pp. 69 & 226)

The device carries a nobleman and his visored foe.

The fall of Adam and Eve heralded all the deadly sins, among them lust. Eve loses the mother-goddess trait, a purity which had disarmed even Satan, and becomes Adam's poetic snare. Her arguments are specious, like Belial's "clothed in reason's garb," and her actions are all purposely seductive. Against his better judgment Adam succumbs to her wiles. Her proximity annuls all his scruples. He is her victim, and through her Satan's. Quarles gives a similar warning. The sapient, though vain Eve, should have been wary of the tempter. She is once enamored of her own beauty, of her image, as she beholds it; the image is hallucinatory but pleasing; and she is beguiled again:

> Look off, let not thy optics be
> Abused: thou seest not what thou should'st
> Thyself's the object thou should'st see,
> But 'tis thy shadow thou behold'st!
> And shadows thrive the more in stature,
> The nearer we approach the light of nature.
>
> (Quarles Emblemes Book
> VI. p. 6)

The sexual urge in Adam and Eve becomes a surging holocaust which propels them with lust's beastiality. They, like Satan, feel themselves attaining divinity, and their fall is complete in as full a sexual orgy as Milton could devise:

> . . . now
> As with new Wine intoxicated both
> They swim in mirth, and fancy that they feel
> Divinity within them breeding wings
> Wherewith to scorn the Earth:
>
> . . . in Lust they burn:
> Till Adam thus 'gan Eve to dalliance move.
>
> now let us play,
> As meet is, after such delicious Fare;
> For never did thy Beauty since the day
> I saw thee first and wedded thee, adorn'd
> With all perfections, so inflame my sense
> With ardor to enjoy thee,
>
> (IX. 1007-32)

Henry Peacham depicts lust in his emblem, Pulchritudo
foeminea, as a naked female astride a Dragon, the
symbol of sin. The scaled dragon's tail is sensuously
coiled and prominent, his foxlike-head shows a lecherous eye, a lolling tongue, and a hooked nose. The
flower-crowned female carries a crystal and a dart
in either hand. One verse reads:

> Her nakednes us tells, she needes no art:
> Her glasse, how we by sight are moovd to
>   love,
> The woundes unfelt, that's given by the Dart
> At first, (though deadly we it after proove)
> The Dragon notes loves poison: and the
>   flowers,
> The frailtie (Ladies) of that pride of
> yours.

> (Peacham, p. 58)

There is nothing subtle about Peacham's emblem of
lust. Whitney on the other hand describes lust with
suavity and savoir faire. In his device and verse
he captures the frame of mind of Milton's Adam and
Eve. In the emblem he shows flames that surround a
marble altar with a lit candlestick and gnats singeing
their wings in flames that rise from the earth,
seemingly in contrition. A snake has threaded its
way through the base of the altar, its tail coiled
on one side and its mouth pressed against an apple
on the other. The scene is superimposed on rolling
hills and a village peaceably nestling in them.

> Even as the gnattes, that flie into the
>   blaze,
> Doe burne their winges and fall into the
>   fire
> So, those too muche on gallant showes that
>   gaze,
> Are captives caught, and burne in their
>   desire :
> And suche as once doe feele this inwarde
>   warre,
> Thoughe they bee cur'de, yet still appeares
>   the scarre.

> For wanton Love althoughe hee promise joies,
> Yet hee that yeeldes in hope to finde it
>   true,
> His pleasures shalbee mated with annoyes;
> And sweetes suppos'd, bee mix'd, with
>   bitter rue:
> . . .

198

        . . .
O love, a plague, thoughe grac'd with
     gallant glosse,
For in thy seates a snake is in the mosse.

Then stoppe your eares, and like Ulisses
     waulke,
The Syreenes tunes, the carlesse often heares:
                                  . . .
The Crocodile, hathe treason in her teares
In gallant fruicte, the core is ofte
     decay'd;
Yea poison ofte in cuppe of goulde assay'd.

                    (Whitney, p. 219)

And this "cuppe of goulde" for Adam is also a bane,
for with it goes his equilibrium and sanity. The
only one who can deliver him, is his poetic snare,
his Circe, Eve. Eve's strength of mind exceeds that
of Adam. Recovery for him would be more
exacting if she were not there to uphold him. Her
inner beauty and confidence, that soothed the
enraged Satan, now in very different circumstances
assauge the troubled and shattered Adam. Her counsel is no longer specious, it is sound and uplifting
and strengthening. She acknowledges her fault and
is rejuvenated nobler than in her state of innocence:

          While yet we live, scarce one short hour
               perhaps,
          Between us two let there be peace, both
               joining,
          As join'd in injuries, one enmity
          Against a Foe by doom express assign'd us,
          That cruel Serpent: . . .
                    both have sinn'd, but thou
          Against God only, I against God and thee,
          And to the place of judgment will return,
          There with my cries importune Heaven, that
               all
          The sentence from thy head remov'd may light
          On me, sole cause to thee of all this woe,
          Mee mee only just object of his ire.

                    (X. 923-36)

The chaotic emotions in their minds are being laid to
rest, as Eve exonerates herself, in spite of her
fallacious judgment later (X. 1000-1). Such words
of penitence can only be expressed by a strong spirit.

                    199

Adam knew his wife when he extolled her before the
fall:

> Greatness of mind and nobleness thir seat
> Build in her loveliest, and create an awe
> About her,

(VIII. 557-59)

Eve's words of contrition reverberate in many emblems.
Peacham entitles one of his emblems Paenitentia, and
shows a rueful female sitting deep in meditation, her
eyes fixed in hope on a life-giving fountain.

> Heere sits Repentance, solitarie, sad:
>
> As greeving for the life,that she hath lad:
>
> Her solemne cheare, . . .
> Denote her anguish, and her greife of soule,
> As often as her life, she doth recount,
> Which Conscience doth, with howerly care
>   enroule,
> The cullor greene, she most delightes to
>   weare,
> Tells how her hopes, shall overcome dispaire.

(Peacham, p. 46)

Milton conveys Eve's sorrow and penitence in lines
that still wring the heart, yet Peacham in another
emblem of Minerva Britanna concedes that no graphic
art can transcribe sorrow:

> Wee eas'ly limme,some lovely-Virgin face,
> And can to life, a Lantscip represent,
> Afford to Antiques, each his proper grace,
> Or trick out this, or that compartement:
> But with the Pencill, who could ere
>   expresse,
> The face of greife, and heartie pensivenes.
>
> For where the minde's with deadly sorrow
>   wounded,
> There no proportion, can effect delight,
> For like a Chaos, all within's confounded,
> Resembling nothing, save the face of night,

(Peacham, p. 114)

Eve is indeed benighted, in Peacham's words, yet
she has shown the strength necessary for recovery.
With John Hall, Eve, along with Adam, can quote St.
Augustine and bewail:

> For I carried my soul as it were torn in
> sunder, and gored with blood, and impatient
> to be carried by me. Aug. Conf. lib. 4.
> Capt. 7.

> Traitor self, why do I try
> Thee my bitterest Enemy?
> What can I beare
> Alas more deare
> Then in this Center of my selfe, my heart?
> Yet all those traines that blow me lie
> there,
> Hid in so small a part.

> How many back-bones nourisht have
> Crawling Serpents in the grave?
> I am alive,
> Yet life doe give
> To myriads of adders in my breast,
> Which doe not there consume, but grow and
> thrive,
> And undisturbed rest.

The Epigram to the poem adds:

> See how these poisnous passions gnaw and feed
> Upon the tortur'd heart in which they
> breed :
> And when (their poison spent) these Vipers
> dy,
> The worme of conscience doth their room
> supply.

(Hall, p. 101-103)

The "worme of conscience" humbles Milton's once self-
assured Eve, but makes her monolithic, greater than
her male counterpart. Her words are well considered
and display a "calm of mind all passion spent." Yet
her judgment is befuddled. She suggests mutual suicide (X. 1000-1) to prevent procreation by irksome
abstinence on their part; and to prevent the suffering that could be in store for their unborn progeny.
Adam wonders at her fortitude and nobility as well

as her words of self-negation but sagaciously allays
her fears and reassures her of God's providence (X.
1012-94). He sees in her an intuitive, heroic greatness, which in him is tempered by reason:

> Eve, thy contempt of life and pleasure seems
> To argue in thee something more sublime
> And excellent than what thy mind contemns:
>
> (X. 1013-15)

Thus repeating Genesis 3.20 where Adam "called his
wife's name Eve" because she was the "mother of all
living," Milton's Adam sums up in Eve all human creation. The words place her on the highest pedestal
a woman would hold until the birth of the second
Adam. But Eve's ego has been deflated: her spirit
is broken, hers is a "sad demeanor meek," as it will
be of the meek Virgin the oxymoronic "Virgin Mother,"
in whom Adam will see himself reinstated and glorified (XII. 379-81). Eve maintains her poise in
spite of Adam's earlier recriminations, until the
final blow of banishment from Eden. In a lamentable
picture Eve is seen at the nadir of despair (XI. 268-
85). The despair is due to a sense of loss and also
to a fear of the unknown. Like Adam, she has to learn
that moderation and the classical golden mean will en-
sure their future and fortify them against trials.
It was her lack of abstinence that created the unhappy situation for Adam and Eve and their posterity
(XI. 476); whenever Adam is in doubt Michael reiterates his and Eve's fault and reminds him of the consequences. She remains the hub of life whether good
or bad. In spite of all her doubts and agonizing,
she has the pioneer spirit which quietly prompts Adam,
"now lead on; / In mee is no delay" (XII. 614-15).
With Adam Eve views the last apocalypse of the
epic:

> They looking back, all th' Eastern side
> beheld
> Of Paradise, so late thir happy seat,
> Wav'd over by that flaming Brand, the Gate
> With dreadful Faces throng'd and fiery
> Arms:
>
> (XII. 643-48)

But part of the apocalypse was also that "The world
was all before them." With Lycidas they could reaffirm their faith in life, for the morrow had "fresh
woods, and Pastures new."

In the emblem books, Milton's masterly assurance
of burgeoning life beyond contrition, is hard to
find. The words and visions were uniquely Miltonic,
though tempered by Genesis 3.19-24.

Henry Hawkin's emblem on "the Moore" codifies
in classical images the duel character of women,
the archetype Eve-Mary; the pictorial snare of Adam
and his redemption:

> The Empresse of the Sea, Latona bright,
> Drawes like a load-stone by attractive
>   might
> The Oceans streames, which having forward
>   runne
> Calles back againe, to end where they
>   beganne.
> This Prince of darknes had ecclipsed Eves
>   light,
> And Mortals, clowded in Cymmerian night,
> Were backwards drawne by Eve, as is the
>   Maine;
> 'Twas only Marie drew to God againe:
> O chast Diana, with thy silver beames,
> Flux and reflux (as in the Oceans streames)
> 'Tis thou canst cause. O draw! and draw
>   me so,
> That I in vice may ebbe, in Vertue flow.

>   (Hawkins, p. 111)

Eve, Adam's snare, is also his salvation.

CHAPTER FIVE

RELIGIOUS AND ETHICAL IDEAS IN PARADISE LOST
AND THE SEVENTEENTH-CENTURY EMBLEM

Milton in Animadversions comments on polarities
that make for soundness: "those two most rational
faculties of human intellect anger and laughter."
Both are evident in Paradise Lost, especially in the
entity of the highest being, God. Reason and wrath
were as much the protestant's code of ethics in the
seventeenth century as labor and application. Just
indignation was an innate and imbedded, church-
oriented, religious consciousness of the age. Milton makes use of it; but he also makes use of another
powerful weapon, laughter, which does not have the
sanction of Protestant ethics. For him laughter is
a mode of expression. God's laughter in Paradise
Lost stems from derision, scorn, sarcasm, fury, self-
confidence, and security. It is at moments when
Satan seems most exultant that God's wrath and laughter are both evoked. Evil is antic and absurd. It
infuriates the rational faculty, but it also amuses
and entertains. Evil and good co-exist. Without
goodness evil is intellectually impossible. They
complement each other as do anger and laughter. If
it were not so man would disintegrate psychologically.
Milton uses both laughter and anger as rhetorical devices early in his prolusions to stress ideas, to
exhort, and show the futility of evil choices.
In Paradise Lost Milton's God exemplifies the mode:

> Mighty Father, thou thy foes
> Justly hast in derision, and secure
> Laugh'st at thir vain designs and tumults
> in vain,

(V. 735-37)

Even Sin knows that God laughs to note evil on the
brink of destroying itself. If the confrontation of
Satan and Death is sinister and horrifying, it is also
comic, and Sin knows its significance. She dramatically sees God's wrath in his laughter:

> O Father, what intends thy hand, she cri'd,
> Against thy only Son? What fury O Son,
> Possesses thee to bend that mortal Dart

204

```
        Against thy Father's head?  and know'st
          for whom;
        For him who sits above and laughs the while
        At thee ordain'd his drudge, to execute
        Whate'er his wrath, which he calls Justice,
          bids,
```

                        (II. 727-33)

God also laughs at man's conjectures and efforts to
probe the secrets of life and the universe. Even
though nature or "Heav'n / Is as the Book of God before thee set, / Wherein to read his wondrous works"
(VIII. 66-78), man's presumption in probing all universal mysteries amuses God. For a seventeenth-century man, curiosity about the controversial Ptolemaic
and Copernican theories was both awesome and exciting
though mysterious. Milton, interested but unsure,
conveniently brushes it aside in Raphael's remark:

```
                  if they list to try
        Conjecture, he his Fabric of the Heav'ns
        Hath left to thir disputes, perhaps to move
        His laughter in thir quaint Opinions wide
```

                        (VIII. 75-8)

God's laughter is evoked by evil and folly. Once
again Milton points out that undue self-pride in man,
ousted by confusion in language diversity, provokes
laughter in Heaven (XII.59). Laughter is a powerful,
ethical weapon of communication in Milton.

        Helen C. White points out that unlike his con-
temporaries, Donne and Herbert, Milton's prayers to
God did not savour of the confessional. His prayer
was for inspiration and light. His approach was not
overburdened emotionally but was intellectual. Usually nascent and primitive evocation of God is emotional. When Milton uses the emotional approach it is a
tool to depict Adam's psychological agony; for himself, he sues for God's light, his emotions subdued
and controlled. God, the Creator, is the inspirer of
creative energy in the artist and has to be invoked.
Milton uses light metaphorically for ethical chiaroscuro effects. The symbolic darkness of the war in
heaven and the darkness of Hell are counterbalanced
by the light of Creation. The story of Creation,
with its primary act the separation of light from

darkness, comes after Milton's own plea for further
enlightenment to complete the remaining half of his
great narrative (VII.21). God's Son and his entourage, the attendant angels, move into Chaos "the vast
immeasurable Abyss / Outrageous as a Sea, dark, wasteful wild" (VII. 211-12), like a scintillating beam
of light. As against the destructive engine of the
war, a pair of creative compasses of the seventeenth
century architect come into focus. The golden compasses emanate their own light as the Son "conglobes"
the universe with a circle of perfection out of
elemental Chaos. Absence of light in the epic is
separation from God and creative light is God. Milton's hell oppresses with its darkness, not with
tortures as in Dante. In Genesis, ethereal and neb-
ulous light is created independent of any luminary
and Milton follows suit. Light is "Ethereal, first
of things, quintessence pure / . . . Spher'd in a
radiant Cloud" (VII. 244-47). Once light is a reality, it becomes the point of departure for all creation, including the abstractly formulated creations
of the mind.

The same inspiration of light informs the work
of the emblematists. Quarles, asks the "great Originall of Light,/ . . . [to] assist / My feeble Quill"
(Hieroglyphikes, p. 3). Man, as the candle, has no
virtue of his own, unless lit by God's "gracious hand"
and "celestiall Flame" (Hieroglyph, p. 7). The light
once his, he can ask, "So guide my heart, my hand, /
That I may doe, what others understand;" (Hieroglyph,
p. 7). John Hall similarly looks for "The Sun's approach, so shall I find / A greater light possess my
mind" (Hall, sig. A.). Wither's Muse inspires him at
night, like Milton's Urania. The idea implicit is
that God illumines the thinker-poet through hours of
contemplation. The caption of the emblem Wither uses
is significant and suggestive: "Before thou bring
thy Workes to Light, / Consider on them, in the
Night." The poem states:

> I, for my seriou'st Muses, chuse the Night;
> (More friend to Meditation, then the Day)
>
> By Night, we best may ruminate upon
> Our Purposes . . .
> And, then, may best into our Selves retire:
>
> (Wither, p. 9)

Milton says to Urania:

> not alone, while thou
> Visit'st my slumbers Nightly, or when Morn
> Purples the East: still govern thou my
> Song,

(VII. 28-31)

Illumination of the mind is imperative to creation. All artists, whether Milton, in his literary greatness, or the emblematists in their religious and ethical zeal, recognize the need for enlightenment and ask for light.

Ruth Mohl points out that "common places" or verities of life were gleaned by students of the sixteenth and seventeenth centuries from the classics and other scholarly works. These were made available not only for knowledge but to help the practice of right expression. Their findings often appeared as theme sentences or sententia, essays, and expositions; the best example being Francis Bacon's Essays. She comments that the kind of topics used by Bacon are also noted in Milton's Commonplace Book.[1] The emblem writers use similar excerpts and concepts for their themes. In format and style their terse aphorisms and poems have infinite diversity, but serve the same purpose as amplified sermons and speeches of their contemporaries; their graphic devices codify the moral and ethical ideas enshrined in "commonplaces."

The Moral Index in Milton's Commonplace Book has 64 entries. Topics such as "Moral Evil," "Of Courage," "Of the Good Man," appear in it. Out of the many entries some captions strikingly reveal themselves in Paradise Lost. The idea of "Moral Evil" covers a variety of foibles, and titillates the mind to discover it in pictures and thoughts clustered in the epic. "Moral Evil" is constantly reiterated in the emblem books.

The moralistic ideas of Paradise Lost center around the theme of subversion, in which the force of evil attempts to undermine goodness at its highest perfection. Hazlitt aptly remarks that Satan's "aim was no less than the throne of the universe."[2] Douglas Bush pins the reason to pride: "The long

account of the war is a picture of ambitious pride
attempting to overthrow righteousness and order and
bringing about utter chaos and destruction."[3] This
egotistic urge of Satan to disrupt order is at the
core of the conflict. Discipline and order are the
traditional hallmarks of the Renaissance. For a
classicist like Milton nothing could be more degenerating than the destruction of God-given order and
degree in man's life on earth or in the cosmos. The
highest virtue was to discipline one's soul for a
good and progressive life. Milton exemplified it in
his own disciplined mind and the rigidity with which
he envisioned every scholar's years of training in
excellence, so seriously yet wittily portrayed in
Of Education. Thus his vital and magnificent Satan
becomes the diabolic energy that is contra-creative.
Instead of moving cyclically in perfection his movements are transverse. Like a double-edged sword he
strikes wherever he thinks the object is most vulner-
able and maims symmetry and order. Early in the epic,
Raphael warns Adam to beware of such a deceptive
force. Its cunning and evil could destroy insidious-
ly. And one of the ways, Milton knows, evil destroys
is by pleasing its victim. Satan's specious speeches
to Emperor Chaos and his flattery of Eve, and Eve's
half truths in her approach to Adam, all designed to
flatter and win, become weapons in the disruption of
order in man, his posterity, and the world.

If Milton as a man of the Renaissance espouses
order, he also advocates justice, which is closely
related to right reason and truth. Milton's God appears a tyrant if one takes into account that he
foresees all, can avert mischief if He so desires,
can save man from ill, but allows events to take
their course and lead to the fall. Once the deed
is done, he shows his ire and wrath and calls for
justice. The whole situation seems paradoxical and
ironical. But another Renaissance idea comes to the
fore: Man is endowed with reason. Created in God's
image, man as the similitude of God has the same power
to exercise his judgment in right choices. It is
evident in Adam's case, for against his better judgment he opts to choose wrong. His will is free, and
using it he breaks the one covenant he had made with
God: a symbol of his loyalty to God. He disobeys.
Adam was already endowed with sapience; he possessed
the knowledge of good and evil long before the actual
fall. He was like God, intelligent and wise. He

needed no fruit of the tree to become clear sighted.
The tree was just a seal and symbol of his pact with
God. The moment Adam saw Eve with the fruit-laden
branch of the tree, he knew that he had to choose
between her and his God. His choice was Eve and
Death. Adam exercised the wrong choice before he ate
of the fruit. If man is the ultimate arbiter of his
choices then God is absolved of all responsibility
for man's acts and God emerges as no tyrant. God's
foreknowledge does not foreordain man's actions. He
is not arbitrarily asking Man to continue the axial
relationship of creature and Creator. If man errs,
the consequences, by laws of nature and polarity,
have to be borne by him. Herein comes justice, the
just consequences of default. Man's disobedience is
the aberration that destroys harmony and order in a
happy, smooth-running hegemony.

Milton's Satan has been an anomaly to many.
Brave, beautiful, adventurous and enterprising, a
good general and leader, compassionate toward his
followers and even toward Adam and Eve at first sight
of their innocent beauty; yet diabolic, egocentric
with misplaced pride, a prevaricator, cowardly, one
not hesitating to identify himself with predatory
beasts and ugly toads, and eventually sinking, with
no volition of his own, to a venomous snake. He is
a complex of virtue and vice, yet never is he seen
untainted It is only reported that he was an archangel of God and close to His throne. There is no
perversion that is not attributed to Satan, even
incest, and the begetting of Death, the fearful personification of man's final dissolution.

In the allegory of Satan, Sin, and Death, Milton has discussed a timeworn question of the early
and mediaeval church: the imperative that man must
fight a continuing battle against ever-threatening
evils before he can brace himself for physical death
and meet his Maker. Satan in Paradise Lost is pleasing yet venomous, Sin is sinister, Death is nebu-
lous and amorphous but threatening; all are mysteriously meanacing abstractions with which man con-
tends. It is a fearful trio pitted against man,
yet man, the similitude of perfection, has a divinity
and Paradise within him that helps him affirm his
faith in himself. Man also has the positive weapon
of reason, which allows him to see a future filled
with possibilities:

209

                    On mee the Curse aslope
        Glanc'd on the ground, with labor I must
          earn
        My bread; what harm? Idleness had been
          worse;
        My labor will sustain me;

                    (X. 1053-56)

        Greatly instructed I shall hence depart,
        Greatly in peace of thought, and have my
          fill
        Of knowledge, what this Vessel can contain;

                    (XII. 557-59)

The epic has a comforting note of faith for Adam and
Eve. They will exercise their reason and choice
again as they step into the "vast profundity" and possi-
bility of an inviting world. They have the assurance
of divine strength without them as within:

          The World was all before them where to
            choose
          Thir place of rest, and Providence their
            guide:

                    (XII. 646-47)

And with confidence, it can be said of Adam as Wither
in his prefatorial verse claims for himself:

            Let it be that, wherein it may be view'd,
            My Makers Image, was in me renew'd
            And, so declare, a dutifull intent
            To doe the Worke I came for . . .

                    (Wither, Sig. A4^V)

     One of the moot ethical ideas that Milton pre-
sents is that both good and evil are present in human
thoughts, and come involuntarily into the mind. Without volition man faces both the pros and cons of
issues, but because he possesses the faculty of
reason he has the choice of rejecting the wrong.
When Eve is distraught by her dream in Book V of
Paradise Lost, Adam comforts her:

                          210

Evil into the mind of God or Man
May come and go, so unapprov'd, and leave
No spot or blame behind:

(V. 117-19)

And quoting Titus i.15 in _Areopagitica_, Milton says:
"To the pure all things are pure, knowledge whether
of good or evill . . . cannot defile if the will and
conscience be not defil'd."[4]

But it is expected that evil should not be ap-
proved or accepted. If evil is not acted upon, it
leaves a person in his pristine state of innocence.
This applies to both God and Man. The temptation is
there, but right reason directs right choice, and
saves the situation. Milton does show that before
committing a wilful act of sin man is prone to it.
Eve has propensities to sin before her fall; she is
not entirely innocent. She is vain and Narcissus-
like momentarily loves her image more than Adam;
she petulantly desires a late night (IX. 657-8) when
Adam explains that time is of the essence. Eve has
a strong will, she admires herself, she out-argues
Adam, though at times speciously, and often gets the
better of him, especially when determined to act as
she pleases. Evil comes into the mind which is pre-
disposed to it, and is seen in action which is not
absolutely righteous. Adam is uxorious long before
he decides to suffer with Eve in her sin. John Hall
aptly writes:

Thus doth depraved man at first begin.
To act his sin,
And put his hand to that his heart
Doth with such opposition thwart,
Half punishing before, thus Serpent sin
To sting and poyson doth at once begin,

(Hall, p. 9)

Milton's human beings, though placed in the state of
innocence in the Garden, are ripe to succumb to
temptation. It creeps on them gradually and insid-
iously, and affects all creation.

William G. Madsen, quoting R. L. Brett, says
that "sense images can convey divine truth; only
when the natural and supernatural are one."[5] Sense

211

images are conveyed metaphorically in poetry. For seventeenth-century poets things were not similar, but were interchangeably the same. "The world was not like an animal, it was animate,"[6] evident when personified nature suffers on account of Adam and Eve's sin. Inchoate nature is one with man. When man disobeys God, nature is the first to show signs of horror "Nature from her seat / Sighing through all her Works gave signs of woe" (IX. 782-83). And when Adam partakes of the forbidden fruit, the impact is worse on Nature: "Earth trembl'd from her entrails, as again / In pangs, and Nature gave a second groan, / Sky low'r'd, and muttering Thunder, some sad drops / Wept at completing of the mortal Sin / Original" (IX. 1000-4). These sense images are closely linked to the idea of affinity and rapport in all creation, so prevalent in primitive mythologies, in which each link in the chain of being is infused with the spirit of the chief Deity. The corollary is that each object, no matter how humble, reveals divine truths. This is true only until a break appears in the continuity of relationships. Once a destructive force is introduced, the rapport is over, and separation and isolation begin. Nature becomes sinister instead of friendly.

> Then we suppose each twig that is behind
>   mov'd by the wind
> Would give a lash, we think a hare
> Flying detests us, if we heare
> A lamkin bleat for milk, we think't doth
>   cry
> Mother, yon man's a sinner, come not nigh:

(Hall, p. 10)

Adam and Eve soon realize that they are bereft, even the animals that gamboled about them now glare at them menacingly (X. 714). And the reader shares the mental agony of the pair.

Milton's treatment of aberrations caused by sin, whether in the personality of Satan or Adam or Eve, or in that of Belial, Moloch and Mammon, shows his understanding of disorders of psychogenic origin. In the chapter on madness and degeneration we noticed the symptoms of psychotic disorders in the characters as a result of guilt. Milton gives all the symptoms of mental imbalance: depression, paronoia,

schizophrenia, delusions, exaggerated fears, jealousy,
egotistic self-pity, emotional pain and misery, weep-
ing, frustration, resentment, self-hate, regrets,
doubts and anxieties, nihilistic and hypochondrical
thought of death, shrinking from the environment,
intolerance, lack of humour, failure to evaluate
reality, delusions of persecution, pleas for mercy,
the paradoxical desire for both death and life,
perplexity and bewilderment, suicidal designs, verbal
abuse, other excuses, superficial arguments, eroti-
cism, stupor,[7] and a feeling of isolation and other
such mental disorders. In other words sin disinte-
grates the harmony of the personality. Sin as personified has all the gnawing fury of the Medusa and
is the cause of dementia and disintegration, as evident in man as in the devils and Adam and Eve:

> But when w' have acted what deprav'd desire
> Did first require;
> The torturer Guilt doth banish fear,
> And sin doth like her self appear
> Arm'd with her venom'd snakes which ready
> stand
> To punish what her self did first command.
>
> By this means conscience disturb'd doth so
> Enraged grow
> That she whips out all peace, so we
> Snatch't from our false securitie
> Are borne by our own tortures, such as ne'er
> The worst offender can from tyrant fear.

(John Hall, p. 9)

To Adam and Eve, once they have acknowledged their
sin, recovery comes, and it is made perfect in the
heavenly grace offered to them: "Man shall find
grace" (III. 227). Adam learns of it in full
measure from Michael, and can triumphantly say, once
reassured that his mental agony is allayed and he is
whole again:

> To God more glory, more good will to Men
> From God, and over wrath grace shall
> abound.

(XII. 477-78)

The ethos of the situation is that union with the

213

in-dwelling divine spirit, once restored through the
acknowledgement of one's fault, erases all the psychotic disorders and gives "calm of mind all passion
spent."

What amazes in Paradise Lost is that life is
never static; there is constant movement. Even when
Raphael is narrating past events, there is a sense of
tremendous energy that propels the animate, inanimate
and abstract alike.

At the core, though himself a constant, is the
principal Mover, God the "essence increate" (III.6):
God, his Son and his Spirit. Theologians may stress
Milton's unitarianism, but in Paradise Lost the three
persons of the Trinity are co-dependent and function
inseparably. They are the source of orderly work in
conjunction with energy. This is evident at crucial
moments, such as the expulsion of the rebel angels,
the momentous time of creation, and the Son's return
from his artistic mission. God's words reverberate:

> Go then thou Mightiest in thy Father's
> might,. . .
>
> He said, and on his Son with Rays direct
> Shone full; hee all his Father full exprest
> Ineffably into his face receiv'd,
>
> (VI. 710-21)
>
> And thou my Word, begotten Son, by thee
> This I perform, speak thou, and be it done:
> My overshadowing Spirit and might with thee
> I send along,
>
> (VII. 163-166)
>
> The Filial Power arriv'd, and sat him down
> With his great Father, for he also went
> Invisible, yet stay'd . . .
>
> Author and end of all things.
>
> (VII. 587-91)

God's "Imperial Throne" is "fixt forever firm" (VII.
585-6), but his energy is never static, and the Godhead reflects it continually in the Father, the Son
and the Spirit. Even at moments when the Father and

the Son speak dramatically in their own voices, it is
as though one mind were weighing the questions before
a decision. Their will is one; they complement each
other as the circular yin and yang of the Chinese
symbol of perfection and unity: "So spake th' Almighty,
and to what he spake / His Word, the Filial Godhead,
gave effect" (VII. 174-5). This brings us to the
core of the Fall. Man in exercising his will contrary
to that of God separates himself irrevocably from the
principle of unity. Man too was God's creative thought
and energy and image, though fashioned of the substance
of the earth. The act of disobedience to God's will
cuts him off from the mystical union which was his
birthright. Once sin enters he has to exercise his
ingenuity and utmost discipline to re-establish the
axial relationship, "Henceforth I learn, that to
obey is best" (XII. 561). In affirming his understanding of the principle of goodness, Adam restores in
himself the motivating energy that was first breathed
into him, and like the Godhead, God and His Son and
the Spirit, he can draw on the divinity within him
for progress and recreation. The energy to construct
and move, displayed by Milton in the epic, is a God-
given energy, a constant motivation to right thinking
and creativity, man's omnipresent asset. Adam's intelligence, his humility and his vision, prepare him
to use this innate power aright in the new situation
and once again converse with his God.

The emblem writers deal with the issues discussed
in the preceding pages. Moral, ethical, and religious
truths were the emblematists' stock in trade, and
didacticism part of their design. If Adam, the Renaissance man, could converse with his Maker and argue
issues with Him (VIII. 370-435), so could the emblematists for they too were working in the same, exciting Renaissance, the Elizabethan and Jacobean
period, in which God and man both mattered. The emblematists in their poems exhibit a love of perfection, like Milton, and continually advise, exhort,
warn to seek excellence. Man's ingenuity and initia-
tive are there, but latent. All man needs is right
direction for right action.

When Quarles offers his Hieroglyphikes, he does
not only, like Shakespeare, offer it as "an Egyptian
dish," but advises his readers to "Fall too; and much
good may't doe you."[8] He knows that man needs
direction and advice in his psychologically troubled

215

state:

> Tost too and fro, our frighted thoughts are
>   driv'n
> With ev'ry puffe, with every Tide
> Of self-consuming Care;
> Our peacefull flame, that would point up
>   to heav n,
> Is still disturb'd, and turnd aside;
> And ev'ry blast of Ayre
> Commits such wast in man, as man cannot,
>   repair.
>
> (Quarles, Hieroglyphikes,
>   p. 12)

And though Quarles refers to man as a "Nothing, all
composed of Doubts,"[9] like Milton he knows that man
has the spark of divinity in him which impels his
recovery:

> Remember, O remember, thou were set,
> For men to see the Great Creator by;
> Thy flame is not thy owne: It is a Det
> Thou ow'st thy Maker; And wilt thou deny
> To pay the Int'rest of thy Light?
> And skulk in Corners, and play least in
>   sight?
>
> [For] . . . this little World of living Clay,
> The pride of Nature, glorified by Art,
> Whom earth adores, and all her hosts obay,
> Ally'd to Heav'n by his Divine part,
> Triumphs
>
> (Quarles, Hieroglyphikes,
>   pp. 32 & 59)

And with John Hall, man can hopefully claim re-established relationship with God:

> Thou (O my sun!) a while maist lie
> As intercepted from mine eye,
> But love shall fight those Clouds, and thou
> Into my purged eyes shall flow,
>
> (Hall, sig. A2)

And in a wonderful metaphysical statement, he examines his oneness with God from whom man has his
being, and who offers his re-ascent:

216

Spring-head of life, how am I now
In-tomb'd in Thee?
How do I since th'art pleas'd to flow,
Hate a dualitie?
How I am annihilated? yet by this
Acknowledge my subsistence is

Still may I rise;

(Hall, p. 54)

Once man has learnt through humility and the annihilation of self that life holds a promise of progress, he can look ahead like Adam and stress the joy
and Protestant ethics of labor. He knows the frustration of sloth. Whitney displays the idea in the
emblem <u>Otiosi semper egentes</u>. Labor, with the horn
of plenty in her right hand and sheaves of corn
crowning her, sits in an ant-drawn chariot, chastis-
ing idleness, an emaciated pauper, who kneels
anxiously nearby:

Here, Idlenes doth weepe amid her wantes,
Neare famished: whome, labour whippes for
    Ire:
Here, labour sittes in chariot drawen with
    antes:
And dothe abounde, with all he can desire.

(Whitney, p. 175)

Recovery is the first step to involvement and success.
Peacham also pursues the idea of work as healthy
for the human soul:

if we doe not exercise our wit,
By dayly labour, and invention still:
In little time, our sloth corrupteth it,
With in bred vices, foule and stincking ill:
That both the glories of our life deface,
And stoppe the source, and head of heavenly
    grace.

(Peacham, p. 68)

Only when Adam uses his reason to assess the utility
of labor, can Providence be his guide.

Another moot thought of the seventeenth century
is that earth is but an emblem of heaven: a symbol

217

and visual experience of that perfection which is incomprehensible. Milton voices it in Raphael's speech:

> and what surmounts the reach
> Of human sense, I shall delineate so,
> By lik'ning spiritual to corporal forms,
> As may express them best, though what if
>   Earth
> Be but the shadow of Heav'n, and things
>   therein
> Each to other like, more than on Earth is
>   thought.

                    (V. 571-76)

Thus the same excellence is expected on earth as in
Heaven, the shadow being the diffused counterpart of
the substance. Conversely spiritual discernment is
required to comprehend the numinous through the concrete. Wither expresses the sentiment in the prefa-
tory verse of his book when ruminating on his portrait:

> A Picture, though with most exactnesse made,
> Is nothing, but the Shadow of a Shade.
> For, ev'n our living Bodies . . .
> Are but the shadowes of that Reall being,
> Which doth extend beyond the Fleshly-
>   seeing;
> And, cannot be discerned, till we rise
> Immortall-Objects, for Immortall-eyes.
> Our Everlasting-Substance lies unseene,
> Behinde the Fouldings, of a Carnall-Screene,
>
> For, as I view, these Townes, and Fields
>   that be
> In Landskip drawne; Even so, methinks, I
>   see
> A Glimpse, farre off, (through Faith's
>   Prospective glasse)
> Of that, which after Death, will come to
>   passe; . . .
>
> Since, Wee, and all God's other Creatures,
>   here,
> Are but the Pictures, of what shall appeare.

                    (Wither, Sig. A4 & A4^V)

According to Milton it is God's way to reveal his

218

laws and give prophetic insights by symbols and pictures, an abstracted, allegorical and powerful medium to convey truths. Michael's mountain-top visions point out that man will learn to rule himself by law. His code of behavior will be guided by the Decalogue, for justice, orderly, communal life and government. These laws will be:

> part such as appertain
> To civil Justice, part religious Rites
> Of sacrifice, informing them by types
> And shadows,

(XII. 230-33)

They will prefigure the promised Messiah, who will be victorious over infernal power, though not without suffering; moreover will continue to suffer vicariously. Man's atonement in sacrifices offered, in comparison, is merely "shadowy expiations weak" (XII. 291). Justice demands a "full, perfect and sufficient sacrifice." Wither puruses the idea in Emblemes (p. 170). The device is reminiscent of the creation of Adam in the Sistine Chapel. Man rests precariously on the peak of a craggy mountain, and seems almost teetering with arms outstretched as though suing for help, while balancing his body. The background shows a faintly etched civilization lit by rays signifying God's prevenient grace, which Wither explains in the verse. After seeking recognition from his fellow man, man realizes that aid can come from Divinity alone.

> Me thinks, in this new-rapture, I doe see
> The hand of God from heaven supporting me,

(Wither, p. 170)

Adam is androgynous before the creation of Eve, like the primeval God of the Hindu pantheon, Brahma. The Vedic Brahma ensconced in a golden, cosmic egg floats on the primeval waters for eons, communicating with himself. Once he emerges from the egg he feels deprived, alone, and frustrated, and so, like the amoeba, by fission divides himself into two, a male and a female entity, but then experiences disunity and joins with the other half to procreate. Brahma and his spouse, Saraswati, the goddess of learning and sapience, then people the heavens and

the earth with gods, human beings and other creatures
down to the ant. If the Hebraic / Christian God
creates Adam in his own image, God is also a hermaphrodite. The moment the female characteristics of
Adam are detached by the extraction of that "Rib /
Crooked by nature" (X. 883) and "that bad woman"
(X. 834) is fashioned into a glorious paragon, duality
comes into that entity of perfection, and results in
the "breaking of the circle," the crack which soon
eases the entry of evil. The angels are androgynous,
their substances coalesce in sensuous delight, but
they exhibit no disharmony, no disjoining. Thus in
the creation of Eve, one wonders if created Man is
morally weakened and unparadised and become prone to
evil. In Milton he maintains the spark of divinity
justly his.

There is a sense of clarity and order in Milton's
moralistic pictures. The emblematists try to maintain an equally comprehensive order in their adages,
though in skill they fall far short of the great
bard. Light, discipline, order, mental elasticity
in philosophical speculation become keys to well-
being if Man uses reason and stays with the golden
mean. Yet all knowledge, all reasoning is crowned
by numinous spirituality and mysticism that cannot
be explained. It approximates to rapport with some
universal energy that alternately crushes and elates
man, with the promise of ultimate well being. Milton
and the emblematists take man through vicissitudes
of moral and ethical being, but return him to his
indestructible self confidence and composure.

FOOTNOTES

[1] Ruth Mohl, John Milton and His Commonplace Book (New York: Frederick Ungar, 1969), p. 23.

[2] William Hazlitt, "On Shakespeare and Milton," Milton Criticism, ed. James Thorpe (New York: Collier, 1950), p. 107.

[3] Douglas Bush, John Milton (New York: Collier, 1964), pp. 148-52.

[4] Hughes, ed. p. 727.

[5] William G. Madson, From Shadowy Types to Truth (New Haven: Yale Univ. Press, 1968), p. 19.

[6] Marjorie Nicolson, The Breaking of the Circle (Evanston: Northwestern Univ. Press, 1950), p. xix.

[7] Arthur P. Moyce & Lawrence C. Kolb, Modern Clinical Psychiatry, 6th ed. (Philadelphia: W. B. Saunders Company, rpt. 1964), pp. 295-317.

[8] Quarles, Hieroglyphikes, p. 1.

[9] Quarles, Hieroglyphikes, p. 44.

221

CHAPTER SIX

THE LITURGICAL AND DRAMATIC ICONS IN PARADISE LOST

The Anglican Book of Common Prayer was instituted
in 1662 as the book of liturgy to be used in all State
churches of England. Certain passages in the Prayer
Book[1] seem strikingly akin to passages in Paradise
Lost. None are taken word for word and incorporated
in the epic, but lines, concepts and turns of speech
indicate conscious or unconscious borrowing on the
part of the poet.

The Prayer Book grew from the liturgies of the
early Church, both East and West, and especially
from the Breviaries of the medieval Church. It became a composite of Scriptural passages and thoughts
and devotions of Church Fathers such as Tertullian,
Cyprian, Basil, Gregory, Hilary, John Chrysostom,
Augustine of Hippo, Ambrose, the Venerable Bede,
Alcuin. The revised edition of 1662 was based on
the First Prayer Book of Edward VI, 1549, and its
second edition of 1552; Elizabeth's Prayer Book of
1559; and James I's of 1604.[2] Milton grew up knowing
the prayer books of the Church.

As a child Milton was brought up in the Anglican
faith. His father had dissented from his own father,
Richard Milton, primarily, as his biographers state,
because of the grandfather's ardent Catholicism and
John Milton senior's adherence to the Church of
England. Milton's father was a good churchman, and
Milton, born and living within a stone's throw of St.
Paul's Cathedral in Bread Street, Cheapside, must have
lisped in church prayers from his infancy and early
childhood. Before he entered Christ's College, Cambridge, Milton had his schooling at St. Paul's, a
church school of the Cathedral. In the English public and church-related schools, attendance at morning and evening prayer was mandatory. The Book of
Common Prayer was used daily in assemblies and chap-
els. Milton, a day scholar at St. Paul's, may not
have participated in all the services through the
day, but Matins and Evensong constituted part of
the school-day schedule. Matins was preceded by the
daily Eucharist, but except for Sundays, attendance
of students was not required at the ritual.

At Christ's College, Cambridge, preparing for
the ministry, Milton was aware of all the disciplines
needed for the priestly office. The mediaeval church
beginning its day with Nocturns or Matins continued
to hold set services until nightfall. There were
eight canonical hours for each day of the year, but
during the English Reformation services of Tierce,
Sext and Nones were deleted; Matins, Lauds and Prime
were combined into Morning Prayer, and Vespers and
Compline into Evening Prayer. In spite of the sim-
plification, such institutions as theological colleges continued the mediaeval discipline. Attendance
at the services was required of divinity students.

With twenty-three and a half years of his life
exposed to words and thought patterns of the Liturgy,
(Milton received his Master's degree on July 3rd,
1632), it was inevitable that Milton should use
phraseology and thoughts of the Prayer Book. This
is also evident in the emblematists. Patterns, concepts, and rhythms of the Book of Common Prayer are
present in their works.

Milton's epic is based primarily on the Bible.
The Book of Common Prayer, drawn from the early
church and saints, also leans on the Bible. At the
turn of the century, John Dowden, Bishop of Edin-
burgh, commented that the lectionary system of the
Book of Common Prayer "secures . . . the orderly reading year by year of the whole Bible," (Workmanship
of the Prayer Book, London: 1899, p. 11), and Samuel
Fuller in Characteristic Excellences of the Liturgy
(Boston: 1845, p. 5) said, "The Liturgy . . . is the
Bible itself in a devotional form." Milton uses the
Bible, but he often picks the Prayer Book, consciously or unconsciously, to illustrate an occasion or a
point. George Newton Conklin explains this ardour for
the Scriptures in the literati of the seventeenth
century:

> Now the seventeenth century, an era of
> enormous erudition almost wholly concerned
> with Biblical scholarship, following the
> twin momenta of Reformation and Humanism,
> stands in the history of Biblical study
> as the great age of philology . . . fed by
> the period's precocious outburst of linguis-
> tic learning, a formidable, complex, and
> brilliant quest for a final, proved, and

irrefutable rendition of the Bible, the
religion of Protestants.[3]

The language of the Bible is poetic and pleasing,
but the spate of religious motifs in the literature
of the seventeenth century might not have been due to
the literati's preoccupation with linguistics and
philology. Rosemond Tuve makes it amply clear that
language in the seventeenth century was an aesthetic
tool for the artists' expression of strongly felt beliefs, and often liturgical utterances of poets carried truths ingrained in them from early years, for
"No cleric of the seventeenth century as liturgically
literate as . . . Milton and brought up on typology
. . ."[4] could be unfamiliar with the significance of
symbols and images in the diction of liturgy. Both
in liturgy and in poetry, conventional situations
required certain usage of language and concepts - a
part of typology, which stemmed from the ideas and
tone of biblical literature. The fact was long
understood by lyricists and ritualistic dramatists
of the Middle Ages, for "poetry had quite as much
kinship with ritual as with drama."[5] Milton's epic
belongs in the tradition of devotional literature,
and he uses the techniques of his forbears, including,
perhaps, the work of the ninth-century Amalarius of
Metz, who "discussed the familiar liturgy as allegory,
and argument . . . destined to result a century later
in the liturgical drama."[6]

Milton may have rejected the Anglican premise
"that the physical church and liturgical ceremonies
and vestments symbolize the inner life of the Christian . . . and also the outward ceremonial aspects of
the Old Law by which the bishops justified the prac-
tices of the Anglican Church,"[7] yet his use of ceremonies and liturgy of the Church in Paradise Lost
show his affinity to the Church of his father and of
his own childhood and youth and the theological
training he underwent at Cambridge. In the Christian
Doctrine Milton acknowledges the theological value
of the Eucharist as a sacrament, though he gives his
own interpretation to the Mass:

> The living bread therefore which Christ
> calls his flesh, and that blood which is
> drink indeed, can be nothing but the doc-
> trine of Christ's having become man in
> order to shed his blood for us; a doctrine

224

which whosoever receives by faith shall as
surely attain eternal life, as the par-
taking of meats and drinks supports our
brief term of bodily existence.[8]

"In its first emergence, ritual appears as a
stylized religious emotion. Spontaneous cries of
joy, outbursts of praise, entreaty, self-absement
seem to represent the earliest response of men to the
incitement of God: and these by repetition gradually
acquire the sanction of a rite. . . . Ritual weaves
speech, gesture, rhythm and agreed ceremonial into
the worshipping action of man; and thus at its best
can unite his physical, mental, and emotional being
in a single response to the Unseen . . . the symbol
or significant image is . . . the point, where physical and metaphysical meet . . . the sensible and
supra-sensible reality."[9] Keeping this statement of
Evelyn Underhill in sight, it can be said with Madsen
that in Paradise Lost Milton is true to his function
as poet-priest; he "creates 'lively images' of
truth,"[10] and dramatically conveys them in liturgical
cadences, to justify God's reality to man.

The rituals of The Book of Common Prayer follow
structured patterns. A combined service of Matins
and the Eucharist begins with a musical prelude and
the ceremonial introit, followed by liturgical
silence, the opening sentences, and the invocation.
The liturgy continues with the General Confession
and Absolution, the Lord's Prayer, Versicles and responses, the Venite Exultemus Domino, Old and New
Testament lessons with the Benedictus es Domine and
the Jubilate Deo; the Creed, Salutation, Collects,
Grace and Homily. Morning Prayer accompanied by
the Eucharist has readings of the Collect, Epistle
and Gospel for the day, with intercessions punctu-
ating the service. The offertory precedes eulogia
or giving thanks over the offered bread, the institution, presentation, and invitation. With the confession and absolution, the Sursum Corda, Sanctus,
and consecration comes the climax of the liturgical
drama, the sacrifice and complete union of devotee
and Deity; and it leads to the catharsis, expressed
in Thanksgiving and in the Gloria in Excelsis. The
Benediction, the Recessional and the postlude bring
the ritual to a close.

Milton's use of the Prayer Book in Paradise Lost

can be stated as correspondence between liturgy and literature; the lyrical use of the Scriptures and narrative events of the epics. Its use is to denote the abstract and express scriptural verities. His borrowings have been reformed to the extent that unless a conscious probe is made of the passages, they elude detection.

In relation to the Scriptures, Milton believed that his mission was identical to that of an ordained priest. He said poets "are of power beside the office of a pulpit, to inbreed and cherish in a great people the seeds of virtue and public civility, to allay the perturbations of the mind and set the affections in right tune, to celebrate in glorious and lofty hymns the throne and equipage of God's almightiness."[11] The "Preface" to the 1662 edition of The Book of Common Prayer states that the compilers of the "Divine Service . . . so ordered the matter, that all the whole Bible (or the greatest part thereof) should be read over once every year"; Milton, the poet-priest, in his epic tries to encompass the entire story of the Bible from Creation to Christ's redemptive action. Michael, in visionary pictures, conveys biblical stories, replete with their lessons, to Adam, and opens the whole panorama of the future to him. The psychological effect is that Adam loses his sense of guilt. The Prayer Book attempts to unburden God's devotees of their paranoia.

The Introit in the liturgical rites has all the dramatic pageantry of a formal procession proceeding to a great hall. The crucifer (like the standard bearer of the rebel angels, Azazel) leads the procession of the choir, the acolytes, and celebrants. At the foot of the altar the standard bearers, choristers, and other functionaries part to allow the chief celebrant, priest or bishop, to proceed to the High Altar. This is the moment when the cadences of the martial music of organ or orchestra die away to a diminuendo, and the priest faces the altar communing silently with the Deity. The silence is as eloquent as the soaring music, and the audience stands awestruck; as though one gigantic mind of priest and people is concentrated in bringing God's presence into focus, and building the rapport which would remain unbroken through the rite.

The introit and the liturgical silence are the

point of departure for the rest of the service. The
first collect in the Eucharistic rite is an invocation. In Miltonic phraseology it asks for God's
cleansing grace for the act of worship:

> Almighty God, unto whom all hearts be
> open, all desires known, and from whom no
> secrets are hid: Cleanse the thoughts of
> our hearts by the inspiration of thy Holy
> Spirit that we may perfectly love thee and
> worthily magnify thy holy name.
>
> (Book of Common Prayer,
> p. 166)

Milton's invocation carries similar thoughts in
Book I. He desires the Holy Spirit to inform and
inspire him, and help him magnify God's name and
justify His actions to his fellow men:

> Thou O Spirit, that dost prefer
> Before all Temples th' upright heart and
>   pure,
> Instruct me . . .
>   What in me is dark
> Illumine, what is low raise and support;
> That to the highth of this great Argument
> I may assert Eternal Providence,
> And justify the ways of God to men.
>
> (I. 17-26)

Likewise Peacham says, "And first with heartie prayer
call on him,/ Whose holy Spirit must guide thee in
the sense," (Peacham, p. 10). The theme is repeated
in another of the opening sentences of the liturgy,
and often said at the beginning of the homily: "Let
the words of my mouth and the meditations of my
heart be always acceptable in thy sight, O Lord
my strength and my Redeemer."

These are serious prayers for God's inspirational guidance, but they also have the dramatic element
of Greek tragedy. The words are prologues to the
sacrifice of praise and thanksgiving. The address is
to an invisibly enthroned and mighty monarch whom
the vate, the poet-priest, humbly petitions. He
asks for both sapience and eloquence to make the
right impact.

227

In the Venite, Exultemus Domino, the priest and
the people call each other, "O Come, let us sing
unto the Lord: let us heartily rejoice in the strength
of our salvation." And in the Te Deum Laudamus of the
"Morning Prayer," the priest and people break into a
song of praise, as the organ peals:

> We praise thee, O God: we acknowledge thee
>   to be the Lord
> All the earth doth worship thee: the Father
>   everlasting
> To thee all Angels cry aloud: the Heavens,
>   and all the powers therein.
> To thee Cherubim and Seraphim: continually
>   do cry,
> Holy, Holy, Holy: Lord God of Sabaoth;
> Heaven and earth are full of the Majesty:
>   of thy Glory.
>
> The Father: of an infinite Majesty
> Thine honourable, true; and only Son;
> Also the Holy Ghost: the Comforter.
> Thou art the King of Glory: O Christ,
> Thou art the everlasting Son: of the Father.
>
>   (Book of Common Prayer,
>   pp. 43-44)

Milton's angels react in a similar fashion, when God
accepts His Son's offer to redeem man. The passages
of the Prayer Book and of Milton are both drawn from
passages of the book of Revelation.

> No sooner had th'Almighty ceas't, but all
> The multitude of Angels with a shout
> Loud as from numbers without number, sweet
> As from blest voices, uttering joy, Heav'n
>   rung
> With Jubilee, and loud Hosannas fill'd
> Th' eternal Regions: lowly reverent
> Towards either Throne they bow, . . .
>
>   thir gold'n Harps they took,
> Harps ever tun'd, that glittering by thir
>   side
> Like Quivers hung, and with Preamble sweet
> Of charming symphony they introduce
> Thir sacred Song, and waken raptures high;
>
>   (III. 344-69)

The angels' song that follows, like the Te Deum, incorporates the central doctrines of Christian belief, which are examined in connection with the Creed
later in the thesis.

St. Robert Bellarmine's book entitled, A Shorte
Catechisme of Card (all) Bellarmine illustrated with
Images, 1614, may have been known to Milton. Bellarmine's method of illustrating the book was to take
essential doctrines incorporated in prayer books, and
quoting them briefly, caption the pictures in his
books. The illustrations relevant to this chapter
are inserted in the thesis, and are self explanatory.
Milton may or may not have been influenced by the
drawings in formulating his verbal pictures, but they
do illustrate portions of the Prayer Book that Milton
introduces in the epic. Bellarmine's icons are in
the emblem tradition, and instruct while they please.
The 1662 Preface of the Book of Common Prayer mentions the purpose of the set rites as "the preservation of peace and unity in the Church; the procuring
of reverence, and exciting of piety and devotion in
the public worship of God." Milton sets out to
achieve a similar goal for his two human characters,
and he achieves it in his unmatched numbers. He
sends Adam and Eve out of the great cathedral of
Eden in accord with each other, their reverence and
devotion for the Deity renewed, in peace of mind;
their piety accepted. Dramatically led by Michael
in a recessional, they leave the presence of beings
preternatural, and with dignity reaffirm belief in life.
Both Milton and the Prayer Book are concerned with
man's spiritual well-being, integral to his physical
life.

The widely scattered passages in Milton which
recall portions of the Book of Common Prayer, vary
from hymns sung by the angels before God's throne,
to words of praise of hell's angels.

Adam and Eve's evening and morning hymns of
praise are akin to the canticles of Evensong and
Morning Prayer; Adam and Raphael's prayer of gratitude for their repast, to that of the Eulogia or the
giving of thanks before the priest administers the
host of the eucharist; the beautiful words of Adam to
Eve, when she is led to him by the Son of God, to
cadences in the marriage ceremony. The verbal patterns in Milton recall pictures and music of several

229

Prayer Book rites and ceremonies. The Preface to
the Prayer Book states, "The Book . . . doth not contain in it anything contrary to the Word of God"
(p. 3); neither does Milton's epic. Both draw on the
Authorized Version of the Bible;[12] but Milton chooses
special passages for special rites. The closest parallel is the use of canticle Benedicite, Omnia Opera
(Book of Common Prayer, pp. 96-97) in the Morning
Prayer of Adam and Eve. The canticle in the Prayer
Book embraces the expanse of the cosmos, and in words
of thankfulness and ringing refrains, asks the
hierarchy of God's creation, from the angels down
to the least, including inanimate nature, to "bless
. . . the Lord: praise him and magnify him for ever."
The song begins with words of the Psalmist, "O All
ye Works of the Lord, bless ye the Lord: praise him
and magnify him for ever. O ye Angels of the Lord,
bless ye the Lord: praise him and magnify him for
ever." The canticle systematically catalogues the
"Heavens," "Waters that be above the firmament,"
"Powers of the Lord," "Sun and Moon," "Stars of
Heaven," "Showers and Dew," "Winds of God," . . .
"Nights and Days," "Light and Darkness," "Lightnings
and Clouds," "the Earth," "Mountains and Hills," "all
ye Green Things upon the earth," "Wells," "Seas and
floods," "Whales, and all that move in the waters,"
"Fowls of the air," "Beasts and cattle," and mankind.
Milton, avoiding all that was not pertinent to pre-
lapsarian Eden, sings the same song, though elaborated:

> Speak yee who best can tell, ye Sons of
>   Light,
> Angels, for yee behold him, and with songs
> And choral symphonies, Day without Night,
> Circle his Throne rejoicing, yee in Heav'n,
> On Earth join all ye Creatures to extol
> Him first, him last, him midst, and without
>   end.

(V. 160 ff.)

Milton's hymn covers forty-eight lines of exquisite
poetry, and like the Matins canticle of worship,
Milton's refrain calls for the repeated use of the
word "praise." Milton's catalogue, along with the
angels and all creatures of the earth, includes "Fairest of Starrs," "Thou Sun of this great World both
Eye and Soul," "Moon, that now meet'st the orient Sun,

now fli'st / With the fixt Starre," the planets or
"yee five other wand'ring Fires that move / In mystic
Dance . . .," "Air," "Mists and Exhalations," "Winds,"
"Fountains and yee, that warble, as ye flow," "all
ye living Souls, ye Birds," "Yee that in Waters
glide, and ye that walk / The Earth, and stately
tread, or lowly creep;" and Man to praise and magnify the "universal Lord" (V. 160-208).

Adam and Eve's evensong in Paradise Lost is
reminiscent of two prayers of the "Solemnization of
Matrimony" in the Book of Common Prayer. Significantly in the benediction of the rite the priest literally recalls "our first parents, Adam and Eve." Adam
and Eve in Milton praise the Creator and ask him for
children:

> Thou also mad'st the Night,
> Maker Omnipotent, and thou the Day,
> Which we in our appointed work imploy'd
> Have finisht happy in our mutual help
> And mutual love, the Crown of all our bliss
> Ordain'd by thee, and this delicious place
> For us too large, where thy abundance wants
> Partakers, and uncropt falls to the ground.
> But thou hast promis'd from us two a Race
> To fill the Earth, who shall with us extol
> Thy goodness infinite, both when we wake,
> And when we seek, as now, thy gift of sleep.

> (IV. 724-35)

The prayers of the marriage ceremony also stress
mutual love and accord along with procreation:

> O Eternal God, Creator and preserver of
>   all mankind,
> Giver of all spiritual grace, the author of
> everlating life; Send thy blessings upon
> these thy servants, this man and this wom-
> an, whom we bless in thy Name; that . . .
> they may surely perform and keep the vow
> and covenant betwixt them made . . . and
> may ever remain in perfect love and peace
> together, and live according to thy laws;
> . . .

> O Merciful Lord, and heavenly Father by

231

whose gracious gift mankind is increased:
We beseech thee, assist with thy blessing
these two persons, that they may both be
fruitful in procreation of children, and
also live together so long in godly love
and honesty, that they may see their
children Christianly and virtuously
brought up to thy praise and honour.

(Book of Common Prayer,
p. 205)

Parallels with other parts of the marriage ceremony
also appear in Paradise Lost. After Eve is moulded
out of Adam's rib and brought to him, as though led
to the altar, Adam sings his epithalmion:

On she came
Led by her Heav'nly Maker, though unseen,
And guided by his voice, nor uninform'd
Of nuptial Sanctity and marriage Rites:
Grace was in all her steps, Heav'n in her
  Eye,
In every gesture dignity and love.
I overjoy'd could not forbear aloud.
This turn hath made amends; thou hast
  fulfill'd
Thy words, Creator bounteous and benign,
Giver of all things fair, but fairest this
Of all thy gifts, nor enviest. I now see
Bone of my Bone, Flesh of my Flesh, my
  Self
Before me; Woman is her Name, of Man
Extracted; for this cause he shall forgo
Father and Mother, and to his Wife adhere;
And they shall be one Flesh, one Heart,
  one Soul.

(VIII. 484-99)

The Book of Common Prayer proclaims that matrimony
"is an honourable estate instituted of God in the
time of man's innocency, . . . which holy estate
Christ adorned and beautified with his presence
. . ." And in the pronouncement of the duties of the
bride and groom, is the biblical injunction, "For
this cause shall a man leave his father and mother,
and shall be joined unto his wife; and they two shall

be one flesh." In the prayer preceding the injunction, the sacrament of marriage is explained as part of the plan of creation: "O God, who by thy mighty power hast made all things of nothing; who also (after other things set in order) didst appoint, that out of man (created after thy own image and similitude) woman should take her beginning, . . . look mercifully upon thy servants, that both this man may love his wife, according to thy Word, . . . and also that this woman may be loving and amiable" (pp. 203-5). Verbal patterns and ideas in Milton can be traced to the rite.

The Christian Doctrine clearly states that "the Apostles creed is the most ancient and universally received compendium of belief in the possession of the Church."[13] The songs of the angels reiterate the creed of the Book of Common Prayer. In a dramatic and ritualistic gesture, the angels bow before God and his Son, casting down their golden crowns in reverence, while their "loud Hosannas" acclaim the Son's offer of Himself as the paschal lamb (III. 372-415). The lines that enshrine the hymn poetically reaffirm the Nicene Creed of the Eucharist, as do devotees repeating their belief in the central doctrines of the Church:

> I believe in one God, the Father Almighty,
> Maker of heaven and earth. And of all
>   things visible and invisible.
> And in one Lord, Jesus Christ, the only-
>   begotten
> Son of God. Begotten of his Father before
>   all worlds, God of God, Light of Light,
> Very God of very God, begotten, not
>   made, Being of one substance with the
> Father, By whom all things were made:
> Who for us men, and for our salvation came
>   down from heaven, And was incarnate by the
> Holy Ghost of the Virgin Mary, And was made
> Man, And was crucified also for us . . .
> He suffered and was buried. And the third
>   day he rose again according to the
>   Scriptures,
> And sitteth on the right hand of the Father.
> And shall come again with glory to judge
>   the quick and the dead. Whose kingdom
>   shall have no end.
>
>   (Book of Common Prayer, p.
>   168)

233

Milton's hymn repeats these ideas in lines such as:
"Thee Father first they sung Omnipotent, / Immutable,
Immortal, Infinite, / Eternal King: thee Author of
all being, / Fountain of Light, thy self invisible
. . . Thee next they sang of all Creation first,/
Begotten Son, Divine Similitude, / In whose conspic-
uous count'nance, without cloud / Made visible, th'
Almighty Father shines, / . . . Hee Heav'n of Heav'-
ns and all the Powers therein / By thee created,
. . . / No sooner did thy dear and onely Son / Perceive thee purpos'd not to doom frail Man / . . . Hee
to appease thy wrauth, and end the strife / Of Mercy
and Justice . . . offered himself to die / For man's
offence" (III. 372-410). And after the Son over-
threw the warring angels and entered the courts of
heaven triumphant, shaded by branching palms, he
advanced to the throne of God, "On high: who into
Glory him receiv'd, / Where now he sits at the right
hand of bliss" (VI. 891-92).

The second half of the Nicene creed is more
fully formulated in Michael's narration of the
events in store for man's salvation, when "Some blood
more precious must be paid for Man, / Just for unjust," (XII. 293-94). Cryptic and precise lines give
a synopsis of the life story of the incarnate Son
(XII. 358-71, 402-29, 436 & 450), and allude to his
final trumph in:

> Then to the Heav'n of Heav'ns he shall
>   ascend
> With victory . . .
>
> Then enter into glory, and resume
> His Seat at God's right hand, exalted high
> Above all names in Heav'n; and thence shall
>   come,
> When this worlds dissolution shall be ripe,
> With glory and power to judge both quick
>   and dead,

(XII. 451-60)

"Then the earth / Shall all be Paradise" (XII. 463-
64). Bellarmine's illustrations give graphic reality
to the doctrines incorporated in the Creed, as does
the Te Deum Laudamus of the Prayer Book. Bellarmine's
icons illustrating the creed appear at the end of this
study.[14]

The Nicene creed was often followed by a homily
or sermon as part of the liturgical service. The
sermon, as Helen Gardner states, was a highly structured speech, where after a brief meditation, a
theme was set, at times with the use of rhetorical
questions, and developed by points until the conclusion. The conclusion was often terse and cryptic.
The theme was supported by quotations from the Bible
and patristic literature, Christian doctrines as well
as psychological appeals to the audience. At times
it was a minute examination of a subject leading to
an ethical or moralistic conclusion. Milton's use
of homiletic persuasion can be gleaned in the speeches
of Raphael and Michael, though the mode persists in
the speech of God, His Son, and Adam. Raphael's
parting words suggest the end of a homily and
benediction:

> Be strong, live happy, and love, but first
>   of all
> Him whom to love is to obey, and keep
> His great command; take heed lest passion
>   sway
> Thy Judgment to do aught, which else free
>   Will
> Would not admit; thine and of all thy Sons
> The weal or woe in thee is plac't; beware.
> I in thy persevering shall rejoice,
> And all the Blest: stand fast; to stand or
>   fall
> Free in thine own Arbitrement it lies
> Perfect within, no outward aid require;
> And all temptation to transgress repel.

(VIII. 633-43)

And in continuation with Adam's comprehension and
acquiesence to divine love, Michael in another homiletic passage, echoing Polonius, exhorts him:

> This having learnt, thou hast attain'd the
> ~ sum
> Of wisdom . . .
>   only add
> Deeds to thy knowledge answerable, add
>   Faith,
> Add Virtue, Patience, Temperance, add Love,
> By name to come call'd Charity, the soul
> Of all the rest: then will thou not be loath

                    To leave this Paradise, but shall possess
                    A paradise within thee, happier far.

                              (XII. 575-87)

Each preacher speaks in his own voice, but they all
appeal to man's psyche and his reason for a
productive life and to find fulfillment. Milton is
using the persuasive method of religious exegesis he
had known since childhood, such as in the book
of St. James where the priest exhorts each segment
of society to the good life.[15]

          After the fall, the euphoria, and recrimination,
and the spread of carnage (like contagion), Adam
and Eve are at the stage when man sues for supernal
grace and pardon and requests to be shriven. This
is where the poem comes nearest to the eucharistic
mass. Adam and Eve pass through the nadir of despair, and rise to the acknowledgement of their sin,
a condition necessary for recovery. "O miserable
of happy! is this the end / Of this new glorious
World, and mee so late/ The Glory of that Glory"
(X. 720-22), cries Adam, and in about one hundred
of the most powerful lines weighs both pros and cons,
trying to see loopholes in the situation. He finds
none. Taxing his reason to capacity does not help,
and Adam acknowledges the enormity of his aberration
and entanglement:

                         all my evasions vain
               And reasonings, though through Mazes,
                  lead me still
               But to my own conviction: first and last
               On mee, mee only, as the source and spring
               Of all corruption, all the blame lights
                  due;

                          (X. 829-33)

Eve addressing Adam in distress at his rejection of
her, is just as conscious of her guilt: "me already
lost, mee than thyself / More miserable; both have
sin'd, but thou / Against God only, I against God
and thee" (X. 928-31). Unlike Adam, Eve, in her
patience, goes a step further towards recovery; she
suggests petitioning God, not for alleviation of
her pain, but Adam's:

                              236

And to the place of judgment will return,
There with my cries importune Heav'n, that
    all
Thy sentence from thy head remov'd may
    light
On me . . .
Mee mee only just object of his ire.

(X. 932-39)

At the very beginning of the rite, the orders of the
Morning and Evening Prayer incorporate verses which
suggest contrition on the devotee's part as he ap-
proaches God's presence: "When the wicked man,
turneth away from his wickedness that he hath committed, and doeth that which is lawful and right,
he shall save his soul alive. Ezekeil 18.27. I
acknowledge my transgressions, and my sin is ever
before me. Psalm 51.3." Similar selections from
other parts of the Scriptures are included in these
passages of guilt-acceptance for the petitioner.
Once the petitioner has admitted his guilt, he has
begun his ascent to grace; and the priest intones,
"The Scripture moveth us in sundry places to
acknowledge and confess our manifold sins and wickedness; . . . with a humble, lowly, penitent, and
obedient heart." Leading to the General Confession,
he asks the congregation to kneel and join him in
saying:

> Almighty and most Merciful Father, We have
> erred, and strayed from thy ways . . . We
> have followed the devices and desires of
> our own hearts. We have offended against
> thy holy laws . . . And we have done those
> things which we ought not to have done
> . . . But thou, O Lord, have mercy upon
> us, miserable offenders. Spare thou
> them, O God, Which confess their faults.
> Restore thou them that are penitent . . .
> That we may hereafter lead a godly, right-
> eous, and sober life.

(Book of C.P. pp. 41-42.

In the Eucharist the priest exhorts, "perceive yourselves to have offended, either by will, word, or
deed, there to bewail your own sinfulness, and to
confess yourselves to Almighty God, with full purpose

237

of amendment of life. [And as Eve instinctively and
intuitively saw, adds] And if ye shall perceive your
offences to be such as are not only against God,
but also against your neighbour; then ye shall recon-
cile yourselves unto them" (Book of C.P. p. 172).
Like Adam and Eve, the Confession avers, "We do
earnestly repent, and are heartily sorry for these
our misdoings; the remembrance of them is grievous
unto us; The burden of them is intolerable . . .
Have mercy upon us, most merciful Father" (p. 175).

Adam and Eve were conscious of God's graciousness in Milton, even at the time of the actual offence, and voiced it in their search for a salve:
"Remember with what mild / And gracious temper he
both heard and judg'd / Without wrath and reviling"
(X. 1046-48), and ". . . his hands / Cloath'd us
unworthy, pitying while he judg'd" (X. 1058-59)..
The Prayer Book, quoting Joel 2.13, had said, "Rend
your heart . . . and turn unto the Lord your God:
for he is gracious and merciful, slow to anger and
of great kindness and repenteth him of the evil."
Emboldened by these thoughts, Adam becomes the suppliant and the devotee, and in language couched in
terms of the Prayer Book, says:

> How much more, if we pray him, will his ear
> Be open, and his heart to pity incline,
> And teach us further by what means to shun
> Th' inclement Seasons, . . .
> Hee will instruct us praying, and of Grace
> Beseeching him, so as we need not fear
> To pass commodiously this life, . . .

> (X. 1060-83)

Having charted their course for recovery, Adam repeats
Eve's suggestion that they repair to the sanctified
spot where God last appeared to them, and like the
communicants at the altar pray for His mercy and grace
kneeling:

> What better can we do, than to the place
> Repairing where he judg'd us, prostrate fall
> Before him reverent, and there confess
> Humbly our faults, and pardon beg, with
>   tears
> Watering the ground, and with our sighs
>   the Air

238

Frequenting,sent from hearts contrite, in
    sign
Of sorrow unfeign'd and humiliation meek.
Undoubtedly he will relent and turn
From his displeasure; in whose look serene
When angry most he seem'd and most severe,
What else but favor, grace, and mercy shone?
    So spake our Father penitent, nor Eve
Felt less remorse: they forthwith to the
    place
Repairing where he judg'd them prostrate
    fell
Before him reverent, and both confess'd
Humbly thir faults, and pardon begg'd, with
    tears
Watering the ground, and with thir sighs
    the Air
Frequenting, sent from hearts contrite,
    in sign
Of sorrow unfeign'd, and humiliation meek.

                (X. 1085-1142)

Thus they in lowliest plight repentant stood
Praying,for from Mercie-seat above
Prevenient Grace descending had remov'd
The stony from thir hearts, and made new
    flesh
Regenerate grow instead, that sighs now
    breath'd
Unutterable, which the Spirit of prayer
Inspir'd, and wing'd for Heav'n with
    speedier flight
Then loudest Oratory:

                (XI. 1-8)

Chastened and shriven after their lowly repentance,
their sacrifice, like incense, is wafted to Heaven.
The Son, their high priest, offers it as oblation to
God for his acceptance and forgiveness:

                to Heav'n thir prayers
 Flew up, nor miss'd the way, by envious winds
Blow'n vagabond or frustrate: in they pass'd
Dimensionless through Heav'nly dores: then
    clad
With incense, where the Golden Altar fum'd,

                239

By thir great Intercessor, came in sight
Before the Father's Throne.

(XI. 14-20)

Milton denounced the ritualistic rites of the Anglo-
Catholic and Roman Catholic Churches as acts of
"formall reverence, and Worship circumscrib'd, where
they hallow'd it, they fum'd it, they sprincl'd it,
they bedeck't it, not in robes of pure innocency, but
of pure linnen, with other deformed, and fantastik
dresses in Palls, Mitres, gold, and guegaw's fetcht
from Arons old wardrobe, or the Flamins vestry: . . .
when the Priest was set to con his motions, and his
postures in Liturgies."[16] Yet he is not averse to
the use of formal worship, replete with incense, in
this dramatic picture of a highly sacred moment, when
the Son confronts the Father with the oblations of
the first two sinners, and becomes the propitiation
for their sins. At moments such as this, God's
throne is enveloped in heady fragrance of incense in
censers of gold. The atmosphere is right for the
Son, Milton's one and only priest, to address his
august Father:

> See Father, what first fruits on Earth are
>   sprung
> From thy implanted Grace in Man, these Sighs
> And Prayers, which in this Golden Censer,
>   mixt
> With Incense, I thy Priest before thee
>   bring . . .
>
>   Now therefore bend thine ear
> To supplication, hear his sighs though mute;
> Unskilful with what words to pray, let mee
> Interpret for him, mee his Advocate
> And propitiation, all his works on mee
> Good or not good ingraft, my Merit those
> Shall perfet, and for these my Death shall
>   pay.
>
> To better life shall yield him, where with
>   mee
> All my redeem'd may dwell in joy and bliss,
> Made one with me as I with thee am one.

(XI. 22-44)

Similarly the priest or bishop intercedes for the
worshipper, and turning to the altar, with the elements of the Eucharist offers them to God, for forgiveness. He chants:

> Almighty and ever-living God, who by thy
> holy Apostle hast taught us to make prayers,
> and supplications, and to give thanks for
> all men; We humbly beseech thee most merci-
> fully to accept our alms and oblations and
> to receive these our prayers, which we offer
> unto thy Divine Majesty; . . . Give grace,
> O heavenly Father . . . to all thy people
> . . . that with meek heart and due rever-
> ence, they may hear, and receive thy holy
> Word, truly serving thee in holiness and
> righteousness all the days of their life
> . . . and may be partakers of thy heavenly
> kingdom:

(Book of C.P. p. 171)

In continuation of the thought, the priest intones
the scriptural words of St. John, "If any man sin, we
have an Advocate with the Father, Jesus Christ the
righteous; and he is the propitiation for our sins"
(1 John 2.1).

God in Paradise Lost accepts the offerings, as
the Son is the high priest and mediator. Revealing
Himself to the Son (and it is only to the Son that
He appears in His full blaze of glory), he signifies
His acceptance:

> All thy request for Man, accepted Son,
> Obtain, all thy request was my Decree:

(XI. 46-47)

This does not exonerate Adam and Eve of the natural
consequences of their sin, but assures them, if they
are found faithful and diligent in good works, of a
"second life" (XI. 64). Absolution is theirs, their
sacrifice is accepted, and they are regenerated. The
priest as the protagonist of this liturgical drama
likewise pronounces a benediction:

241

Almighty God, our heavenly Father, who of
his great mercy hath promised forgiveness
of sins to all them that with hearty repentance and true faith turn unto him;
Have mercy upon you; pardon and deliver
you from all your sins, confirm you in all
goodness, and bring you to everlasting
life.

(Book of C.P. p. 176)

This leads to the paean of praise and thanks. The
priest faces the altar, as though communicating with
his unseen God, and calls on the people to thank the
Deity:

Therefore with Angels and Archangels, and
with all the company of heaven, we laud and
magnify thy glorious Name, evermore praising
thee, and saying, Holy, holy, holy, Lord
God of hosts, heaven and earth are full of
thy glory: Glory be to thee, O Lord most
High. Amen.

(Book of C.P. p. 176)

The song, based on Revelation, recalls Milton's passages in Books III and VI; the jubilant angels extolling the Son in his triumph, both moral, where he
offers himself as an expiation for the sins of man,
and physical in his victorious overthrow of the evil
angels. And in identical cadences, Milton makes his
angels sing when the "Filial Power" completes his
acts of creation, and returns to "th' Imperial
Throne / Of Godhead," mystically and numinously joining his Father, who though enthroned, had accompanied
the Son on his mission of creation (VII. 585-89).
The full orchestration of harp, pipe, dulcimer,
organ, "All sounds on Fret by String or Golden Wire /
Temper'd with soft Tunings, intermixt with Voice /
Choral or Unison;" (VII. 595-99), is overwhelming at
this juncture. The music fills the cosmic vault as
the fumes and fragrance of incense in Golden Censers,
rise in celebration of the event. The song of the
angels is reverberatingly beautiful:

Great are thy works, Jehovah, infinite
Thy power; what thought can measure thee
or tongue

242

Relate thee; greater now in thy return
Than from the Giant Angels; thee that day
Thy Thunders magnifi'd; but to create
Is greater than created to destroy . . .

So sung they, and the Empyrean rung,
With Halleluiahs.

(VII. 602-34)

Again when God foretells the Son's final victory over
Satan, Sin and Death, and man's eventual reinstate-
ment, the angels sing in priase:

the heav'nly Audience loud
Sung Halleluiah, as the sound of Seas,
Through multitude that sung: Just are thy
    ways,
Righteous are they Decrees on all thy Works;
Who can exentuate thee? Next, to the Son,
Destin'd restorer of Mankind, by whom
New Heav'n and Earth shall to the Ages rise,
Or down from Heav'n descend.

(X. 641-47)

The Eucharist also ends with a paean of praise and
gratitude for the blessing of a new lease of spiritual life. The congregation, having knelt in silence
during the last prayers, and concentrating on the
mystical presence of God, the focal point, rises with
the last "Amen." The organ peals the Gloria, the
censers swing, and the anthem rings:

Glory to God on high, and in earth
peace, good will towards men. We praise
thee, we bless thee, we worship thee, we
glorify thee, we give thee thanks for thy
great glory, O Lord God, heavenly King,
God the Father Almighty. O Lord, the only-
begotten Son Jesus Christ; O Lord God,
Lamb of God, Son of the Father, that tak-
est away the sins of the world, receive our
prayer. Thou that sittest at the right
hand of God the Father, have mercy on
us. For thou art holy; thou only art the
Lord; thou only, O Christ, with the Holy

243

Ghost, art most high in the glory of God
the Father. Amen.

(Book of C.P. p. 180)

The priest gives the blessing.

Milton's angels sing the Gloria in excelsis on
the occasion of the Son's acceptance of the Father's
behest to create a new race of men. The idea in Milton is double purposed. When the angels are heard
singing the Gloria by the shepherds in the fields of
Bethlehem, their words do not announce the advent and
the nativity but proclaim peace and good-will that
the God-man has brought. Symbolically their song
conveys the regeneration and creation anew of Man in
his prelapsarian image, and the generation of a new
race of human beings. Milton, in words reminiscent
of both the Gloria and the Magnificat, writes:

> Glory they sung to the most High, good will
> To future men, and in their dwelling peace;
> Glory to him whose just avenging ire
> Had driven out th'ungodly from his sight
> And th' habitations of the just; to him
> Glory and praise, whose wisdom had ordain'd
> Good out of evil to create, instead
> Of Spirits malign a better Race to bring
> Into their vacant room, and thence diffuse
> His good to Worlds and Ages Infinite.
> So sang the Hierarchies:

> (VII. 182-92)

The strain confirms God's prevenient grace to Man in
the epic and the Eucharist. With this beatitude the
devotee leaves the place of worship.

Raphael's salutation to Eve in the epic recalls
Gabriel's salutation of the Virgin. In her pristine
innocence Eve typifies the Virgin, and Raphael can
greet her in Biblical terms:

> On whom the Angel Hail
> Bestow'd, the holy salutation us'd
> Long after to blest Marie, second Eve.
> Hail Mother of Mankind, whose fruitful Womb
> Shall fill the World more numerous with
> thy Sons
> (V. 385-89)

244

In spite of Eve's frailty, the confidence in her was
not misplaced. Adam had gauged her potential after
the traumatic fall, and her eagerness to make amends,
and had assured her of God's mercy soon after their
prayer of contrition:

> yet this will Prayer,
> Or one short sigh of human breath, up-borne
> E'vn to the Seat of God. For since I sought
> By Prayer th' offended Deity to appease,
> Kneel'd and before him humbl'd all my heart,
> Methought I saw him placable and mild,
> Bending his ear;

(XI. 146-52)

Emboldened by this acceptance of them by God, Adam can
elevate Eve in his salutation of her to a position
which is justly hers. He salutes her as the august
and the first female principle, the awesome earth-
mother and the primeval Virgin. Like Raphael he
greets her:

> Hail to thee
> Eve, rightly call'd Mother of all Mankind,
> Mother of all things living, since by thee
> Man is to live, and all things live for Man.

(XI. 159 61)

The nativity story from Michael, brings the same salutation to Adam's lips for Mary, the second Eve, a
saint and epitome of womanhood:

> Virgin Mother, Hail
> High in the love of Heav'n, yet from my
>   loyns
> Thou shalt proceed, and from thy Womb the
>   Son
> Of God most High; so God with man unites.

(XII. 379-82)

Milton is recalling the Magnificat of the Evening
Prayer in these passages of his poem. In contrast to
the early self-assured utterances of Eve, the Magnificat is a song of humility. Mary sings:

245

My soul doth magnify the Lord: and my spirit
    hath rejoiced in God my Savior
For he hath regarded: the lowliness of his
    hand-maiden.
For behold from henceforth: all generations
    shall call me blessed.
For he that is mighty has magnified me:
    and holy is his Name.

(Book of C.P. p. 53)

Contrite and humble, Eve, assumes the same stance as
the Virgin, when Adam praises her as the very source
of life. Her reply to him is her own Magnificat:

    To whom thus Eve with sad demeanor meek.
    Ill worthy I such title should belong
    To me transgressor, . . .
    But infinite in pardon was my Judge,
    That I who first brought Death on all,
        am Grac't
    The source of life;

(XI. 162-69)

        Milton's epic does not follow the liturgical pat-
tern of the Book of Common Prayer, but passages of Paradise
Lost, like those discussed above and as Thomas B. Stroup
points out, seem convincingly influenced by the rites and
ceremonies and verbal turns of the Book of Common Prayer.
Bellarmine's illustrations give the iconographic pattern of
some of the passages, especially those connected with
the creed. Liturgy depends on its ritualistic, visual appeal as on its doctrinal precepts and the dramatic. From the introit to the end, liturgy, as a
Divine Office and not the Eucharist alone, becomes a
highly motivated play. Each action and movement and
utterance, the gestures, the juxtaposition of the
priest and congregation, the acolytes, the deacons and
lay readers, spell drama. The Eucharist enacts the
great, historical tragedy of Christ on the cross, and
the rejuvenating power of the sacrifice of love. Milton's epic though not fashioned as a liturgical drama
is a didactic play, doctrinal yet aesthetically
pleasing. In it preternatural beings move through
cosmic space, and expunge all disbelief. The fact remains that Milton's work cannot be disassociated from
his creed and reality. His epic pulsates with organic

246

life and drama.

Before the fall in the epic all the characters,
including Adam and Eve, are supernatural. Their
salubrious state calls for little dramatic action,
until the arch-enemy steps into the garden and Iago-
like plots the fall. After that there is no lull in
the dramatic action, nor in the dramatic effectiveness
of the characters. God, the Son, Michael, the other
angels, and now the very human Adam and Eve are ani-
mately involved. The tragic action proceeds to its
denouement, yet leads to recovery and a reaffirmation
of life, though life no longer is "without Thorn the
Rose" (IV. 256).

The drama begins in the liturgical rite with the
processional introit, enacts the rites of praise and
sacrifice involving God's unseen presence, the priest
and devotees; and ends with the recessional. Milton's
epic has the same elements. It has its entrances and
exits like the liturgy, its ministry of angels, its
God-priest', devotees, and sacrifice. In Milton the
backdrop is cosmic; the liturgy moves in a cosmic
aura though mostly confined to the precincts of a
temple. The music of the verses sound antiphons and
tropes of the liturgy. Some songs of the epic have
the tonal quality of the sixth-century Gregorian
chants; the words conveying situations and actions
for the progressive movement of the narrative as in
the ritual. The crescendo builds emotionally to the
point of sacrifice both in the liturgy and the epic.
The exhortations, prayers and absolutions all prepare
the devotees and communicants for the final sacrifice.
In taking the bread or wine, the symbolic body and
blood of Christ, the individual in the liturgical
ritual sacrifices his will completely in acquiescence
to the will of God. Milton's human beings also empty
themselves in orisons to God in hope of winning
back a measure of his grace. These are moments of
catharsis in both the liturgy and the epic. Emotions
that have been escalating to a peak suddenly find an
outlet in completion. The result is a sense of
exhaustion with peace, and a renewal and continuation
of faith. Tragedy takes a turn for comedy. With
Joseph Campbell it can be said, man can laugh with
the gods, for life is not discharged.

Mystery and Miracle plays in Medieval England
were announced by banns, days before the performance,

247

inviting the towns to witness the sacred entertainment. Similarly the opening sentences of the liturgy invite the congregation to partake of the dramatic moments of the ritual. Milton's epic like the classical epics, effortlessly involves the reader through its prologues, the situations and episodes, and the dialogue, until devotee-like the reader loses his identity and is absorbed in the poem. In the liturgy there is dramatic rapport between the priest and the audience.

The actor-spokesman the priest kneels or faces the audience or exhorts and praises God, and the tempo of the liturgical phrases enthrall the listeners until they identify themselves completely with the priest, their mediator. The movements of the priest in the sanctuary become part of the drama, and are significantly representative of spiritual verities, and help the devotees to align their thoughts with the priest's, prior to the ultimate sacrifice. "The Eucharistic rite, is however, distinctly the rehearsal of the drama of redemption, rising to its climax in the Memorial of the Institution, and the Invocation of the Holy Spirit - in other words, the consecration of the Eucharist."[17] In the epic there is continuous flux. The scenes hover between Heaven and Hell, Chaos and Paradise. The movement is vertical, horizontal, and diagonal, which helps to make the drama pulsatingly dynamic and gripping. Many a time the words and phrases of the liturgy and the epic correspond, and exert identical awesome influence. And not only the words evoke different responses and emotions, but the rhythms and cadences. Milton's extended narrative poem then becomes a massive act of devotion. Through the words of God, His Son, Raphael and Michael, Milton sermonizes, and especially in the last book of the epic, where he formulates didactic pictures to illustrate his thoughts. Artistically the verbal anecdotes of Milton fit the structural unity of the plot, and do not appear as digressions as in the primary epics of Homer.

The liturgy is more akin to the Aristotelian theory of the drama, in which the plot adheres to the three unities of time, place and action; the epic transcends time and space. It moves in eternity and the cosmos is its stage. But both the epic and the liturgy deal with the numinous in realistic terms

248

and call for complete suspension of disbelief on
the part of their devotees. It may be because for
Milton and the ritualist their literature deals with
living reality and is part of their creed. Like the
mystery and morality plays, the liturgy and the epic
are based on the allegory of good and evil with their
corollaries; forgiveness with mercy and justice, or
damnation with sin and death. And as in the morality
plays, the struggle is an inward war between the angelic and the demonic in man. Inevitably in response
to the comedy of life, the angelic wins and man renews himself in majectic self-assurance. The communi-
cant and Adam both prevail over death and dissolution.
God, His Son, the Virtuous angels, and Satan, Sin and
Death and the Vices in the form of the fallen angels,
are all central to the theme of the epic and the
liturgy.

Alfred W. Pollard's comments on the liturgical
origin of religious plays is worth quoting; for the
statement illustrates the drama of Milton's epic and
its liturgical connection; its use of God and the
Son, and of abstractions like Death:

> In the so called Coventry cycle the didac-
> tic speeches . . . are delivered by an
> allegorical personage called Contemplacio.
> Death is personified, and a play on the
> Salutation is prefaced by a long prologue
> in heaven, in which the speakers are (be-
> sides Deus Pater and Deus Filius), Veritas,
> Misericordia, Justicia, and Pax. This
> tendency towards the personfication of
> abstract ideas is a mark of late date in
> the history of the Miracle Play . . . based
> on the Bible narrative, the Apocryhal Gos-
> pels, and the Medieval Legends . . . setting
> forth the goodness of the Lord's Prayer and
> the Creed."18

Pollard adds that these plays were performed in the
sixteenth and the seventeenth centuries when the popularity of religious drama was at its height and
stressed the moral and sacramental teaching of the
Church. The Castell of Perseverance is the earliest
extant morality play; Milton may have read it if not
seen it performed. It deals with:

249

the spiritual history of Humanum Genus from
the day of his birth to his appearance at
the Judgment Seat of God, to personify the
foes by whom his pathway is beset, the
Guardian Angel by whose help he resists
them, and the ordinances of Confession and
Penance by which he is strengthened in his
conflict, this was the playright's object;
. . . The opening pageant of mundus, Belyal
and Caro; the World, the Devil, and the
Flesh, each boasting of his might; the
appearance of Humanum Genus, naked save
for the chrism cloth on his head, and conscious of his helplessness; the first struggle for his soul of his Good and Bad Angels,
and the victory of the latter, make up an
impressive prologue, which ends with the
lament of Bonus Angelus, chanted to music.

In the next division of the play Mankind is presented to Mundus, to whom he
professes allegiance, and is confided to
the care of Pleasure, Folly, and Backbiting
(Voluptas, Stultitia, Detreccio) and ultimately to Belial and Caro, and the seven
deadly Sins, each of whom enters with an
appropriate speech. Then Mankind's Good
Angel calls to his aid Confessio and
Schrift, and with the help of Penitencia
the sinner is converted and reconciled and
safely lodged in the Castle of Perseverance![19]

In the liturgy of The Book of Common Prayer the act-
ors are the priests and the devotees; in Milton, God,
His Son, the good and bad angels, and Adam and Eve.
The plot is traditional, the action centering round
Man's fall and salvation. Milton spares none of the
dramatic techniques to make his epic pulsate with
life. He uses beautiful settings, each superbly
appropriate to the scene enacted, prologues, timely
entry and exits, soliloquies, a great deal of movement
with a few statuesque poses, fascinating dialogue,
suspense, and scenes varying from the idyllic, serene
and tranquil to the intense, emotionally charged leading to a catharsis when the reader with Adam and Eve
can relax and reaffirm faith in life. An amazing
feature of the epic is that each character speaks in
his own voice. The voices are seldom harsh but
invariably musical and always distinctive. "The Son

is the voice of love and mercy and his speeches embody
a special recognizable rhythm. The speaking roles of
God and the Son provide some celestial drama, although,
in dividing the attributes of Deity, they can have the
effect of making God seem harsh," says Douglas Bush.[20]
The long debates are engrossing, for each shows a
vitality commensurate with its speaker, and the whole
is a panoramic drama that enthralls from the opening
of Book I to the close of Book XII.

The discipline that Adam and Eve undergo is that
of the ritual of the liturgy. Having lost their innocent bliss and encumbered by guilt, they atone for
their sins by contrition, penance, and confession.
Their reward is a vision, though a great deal of it
horrifying because of the carnage. Their hope is the
future and anticipation of a new life. Their quest
is knowledge.

A striking picture of this dramatic epic is the
mystical dance of the angels. Its orbits and geometrical designs recall the concelebration of the
eucharist in some churches. The ritual is performed
by three or more priests. The movements of the
priests are conducted in unison and are highly rhyth-
mic, and the whole ritual, along with the musical in-
tonation, takes on the character of a sacred ceremony
offered to the Deity in praise and thanksgiving.
Milton's emblematic picture moves with the grace of
the concelebrants round the altar:

> That day, as other solemn days, they spent
> In song and dance about the sacred Hill,
> Mystical dance, which yonder starry Sphere
> Of Planets and of fixt in all her Wheels
> Resembles nearest, mazes intricate,
> Eccentric,intervolv'd, yet regular
> Then most, when most irregular they seem:
> And in their motions harmony Divine
> So smooths her charming tones, that God's
>   own ear
> Listens delighted.

(V. 518-27)

The seventeenth century believed in the music of the
spheres and the cosmic dance, and the Church emulated
it in its own ritualistic and dramatic worship; Milton's angels are an admixture of the Platonic and the

251

Christian as they adulate their Maker in song and
dance. Their stately arabesques spell praises of God.

Central to the liturgy and the epic is man. The
eucharist is a corporate form of worship, yet each
devotee communicates with the Deity as an individual.
Adam, though the prototype of all mankind, sees himself as an individual entity while sharing Michael's
visionary pictures and narrative. In the end it is
Adam who leaves the garden of Eden not mankind. Both
the liturgy and the epic presuppose the individual as
the hero. The sacrifice of his will he offers God,
is his own choice. Like many tragic heroes he goes
through a period of doubt before the last act of
acquiescence to God's will and acceptance of his
mission. The liturgy dismisses the devotee with
"Go forth in Peace"; the epic also ends with a
benediction, for Providence is their guide (XII. 647).

The dramatic element in Milton has been explored
many times through the centuries. His Commonplace
Book has been cited for the plays he had envisioned
writing. In Paradise Lost he has captured the pith
of drama and made it as didactically moving as the
dramatic rituals of the Church. A few of the dramatic techniques Milton uses were noted, but some call
for specific comment as they add greatly to the eloquence of the epic. A powerful, aesthetic tool is
the soliloquy. Had it not been for this Iago-like
technique used for the Arch-fiend, half the joy of
knowing Satan would be lost. He reveals himself
more in communing with himself aloud than in his
grandiloquent speeches. His villainy, his cowardice,
his fear of acknowledging defeat, his knowledge that
God is invincible but can be hurt vicariously, his
penitent nostalgia for heaven, and his thoughts on
the futility of repentance, all give him dramatic
proportions of great power. The soliloquies come
as shocks. The grand rebel seems admirable on first
reading Books I and II; his magnitude of mind and
body is overwhelming. Soon his thoughts condemn
him; his suavity peels off like veneer, and the
reader is left with the diabolic, cantankerous,
puny creature illustrated so imaginatively by Paul
Doré. Satan, the epitome of male beauty and glory,
begins to grow claws and hooves and horns.

Adam's dramatic flaw is not hubris, but inordinate love for Eve. Douglas Bush points out that

252

if Eve has a Narcissus complex, Adam's pursuit of her,
when she first shies from him, recalls Apollo's desire for Daphne. Both display their hamartia early
in the epic. Adam's description of Eve to Raphael
gives an inkling of what the action will involve.
Adam's effusiveness startles the reader, for Adam
seems to be losing a sense of proportion. He enshrines Eve in an omniscience that belongs to God. Even
prior to his tasting the fruit, Leland Ryken argues,
Adam's sexual desire for Eve, though innocent, is
excessive and lustful.[21] Ironically the angel sees
it while Adam does not. Adam clothes Eve with angelic virtues as God is surrounded by angels. His
statements are full of dramatic irony:

> here passion first I felt,
> Commotion strange, in all enjoyments else
> Superior and unmov'd, here only weak
> Against the charm of Beauty's powerful
> glance.
>
> when I approach
> Her loveliness, so absolute she seems
> And in herself complete, so well to know
> Her own, that what she wills to do or say,
> Seems wisest, virtuousest, discreetest,
> best;
> All higher knowledge in her presence falls
> Degraded, Wisdom in discourse with her
> Loses discount'nanc't, and like folly shows;
> Authority and Reason on her wait,
> As one intended first, not after made
> Occasionally; and to consummate all,
> Greatness of mind and nobleness thir seat
> Build in her loveliest, and create, an awe
> About her, as a guard Angelic plac't.

(VIII. 530-59)

After a speech like that Raphael's chagrin and dramatic retort are inevitable and understandable. Had he
been human his words might have been more caustic,
for Milton could well spar with words. But being
the affable angel and speaking as himself, Raphael
anxiously warns Adam. Like the emblematists, personifying wisdom, he entreats Adam to hold fast to
sapience and not belittle his own worth:

To whom the angel with contracted brow.
Accuse not Nature, she hath done her part;
Do thou but thine, and be not diffident
Of Wisdom, she deserts thee not, if thou
Dismiss not her, when most thou need'st
    her nigh,
By attributing overmuch to things
Less excellent, as thou thyself perceiv'st.
            . . . weigh with her thyself;
Then value: Oft-times nothing profits more
Then self-esteem, grounded on just and right
Well manag'd . . .
But if the sense of touch whereby mankind
Is propagated seem such dear delight
Beyond all other, think the same vouchsaf't
To Cattle and each Beast . . .
In loving thou dost well, in passion not,

(VIII. 560-88)

Adam is reproved by Raphael for his naivity and
uxuriousness and forewarned of what could transpire
if he neglects the warning. Adam neglects it and
falls.

Milton uses his aesthetic love of the dramatic
and his familiarity with liturgical literature in
the long morality Paradise Lost, and reveals the
cyclic nature of life in man; his fall, and rejuvenation and communion with God. He speaks through
poetry, for poetry appeals where argument fails; and
justifies God to man.

254

FOOTNOTES

[1] The Book of Common Prayer henceforth will be referred to as the Prayer Book.

[2] John Dowden, Workmanship of the Prayer Book (London: 1899), p. 9.

[3] George Newton Conklin, Biblical Criticism and Heresy in Milton (New York: Columbia University Press, 1949), p. 2.

[4] Rosemond Tuve, A Reading, George Herbert (Chicago: University of Chicago Press, 1952), p. 27.

[5] Tuvo, p. 36.

[6] Allen Cabaniss, Liturgy and Literature (Alabama: University of Alabama Press, 1970), p. 16.

[7] W. G. Madsen, From Shadowy Types to Truth (New Haven: Yale University Press, 1968), p. 51.

[8] Christian Doctrine, I. i.

[9] Evelyn Underhill, Worship (New York: Harper, 1937), pp. 33-40.

[10] Madsen, p. 82.

[11] Hughes, ed., The Reason of Church Government, p. 669.

[12] James H. Sims, The Bible in Milton's Epics (Gainesville: University of Florida, 1962), p. 4.

[13] Hughes, ed. p. 964.

[14] See pages 279 ff.

[15] Allen Cabaniss, Liturgy and Literature (Alabama: Un. of Ala. Press, 1970), p. 15.

[16] Of Reformation, J. Max Patrick, ed. p. 42.

[17] F. Gavin, "The Eucharist in East and West," Liturgy and Worship, ed., W. K. Lowther Clark (London: S.P.C.K., 1933), p. 103.

255

[18]Alfred W. Pollard, English Miracle Plays, Moralities, and Interludes (Oxford: Clarendon Press, 1890 & 1954), pp. xxxix - xlvi.

[19]Pollard, pp. xxxix - xlvi.

[20]Douglas Bush, John Milton (New York: Collier, 1967), p. 156.

[21]Leland Ryken, The Apocalyptic Vision in Paradise Lost (Ithaca: Cornell Univ. Press, 1970), pp. 142-145.

CHAPTER SEVEN

CONCLUSION: A SYNOPSIS OF THE ARGUMENT IN

THE PRECEDING CHAPTERS

Having examined Milton's magnum opus in connection with the emblems and the liturgical tradition of the Anglican Church, we can quote Gombrich's rhetorical question, "What is it . . . the true poet imitates? In his object the visible world of ours or rather the intelligible world?"[1] The obvious answer is both. It is the visible cosmos that triggers the conceptual, so often seen in Paradise Lost, where light, for example, is an attribute of God, darkness of the Devil; Sin, an embodiment of an abstraction. The visible and invisible are complementary, and pictures have a covert significance. Rosemary Freeman states, "In seventeenth-century terminology it was generally the picture alone that was the 'Emblem', the motto was called the 'Word', and the poet added Verses or 'moralised the emblem.'"[2] The output consists of the Figura and Lemma or Vox, where the visible and the abstract combine to instruct. In the emblematists, often, there is little coherence between the picture and the poem; usually the picture is a point of departure for a series of thoughts that follow. Milton occasionally follows a similar pattern and stresses the verities of life while elucidating his thoughts. But unlike the emblems, Milton's pictures, however far-fetched, pulsate with vibrancy and are consistently appropriate to the didactic element they convey. They make one willingly suspend disbelief and see in them "a kind of understanding and wisdom and substance given all at once;"[3] their motto built within them.

Mario Praz in Mnemosyne avers that art is an expression from within, that it is not analytical but synthetic, and therein lies its power. A poem and picture may complement each other, but neither one can replace the other, because in themselves each is the synthesis of the artist's dreams and ideas and is uniquely itself.[4] Yet the emblem writers try to show correspondences and parallelisms between the visual device and the verbal poem. That they succeed is evident from their popularity in the seventeenth century. To see the resemblance between the picture

257

and the poem requires stretching the aesthetic and
poetic imagination to the point of stress, but the
inspiration behind the works never fails to convince
of the sincerity and veracity of the poet-artists,
or their belief in their mission. Milton's verbal
pictures insinuate mottos, except when he becomes
didactically overt, as when conveying Satan's blatant
hypocrisy, his metamorphosis as a cherub at a time,
in reality, when he is most diabolic; or when Raphael
gives advice to Adam, asking him to remember that he
is God's masterpiece and carries divinity within
him while Eve is lower in the great Chain of Being.
Like the exhortations of Man by the emblematists,
Adam is advised to be obedient, to seek knowledge
but not probe hidden mysteries; to love his wife
though not to excess. Milton is openly didactic in
the horrendous spectacle of war and madness, and its
aftermath; in Eve's tempting Adam to spiritual and
physical death; in the conflict of Adam's carnal
love for his wife and his reason; Adam's need of
supernal grace and divesting himself of self-pity and
self love; in Michael's upbraiding of Adam and giving him visions of horror (with few respites) though
reassuring him of ultimate and generic salvation in
the second Adam; in Eve's fortitude, endurance and
stamina; in the heavenly circles of the angels and
the circle of perfection of the new-made world against
the dolorous flames of hell and the cacophony of
Chaos; and in the rapport of God and His Son. Step
by step, in sequential arrangement of episodes,
Milton teaches through his art.[5] Even his mazes become directions to the ultimate understanding of the
God-man relationship. The emblematists touch many
phases of existence, not in any well defined order,
but to fathom and elevate man's spiritual life.
Milton's cosmic view encompasses an organised and
structured heaven, earth, and hell. His word pictures are drawn so vast that the mind stops discern-
ing limits, and soars and sinks with the poet through
timelessness and eternity, forgetting corporeal
limitations. If the Ptolemaic and Copernican sys-
tems and geographical boundaries in the epic limit
the movement, it is only in passing. The scope of
the poem transcends all graphic boundaries and shows
the profundity of the Renaissance, Miltonic mind.

Milton's works have been studied for their
pictorial quality and often been related to the
High Baroque and Rococo in art; but have not often

258

been associated with iconology. C. S. Lewis noticed
emblems in Comus,[6] G. E. Wilson mentioned "Emblems
in Paradise Regained" and Mario Praz in Milton's
prose.[7] The preceding chapters have shown that,
whether consciously or unconsciously, Milton frequently uses the iconological and emblematic mode in Paradise Lost. Thus Milton is not unaffected by the
popular emblems; he follows the emblematic technique
when suited to his purpose. The realism of his icons
is so pronounced that one can be thrown off the
quest for emblems in the epic, and feel it a sacri-
lege to compare his incomparable poetry to stock
images of Renaissance iconography and emblem books,
yet the connection when found is pleasurable. Milton's work is many-faceted and too complex to be
categorized. A compendium of classical thoughts and
myths, Hebraic-Christian narratives and beliefs,
theology of the Church Fathers, liturgical passages
from Church-related rites and observances, philosophical truths, historical events and legends, political
innuendoes and contemporary activities, highly subjective autobiographical sketches, and all available
knowledge, Milton's is an unmatched work of art. His
poetry and his clarity of sight and his rationality,
uplift and amaze. With Chaucer and Shakespeare, Milton still smiles indulgently on a doting world, and
believes in man's divinity.

     "Thomas Macaulay . . . stated that Milton's
images depend 'less on what they likely represent than
on what they remotely suggest,' and that 'the art of
his description lies in its suggestiveness.'"[8] The
emblematists operate likewise, highlighting their
concerns in conceptual, suggestive images. The emblem writers and Milton are poet-priests. To them
God, the Son, angels and Heaven; Satan, Sin, the
devils and Hell, are as much a reality as Man and
Death. They have the medievalist's preoccupation
with man's soul, and impress the fact in icons and
verbal pictures.

     Milton and the emblematists, living in the same
era and being exposed to the same traditions and patterns of thought, express themselves in the visionary,
poetic mode, often in "costliest emblems." The emblem
writers may again be relegated to the stack rooms, but
Milton will militantly and graciously continue to
reign in the intellectual and aesthetic mind.

                              Shahla Anand

FOOTNOTES

[1] E. H. Gombrich, Symbolic Images (London: Phaidon, 1972), p. 157.

[2] Freeman, pp. 37-38.

[3] Gombrich, p. 158.

[4] Mario Praz, Mnemosyne (Princeton: Princeton University Press, 1970), p. 3.

[5] Roy Daniells, Milton, Mannerism and Baroque (Toronto: Un. of Toronto Press, 1963).

[6] C. S. Lewis, Spenser's Images of Life (London: Cambridge Un. Press, 1967), p. 11.

[7] Gayle E. Wilson, "Emblems in Paradise Regained," Milton Quarterly, VI, No. 4.

[8] Ryken, p. 187.

A SHORTE CATECHISME

Of Card.ᵃˡˡ Bellarmine

illustrated with the

IMAGES.

In Augusta.

VVith Licence of Superiours.

1614.

(℔ · 8ᵛ · B · 180 · ; · ⅱ

261

M. *VVhat meaneth* Vnitie *&* Trinitie *of*
God?

S. It menaeth that in God there is one only
Diuinitie, or, as we saie, Essence and diuine
nature, which neuertheles is in three diuine persons, that are called *Father, Sonne* and
boly Ghoß.

A 5   Wberfore

IV.

Heauen.

II.

And in IESVS Chriſt his onlie Sonne our
Lord.

Whoe

Enuie, to vvhich is oppofite brotherlie loue.

G 3 **Slouth.**

Couetousnes,to vvhich is contrarie
Liberalitie.

G   Leche

I.

Pride, to which is contrarie Humilitie.

Couetouſ-

Angre, to vvhich ir oppofite Patience.

G 2   Glou-

III.

Hell.

Women

VIII.

I beleeue in the ho'y Ghoſt.

The

M.   *Say the Creede.*

I.

S. I beleeue in God the Father almightie,
    Creator of heauen and earth.

And

II.

Carnall finne againft nature.

Oppreffion

V.

Gloutonie, to vvhich is oppofite Ab-
ftinence.

Enuie,

Lecherie, to vvhich is oppofite
Chaftitie.

Angre,

6.

Finall impenitence.

Hovo

I.

Death.

Iugd.

4.

Enuie at an other mans grace.

Obsti-

V.

Thou shalt not murder.

Thou

M. *Hovv manie be the sinnes that crie vengeance in the sight of God?*

S.   They be foure.   I.

VVillfull murder.

Carnall

VI.

And leade vs not into tentation.

C 2   But

VII.

But deliuer vs from euil, Amen.

Whoe

From thence he shall come to iudge the
quicke and the dead.

B 2　　　　Ibeleeue

II.

Iudgment.

H 2 Hell.

XII.

Life euerlasting. Amen.

Whee

BIBLIOGRAPHY

Adams, R.M. Milton and the Modern Critics. Ithaca: Cornell University, 1955; rpt. 1966.

Allen, Don Cameron. Image and Meaning: Metaphoric Tradition in Renaissance Poetry. Baltimore: John Hoplins, 1960.

_____. Mysteriously Meant: The Rediscovery of Pagan Symbolism and Allegorical Interpretation in the Renaissance. Baltimore: John Hopkins, 1970.

Anand, Shahla. A Potpourri of Thoughts on English Literature. New York: Vantage Press, 1975.

Appleton, L.H. & Bridges, M. Symbolism in Liturgical Art. New York: Charles Scribner, 1959.

Aptekar, Jane. Icons of Justice. New York: Columbia University, 1969.

Ayres, Philip. Emblemata Amatoria 1683. Facsimile. Menston, Yorkshire: Scolar Press, 1969.

Ascham, Roger. The Scholemaster 1570. Facsimile. Menston: Scolar Press, 1967.

Banks, Theodore Howard. Milton's Imagery. New York: Columbia University, 1954.

Barker, Arthur. Milton: Modern Essays in Criticism. New York: Oxford University, 1965.

Bellarmine, St. Robert. A Short Catechisme 1614. Facsimile. Menston: Scolar Press, 1973.

Bender, John B. Spenser and Literary Pictorialism. Princeton: Princeton University, 1972.

Bodkin, Maud. Archetypal Patterns in Poetry. London: Oxford University, 1934, rpt. 1968.

The Book of Common Prayer . . . according to the use of The Church of England. London: 1662.

Brinkley, Roberta Florence. Arthurian Legend in the Seventeenth Century. New York: Noble Offset, 1970.

Browne, Sir Thomas. Religio Medici. Cambridge: Cambridge University Press, 1953.

Bush, Douglas. English Literature in the Earlier Seventeenth Century. London: Oxford University, 1962.

_____. Mythology and the Renaissance Tradition in English Poetry. New York: W.W. Norton, 1932, rpt. 1963.

Cabaniss, Allen. Liturgy and Literature. Alabama: Un. of Alabama, 1970.

Catalogue of an extensive collection of books of emblems. May 1884. Lond (1884)8.

Cirlot, J.E. A Dictionary of Symbols. Trans. Jack Sage. New York: Philosophical Library, 1962.

Clark, Sir George. The Seventeenth Century. London: Oxford University, 1929, rpt. 1970.

Comenius, Jan Amos. A Reformation of Schooles 1642. Facsimile. Menston: Scolar Press, 1969.

Conklin, George N. Biblical Criticism and Heresy in Milton. New York: Columbia Un., 1949.

Cope, Jackson I. The Metaphoric Structure of Paradise Lost. Baltimore: John Hopkins, 1962.

Cowley, A. A Proposition for the Advancement of Experimental Philosophy, 1661. Facsimile. Menston: Scolar Press, 1969.

Croll, Morris W. "Attic" and Baroque Prose Style. eds. J.M. Patrick, et al. Princeton: Princeton University, 1966.

Crouch, Nathaniel. Delights for the ingenious. London 1684. Printed for Nathaniel Crouch at the Bell in the Poultry near Cheapside, 1684.

286

Curry, Walter Clyde. Milton's Ontology Cosmogony and
    Physics. Lexington: University of Kentucky,
    1966.

Daniells, Roy. Milton Mannerism and Baroque. Canada:
    Toronto University, 1963.

Davidson, Gustav. A Dictionary of Angels. New York:
    Collier, 1967.

DeMontenay, Georgette. Emblemes ou Devises Chresti-
    ennes, 1571. Facsimile. Menston: Scolar Press, 1973.

Douglas, Mary. Natural Symbols: Exploration in Cos-
    mology. New York: Pantheon, 1970.

Doughty, W.L. Studies in Religious Poetry of the
    Seventeenth Century. Port Washington: Kennikat,
    1966.

Dowden, John. Workmanship of the Prayer Book. Lon-
    don: 1899.

Duvignaud, Jean. The Sociology of Art. trans. T.
    Wilson. New York: Harper & Row, 1967.

Earl, John. The Autograph Manuscript of Micromos-
    graphie 1628. Facsimile. Menston: Scolar
    Press, 1966.

Egerton MS 203 Paradise Lost.

Emblemata. Scripture emblems taught in the household
    by a Sunday School Teacher. 1868.

Every, George. Christian Mythology. London: Hamlyn,
    1970.

Fish, Stanley E. Surprised by Sin. Berkley: Uni-
    versity of California, 1971.

Fixler, Michael. Milton and the Kingdoms of God.
    Northwestern, 1964.

Fletcher, Angus. Allegory: The Theory of a Symbolic
    Mode. Ithaca: Cornell University, 1964.

Freeman, Rosemary. English Emblem Books. New York:
    Octagon, 1970.

287

Fremantle, Anne, ed. The Protestant Mystics. New
    York: New American, 1965.

Frye, Northrop. Fables of Identity. New York: Har-
    court Brace, 1963.

_____. Knight, L.C., et al. Myth and Symbols.
    Lincoln: University of Nebraska, 1967.

Fuller, Samuel. Characteristic Excellence of the
    Liturgy. Boston: 1865.

Gardner, Helen. A Reading of Paradise Lost. Oxford:
    Oxford, 1965.

_____. Religion and Literature. New York: Ox-
    ford University, 1971.

Gavin, F. Liturgy and Worship. London: S.P.C.K.,
    1933.

Giamatti, A. Bartlett. The Earthly Paradise and the
    Renaissance Epic. Princeton: Princeton Univer-
    sity, 1966.

Green, Henry. Andrea Alciati and His Book of Emblems.
    New York: Burt Franklin, 1872.

_____. Shakespeare and Emblem Writers. London:
    Trubner, 1870.

Grierson, Herbert. Cross Currents in English Liter-
    ature of the Seventeenth Century. 1929, rpt.
    Baltimore: Penguin, 1966.

Guthrie, W.K.C. In the Beginning. Ithaca: Cornell
    University, 1965.

Halkett, John G. Milton and the Idea of Matrimony.
    New Haven: Yale University, 1970.

Hall, John. Emblems with Elegant Figures 1658. Fac-
    simile. Menston, Yorkshire: Scolar Press,
    1970.

Hanford, James Holly. John Milton: Poet and Humanist.
    Cleveland: Western Reserve University, 1966.

_____. Milton. New York: Appleton Century Crofts,
    1966.
288

_____. Milton: Goldentree Bibliographies. New York: Appleton Century Crofts, 1966.

_____. A Milton Handbook. New York: Appleton Century Crofts, 1954.

Hawkins, Henry. Partheneia Sacra 1633. Facsimile. Menston: Scolar Press, 1971.

Hesiod, Theoginis. trans. D. Wender. Baltimore: Penguin, 1973.

Hill, Christopher. Puritanism and Revolution. 1958; New York: Schocken Books, 1970.

The Holy Bible: King James Version, 1611. London: Cambridge University, n.d.

Honig, Edwin. Dark Conceit: The Making of Allegory. New York: Oxford University, 1966.

Huckabay, Calvin. John Milton: An Annotated Bibliography 1929-1968. Pittsburgh: Duquesne University, 1969.

Hughes, Merritt Y. ed. John Milton: Complete Poems and Major Prose. New York: Odyssey Press, 1957.

Ingram, W. and Swaim, K. A Concordance to Milton's English Poetry. Oxford: Clarendon Press, 1972.

In tercets King Charles I long poem written in captivity.

Jenner, Thomas. Emblemata 1651.

Johnson, Samuel. "Milton," Lives of the Poets. ed. K. Deighton. London: Macmillan, 1949.

Keats, John. Poetical Works. London: Collins, n.d.

Kermode, Frank, ed. The Living Milton. London: 1960.

Lee, Rensselaer W. Ut Pictura Poesis, The Humanistic Theory of Painting. New York: Norton, 1967.

Levin, Harry. The Myth of the Golden Age in the Renaissance. New York: Oxford University.

289

Lewis, C.S. The Allegory of Love. London: Oxford, 1936; rpt. 1971.

_____. A Preface to Paradise Lost. London: Oxford, 1942, rpt. 1971.

_____. Spenser's Images of Life. London: 1967.

Lovejoy, Arthur O. The Great Chain of Being. Cambridge, Mass.: Harvard University, 1967.

Lyons, Bridget G. Voices of Melancholy. New York: W.W. Norton, 1975.

M., E. Ashrea: or the grove of beatitudes, represented in emblems 1665. Facsimile. Menston: Scolar Press, 1970.

MacCaffrey, Isabel Gamble. Paradise Lost as Myth. Cambridge, Mass.: Harvard University, 1967.

MacLean, H. ed. Edmund Spenser's Poetry. New York: W.W. Norton, 1968.

Madsen, William G. From Shadowy Types to Truth. New Haven: Yale University, 1968.

Mazzeo, Joseph Anthony. Renaissance and Revolution. New York: Pantheon, 1967.

_____. Renaissance and Seventeenth Century Studies. New York: Columbia University, 1968.

Milton, John. The Anti-Prelatical Pamphlets 1641-1642. Facsimile. Menston: Scolar Press, 1968.

_____. The Divorce Tracts, Areopagitica, and Of Education 1644-45. Facsimile. Menston: Scolar Press, 1968.

_____. Poems. Reproduced in Facsimile from the Manuscrip in Trinity College, Cambridge, Cambridge With a Transcript. Menston: Scolar Press, 1972.

Miner, Earl. Seventeenth Century Imagery. Los Angeles: University of California, 1971.

Mohl, Ruth. John Milton and His Commonplace Book. New York: F. Ungar, 1969.

Moyce, A.P. and Kolb, L.C. Modern Clinical Psychiatry. Philadelphia: Saunders, 1964.

Murray, Patrick. Milton: The Modern Phase. London: 1967.

Murrin, Michael. The Veil of Allegory. Chicago: Chicago Un., 1969.

Nicolson, Majorie Hope. The Breaking of the Circle. Evanston: Northwestern University, 1950.

_____. John Milton: A Reader's Guide to His Poetry. New York: Farrar-Strauss, 1963.

Nicolson, Marjorie Hope. Mountain Gloom and Mountain Glory. 2nd ed. New York: Norton, 1963.

Oras, Ants. Blank Verse and Chronology in Milton. Gainesville: University of Florida, 1966.

Osgood, C.G. The Classical Mythology of Milton's English Poems. New York: Henry Holt, 1900.

Ovid. Metamorphoses. trans. M.M. Innes. Baltimore: Penguin, 1953.

Osborne, Harold, ed. The Oxford Companion to Art. Oxford: Clarendon, 1970.

Panofsky, Erwin. Studies in Iconology. New York: Harper & Row 1939, rpt. 1972.

Paradise Lost A Poem Written in Ten Books by John Milton 1667. Facsimile. Menston: Scolar Press, 1972.

Paradise Regained A Poem in IV Books, To which is added Samson Agonistes 1671. Menston: Scolar 1968.

Parker, William Riley. Milton A Biography. 2 vols. Oxford: Clarendon Press, 1969.

Partridge, A.C. The Language of Renaissance Poetry. London: Andre Deutsch, 1971.

Patrides, C.H. Milton's Epic Poetry. Baltimore:
Penguin, 1967.

Patrick, J.M. ed. The Complete Prose Works of John
Milton. Vol. V. Part I & II. trans. P.W.
Blackford. New Haven: Yale, 1971.

Peacham, Henry. Minerva Britanna 1612. Facsimile.
Menston: Scolar, 1973.

Pickering, F.P. Literature and Art in the Middle
Ages. Coral Gables: University of Miami, 1970.

Poems of Mr. John Milton, Both English and Latin
Compos'd at several times. (Poems 1645 Lycidas
1638). Facsimile. Menston: Scolar, 1970.

Pointon, Marcia. Milton and English Art. Toronto:
Toronto University Press, 1970.

Pollard, A.W. English Miracle Plays, Moralities,
Interludes. Oxford: Clarendon, 1954.

Potter, Lois. A Preface to Milton. New York: Charles
Scribner's, 1971.

Praz, Mario. The Flaming Heart. Glouster: Peter
Smith, 1958; rpt. 1966.

_____. Mnemosyne: The Parallel Between Literature
and the Visual Arts. Princeton: Princeton University, 1970.

_____. Studies in Seventeenth Century Imagery.
2nd ed. Roma: Edizioni di Storia E Letteratura,
1964.

Prince, F.T. The Italian Element in Milton's Verse.
Oxford: Clarendon Press, 1954.

Puttenham, George. The Arte of English Poesie 1589.
Facsimile. Menston: Scolar, 1968.

Quarles, Francis. Complete Works. ed. Alexander B.
Grossart. New York: AMS Press, 1967.

Quarles' Emblems. Ed. Charles Cowden Clarke. London:
Cassell. Petter Galpin & Co., n.d.

Quarles, Francis. 1592-1644 For A selection of em-
    blems from H. Hugo Pia desideria. Hugo (her-
    mannus).

Quarles, (Francis). Hieroglyphikes. 1638.

Quarles, Francis. Hieroglyphikes of the life of man
    1638. Facsimile. Menston: Scolar Press,
    1969.

_____. Emblems. Introduction: George Gilfillan.
    ed. Charles Cowden Clarke. London: Cassell,
    Peter, Galpin, n.d.

Rajan, B. Paradise Lost and the 17th Century Reader.
    Ann Arbor: University of Michigan, 1947, rpt.
    1967.

Raleigh, Sir Walter A. Milton. 1900, rpt. New York:
    Benjamin Bloom, 1967.

Ricks, Christopher. Milton's Grand Style. London:
    Oxford University, 1967.

Robinson, Forrest G. The Shape of Things Known.
    Cambridge, Mass.: Harvard University, 1972.

Rose, Mark. Shakespearean Design. Cambridge: Harvard
    University, 1972.

Ryken, Leland. The Apocalyptic Vision in Paradise
    Lost. Ithaca: Cornell, 1970.

Samuel, Irene. Dante and Milton. Ithaca: Cornell
    University, 1966.

_____. Plato and Milton. Ithaca: Cornell Un.,
    1946, rpt. 1965.

Sanders, N.K. trans. The Epic of Gilgamesh. Balti-
    more: Penguin, 1968.

Shakespeare, W. The Complete Works. ed. Hardin Craig.
    Chicago: Scott-Foresman, 1951.

Shumaker, Wayne. Unpremeditated Verse: Feeling and
    Perception in Paradise Lost. Princeton: Princeton
    Un., 1967.

293

Sims, James H. The Bible in Milton's Epics. Gainesville: University of Florida, 1962.

Steadman, John M. Milton and the Renaissance Hero.
Oxford: Clarendon Press, 1967.

_____. Milton's Epic Characters. Chapel Hill:
N. Carolina, 1968.

Stevens, David H. A Reference Guide to Milton from
1800 to the Present Day. Chicago: 1930.

Stroup, Thomas B. Religious Rite & Ceremony in Milton's
Poetry. Lexington: Un. of Kentucky, 1968.

Summers, Joseph H. The Lyric and Dramatic Milton.
New York: Columbia University, 1967.

_____. The Muses Method. London: Chatto & Windus,
1962.

Taylor, George Coffin. Milton's Use of Du Bartas.
New York: Octagon Books, 1968.

Thrope, James. Milton Criticism. New York: Collier,
1950, rpt. 1969.

Tillyard, E.M.W. The Elizabethan World Picture. New
York: Modern Library, 1962.

_____. Milton. New York: Collier, 1967.

Tuve, Rosemond. Allegorical Images. Princeton:
Princton Un., 1966.

_____. Elizabethan and Metaphysical Imagery.
Chicago: Chicago Un., 1968.

_____. A Reading, George Herbert. Chicago: Un.
of Chicago, 1952.

Underhill, Evelyn. Worship. New York: Harper, 1937.

Virgil. Aeneid. trans. W.F.J. Knight. Hammondsworth: Penguin, 1968.

Visiak, E.H. The Portent of Milton. New York:
Humanities Press, 1968.

Waldock, A.J.A. Paradise Lost and its Critics. Cambridge: 1961.

Webster's Third New International Dictionary, ed.
    P.B. Gove. Springfield: Mariam, 1968.

West, Robert H. Milton and the Angels. Athens:
    University of Georgia, 1955.

Westfall, Richard S. Science and Religion in the
    Seventeenth Century England. Ann Arbor: Uni-
    versity of Michigan, 1973.

Weston, Edward. The Patterne of all Pious Prayer
    1636. Facsimile. Menston: Scolar Press, 1973.

White, Helen C. The Metaphysical Poets: A Study in
    Religious Experience. New York: Collier-Mac-
    millan, 1966.

Whitney, Geoffrey. A Choice of Emblemes,
    1586. Facsimile. Menston: Scolar Press, 1973.

Wither, George. A Collection of Emblemes, 1635.
    Facsimile. Menston: Scolar Press, 1968.

A Short Biographical Sketch of

Shahla Anand

Shahla Anand was born and raised in Lucknow during the
height of India's struggle for freedom. Though her first interest
was English literature, like many of her youthful and idealistic
contomperaries, she sacrificed a brilliant career and plunged
into active social work in the villages and slums of Northern
India and Bombay.

She married Kenneth D. W. Anand, a specialist in comparative
religion and especially Islamics, who later became the second
Anglican (Episcopal) Bishop of the see of Kashmir Punjab, and
Himachal Pradesh. After India's independence, though still
actively involved in community service and holding   offices in
national service organizations, Shahla reverted to her first
love, literature, and taught at colleges of Delhi, Calcutta,
and Punjab Universities. Eleven years ago she came to the
U. S. A., where she had studied, and had been invited since for
lecture tours by different organizations. Her husband joined
her two years later, and subsequently was appointed Assistant
Bishop of the Episcopal Diocese of Newark. He served the Diocese
until his death in 1975. Shahla has been employed at Montclair
State College, in the Department of English, for almost ten
years.

Anand's schooling was at Isabella Thoburn College,
Lucknow University; Selly Oak Colleges, Birmingham, U. K.;
Agra University; Columbia University, New York; and New York
University. Having won acclaim for writing in school and
outside, and having been an associate editor of The Indian
Home, Bombay, in her early married life, and also having been
responsible for reports for various agencies since her college
days, Shahla turned to serious writing. Her first book,
A Potpourri of Thoughts on English Literature, appeared in
1975. It was well received, and had a second printing in 1977.
Of Costliest Emblem: Paradise Lost and the Emblem Tradition
should prove as stimulating. Shahla got her love for Milton
from her grandfather, Isa Charan Sada, poet, Milton scholar
and linguist. Along with his published poetry, Sada translated
Milton's major poetical works into Urdu poetry. But Shahla claims
that the greatest influence in her appreciation of Milton was
Professor Marjorie Hope Nicolson at Columbia University.
Along with attending Miss Nicolson's Milton and Seventeenth
Century courses, Shahla had the extra privilege of being Miss
Nicolson's advisee. Since then Shahla studied under the
guidance of Professors J. Max Patrick and Anthony Low, two
outstanding, contemporary Seventeenth Century and Milton scholars.

SHAHLA ANAND